A Psalm in Jenin

Brett Goldberg

To Eve and Isa

Contents

FOREWORD

The stories of the Bible, in their power and simplicity, are woven together like an ancient tapestry. Actions are described with minimalist precision. Dialogue is exact, alluding to the essence of things, hinting at the internal worlds of the Bible's characters. Interpretations as to the thoughts and feelings of the Bible's characters are left to future readers.

It is the Book of Psalms that provides us with the key to understanding the internal worlds of the Bible's characters. In each Psalm, we hear the voice of a tortured soul in search of meaning. It is no wonder that this internalized echo of the Biblical heroes has formed a major part of the liturgy of synagogues and churches for two millennia. The Book of Psalms has become a universal expression of the internal world of every being created in the image of G-d.

Once again, the Children of Israel, here in the land of the Bible, face their own battle for survival, as did their forefathers. Once again, we hear stories woven of a tapestry similar to that of the Bible. Stories, that without their Psalms, without their internal counterparts, would sound like simplistic distortions.

A Psalm in Jenin is a snapshot of the internal worlds of these young men. The book guides us faithfully through encounters with young men for whom the battle cry is the furthest thing from their essence. Young men who from their earliest years were raised to value sensitivity and love of their fellow man. And as one reads in these 'Psalms', not even the horrors of the Middle East conflict can change this fundamental approach to life.

I had the honor of accompanying many of these men through their formative years. I have followed their growth as men of outstanding Jewish and universal values, men motivated by a desire to bring about a better world.

In recent times, they have found themselves in an opposite reality. These gentle young men who, as their forefathers, love nothing more than study. These young men whose internal worlds are a mirror of the Bible's values and ethics. These young men who see the Bible as the DNA of their own identities. Indeed, their uniquely Israeli identities are the essence of the Biblical character Israel, as depicted in the mythic vision of Genesis 32. It is there that the name Israel first appears.

On that night of heavy darkness and unfathomable isolation, the forefather Jacob was made to engage for long hours in a grueling struggle, a dialogue of bodies without human voices, with a man who injures him. That 'man' was an angel fulfilling a mysterious mission.

Only the Book of Psalms is able to touch upon that which happened within Jacob's soul – his exhaustion, his search for meaning, his cry for the strength to persevere.

With the first light of dawn, as the darkness slowly recedes, Jacob can finally acknowledge his own survival. He has triumphed. "Release me, for the sun has risen", the angel beseeches him. But Jacob is not yet ready to release the angel from his grip. "I will not release you until you bless me," he demands of his opponent.

He demands the blessing of his enemy. For Jacob, the removal of darkness does not suffice to bring light. In this struggle, the victory of one of the sides was not enough to bring about its end. Jacob's struggle was unique and of great significance to future generations, for it was his enemy 's blessing that transformed him into Israel.

The heroes of this book, modern Israeli young men, embody the name Israel. Their world is formed by the spirit of their forefather who sought the blessing of his enemy, an enemy who like them is among G-d's creations.

Dr. Haim Peri
Director, Yemin Orde Youth Village

CHAPTER 1 The Room

Sleep always brought him back to that same cramped room in Jenin. Somehow, the entire platoon had crammed into that tiny apartment. They nailed carpets over the open windows, plunging the hideout into total darkness. The carpets afforded little protection against grenades or makeshift bombs, but kept them out of the sights of enemy snipers. Lights were forbidden, as was anything other than an occasional whisper. Sleep took place in fits and starts, at best an hour or two before an explosion shook them awake. He squeezed his toes against each other to relieve the itch. It had been almost a week since he had showered or taken his boots off.

Someone was making noise. It sounded like crying. "Quiet, they'll hear us!!" Doron whispered. The noise continued. "Quiet!" he hissed. Still, the noise, louder now and more insistent. He grabbed for his rifle. It wasn't there. He felt naked and vulnerable. Where was his weapon?

He came to. It was his nine-month old son Ofek crying in his crib. He went to the crib and held Ofek to his chest. Tears streamed down his own face as he rocked his child to sleep. I will hold him forever, Doron thought. I will hold him until he feels real. I will hold him until I have reclaimed him.

He was home for two weeks now, but every night he awoke in Jenin. He couldn't sleep for more than an hour or two without awakening in a sweat. Usually, he would gain his bearings within a couple of minutes. The other night, awakening to the sound of a helicopter, it took longer. He was certain that he was still in Jenin.

He was a reservist for over ten years now. In the past, he had always been able to reclaim his life after each stint of reserve duty. Even a year and a half ago when Amir was killed. Somehow, every year, he shook off his soldier self and became a civilian again and it felt real. He had adjusted to the rhythm of being called back once a year, to his brothers, to his second family. But now he was being called back every night, every few hours.

Each morning, he tried to take hold of this good life again. His wife Liron, his three children, his students. He tried to reclaim this good life and make it feel real. But each night it fell away like an illusion and he was back in that room again. It was always Friday night, right after Barak, Itzik, and Maor made it back to the house. Without injury, except for Itzik's cheek wound. The enemy had an approximate idea of where the platoon was now. They were probing for the exact house.

Enemy gunmen fired into the house two doors down. The walls shook as they tossed in a *mit'an*, a makeshift bomb. The men wanted to return fire, but Maor and Doron motioned for them to lay still. A machine gun fired into the adjacent house. A *mit'an* exploded in the yard outside. Still, no fire through their windows. Doron prayed that Effy Cohen, stationed at the window closest to the yard, would somehow know not to return fire. Silence. Doron remained motionless, only his lips moving as he prayed.

He knew it was going to be a long night. He didn't know that it was going to be endless.

CHAPTER 2 The Events of Jebaliah

Doron grew up in Bat Yam, Tel Aviv's southern suburb. He was the second of four children. His parents arrived in Israel in 1954, his father from Morocco, his mother from Egypt. His father had studied in a yeshivah in Morocco, but abandoned his studies to become active in the secular *Shomer Hatzair* youth movement and the Moroccan *Aliyah*. His mother, a teacher, thought of herself as secular in the early years but always kept a kosher home. With each passing year, Doron's family became more observant. To Doron, this gradual process of *tshuvah* felt very natural. It began with his education in a religious elementary school and gained momentum as he grew older.

Doron saw more of his father than most children. A policeman, he worked part-time as a security guard on school trips. By the time Doron was a teenager, their Bat Yam neighborhood began to change for the worse. His parents worked long overtime hours to move to a better neighborhood and pay for Doron's yeshivah studies. Sometimes, his father's overtime hours actually worked out well for Doron and his friends. When he worked as a security guard at the local soccer games, they could always count on good seats.

Doron's maternal grandfather, Saba Nissim, was tall and built like an ox. In Egypt, he was a longshoreman on the docks of Cairo. He was from a secular family and never learned to read or write Hebrew. In Israel, where he worked as a janitor, he never mastered the language beyond the point of a few phrases. But none of that interfered with the powerful connection that Doron felt with Saba Nissim.

Izzayak, Saba? Doron would greet him in Egyptian Arabic. Saba Nissim would answer in a mixture of Hebrew and Arabic, *Hamdulilla, Baruch Hashem, Mabsuut.* Praise be to G-d (Arabic), may G-d be praised (Hebrew), I am happy (Arabic). Doron could clearly sense Saba Nissim's strong faith even though they had little by way of common vocabulary.

In later years, when Saba Nissim passed away, Doron wrote a small book for his children telling the story of Saba Nissim's life. During the *shivah*, the week of mourning, he collected stories from relatives.

One story involved Saba Nissim's exploits in Egypt. After the second World War, he took up a collection of blankets and other necessities for the penniless Jewish refugees from Europe who huddled in the Central Synagogue of Cairo awaiting entry to Palestine. Some of the wealthier Cairene Jews gave willingly. Those who did not, gave unknowingly. Saba Nissim would sneak around to their backyards and take as a donation whatever happened to be hanging on their clothes line. His friends called him the 'Jewish Robin Hood of Cairo'.

Doron was in tenth grade in 1984 when Operation Moses, the first mass rescue of Ethiopia's Jews, took place. Two apartment buildings in his neighborhood quickly filled with Ethiopian immigrants. Every day on his way home from yeshivah he'd see Ethiopians of all ages milling in the parking lots looking plaintive and lost. Curious, he approached them one afternoon. One of the youngsters led Doron to his family's apartment. The family was struggling with the assembly of a do-it-yourself bed given to them by the Jewish Agency. The instructions were in Hebrew and English. Doron found a payphone and called his friends.

"Bring screw drivers and pliers," he instructed them. The younger Ethiopian children had already acquired a smattering of Hebrew, but not enough to understand the assembly instructions for the beds. Doron and his crew went from apartment to apartment, showing them with gestures how to assemble the do-it-yourself beds.

From that day on, Doron would sneak out of *Seder Erev*, the evening homework session at his yeshivah, and visit with the Ethiopians. He learned the importance of drinking *bunna*, the thick Ethiopian coffee, with the elders before tutoring the children. He and his fellow students held tutoring sessions in the building's bomb shelter. One day, the children didn't come. In the parking lot, Doron ran into eight year old Uzi and fifteen year old Asher. They were regular visitors in his house.

"What's going on? How come no one's coming to the homework sessions anymore?"

"We can't, our fathers will beat us."

"What do you mean?"

It had to do with the painful conversion issue. Although Ethiopia's Jews had steadfastly clung to their faith for over two millenia, Israel's religious establishment was requiring Ethiopian Jews to undergo symbolic conversions. The parents were afraid that the *kippah*-clad yeshivah students were there to take their children from them.

"Listen to your parents," Doron told them. He didn't want to make things worse than they already were. Eventually, the issue was resolved and the tutoring sessions resumed.

When it came time for his army service, Doron volunteered for a *Nahal* unit. The Nahal Infantry Brigade, which combined military and agricultural training, dated back to the days when the country desperately needed both farmers and soldiers. Nahal soldiers were crack infantrymen, but also spent time cultivating fields and tending greenhouses. A Nahal infantry unit would eventually become a *gar'in*, or seed. Such 'seeds' were planted in small outposts that were designated to grow, or be 'civilianized' into full fledged communities. Many thriving kibbutzim began as Nahal *gar'inim*. Doron's unit was formed on kibbutz Rosh Zurim, where they underwent their agricultural training. It was there that he met Liron, his future wife.

Doron was among those chosen from the unit to be sent on to Commander Training School. He graduated Outstanding Cadet. After Commander School, he was invited to undergo an additional round of special training. A new unit was being formed, a special Engineering Company that would be attached to an infantry battalion. It was the first such Engineering Unit in the Nahal Brigade, and was called the *Pal-Han,* the Engineering Company. This "spearhead" unit was designed to go ahead of the general infantry to sweep for mines, put bridges in place, and remove obstacles.

With the outbreak of violence in the late eighties, keeping the peace took precedence over agriculture for many Nahal units. In 1989, Doron was assigned to serve as a squad leader in a unique Nahal company of soldiers with an artistic bent. Itamar, the Company Commander, was a gifted painter. Doron's best friend Moti was a clarinetist. Doron himself was the poet of the group.

The unit was assigned to a tiny outpost in the center of Jebaliah, a teeming refugee camp in the Gaza Strip that erupted daily into spasms of violence. It was hell on earth. Open sewage ditches crisscrossed the dense neighborhoods and giant rats rummaged leisurely through mounds of garbage. A wire fence was all that separated the tiny Nahal outpost from the camp's 50,000 hostile inhabitants.

The soldiers soon became familiar with the inhabitants of the neighborhood surrounding the outpost. After a few weeks, the locals knew each soldier by name. Doron studied his new neighbors with the same fascination as that with which he had studied successive waves of new immigrants in Bat Yam.

The older men in the neighborhood sat outside their low houses, drinking tea and playing backgammon. Behind their backs their fingers worked meticulously, counting their *masbaxa* beads. Doron and his men found they had a common language with the elders. Most had worked in Israel and knew Hebrew. From Saba Nissim, Doron had a rudimentary grasp of the Egyptian Arabic spoken in Gaza. He tried to reason with the old men to keep the youths from throwing stones.

"What's the point?" he cajoled them. "They're children. They're only going to get hurt."

The elders would shrug politely and offer drinks to the soldiers. One of them, Abu Jamil, even spoke a passable Yiddish and had attended many weddings in Israel. *Voos ken men tun*, he would answer in Yiddish. Nothing to be done.

Doron was struck by Abu Jamil's uncanny resemblance to Saba Nissim. Saba Nissim with a *kafiyyeh*, he mused. They spoke alike too, that same Egyptian dialect.

When on leave in Bat Yam, Doron would often share stories from his service in Gaza with Saba Nissim. After pondering each story, Saba Nissim always summed up the experience with one of his two-word phrases. *Kabdehu v'Chashdehu*. The accumulated ambivalence of twenty-odd centuries spent as guests in neighboring lands. "Show respect, but never turn your back."

Doron had long conversations with Itamar on the nature of hatred. How can these small children hate us without knowing us? At least with the elders, Doron and his soldiers could discuss practical matters. The mechanics of existence. Doron wanted to believe that their rapport was genuine, but then again, the children's hatred must have come from somewhere. Did the situation breed the hatred, or did the hatred breed the situation? The educational system in Gaza was foreign to him. In his yeshivah studies, he had always been taught that question marks were more important than exclamation points. He and his friends were constantly questioning everything: their teachers, the scriptures, themselves. But here, as he passed by the local schools on patrol, he saw that learning took place by rote. When searching through students' knapsacks for weapons, he would often find pictures of Israeli soldiers impaled by bloody daggers.

He showed one of the notebooks to Itamar. "Can you believe this stuff?"

Itamar seemed to understand. "If you were in their situation, would you behave any differently?"

A severely retarded twelve year old took to spending long hours each day near the outpost gate. For lack of a better name, the soldiers called him Jimmy. The sentries watched him outside the compound every day, rummaging through the garbage in search of food. He liked the finely chopped Israeli salads, which he scooped out of the dumpster and ate with his hands. It was hard to watch. The soldiers asked Doron for permission to leave him hot meals. The company quickly adopted the young boy. Jimmy was the only local who was allowed to approach the outpost. The soldiers always had something for him. Whenever a care package arrived from home, the soldiers would set aside treats for Jimmy. As the months went by, he became more and more significant to the isolated young men. For a few minutes each day, they felt human. He became the company icon. One of the soldiers, a caricaturist, drew a sketch of Jimmy which was emblazoned on T-shirts for the entire unit.

Doron knew that someone was taking care of the boy, for twice a day Jimmy would reappear in clean clothes. Once, he followed Jimmy home from the base and met his mother. He learned the boy's real name. It was Anwar. *Majnoon, majnoon. Min Allah*, she pointed to her head. Crazy. From God.

At the next company briefing, Itamar warned the troops to stay away from the retarded child and to not let him near the compound. The soldiers reacted in an uproar. Jimmy was an exception, they protested. Should he be punished for the actions of others? Was that humane?

"It's for his own good," Itamar said. "They mentioned him specifically at the last intelligence briefing. It hasn't escaped the notice of certain parties that he's allowed to get close to the base. We've received an alert that he's about to be wired with explosives."

There was silence as the message sank in. Doron felt himself about to be sick and left the room. Thereafter, the soldiers left Jimmy's food in a spot far from the base and threw him candies from the jeep as they drove by. They could see him from a distance, whimpering.

When riots broke out, Jimmy would plant himself in between the stone throwers and the soldiers. "*Salaam, salaam!*" he would cry. Peace. Peace. Often rocks hit him, and he doubled over. But Doron never saw him cry. After one particularly violent demonstration, Jimmy remained in a fetal position on the ground after the crowd had dispersed. The company medic wanted to examine him for injuries, but Jimmy refused to let the medic touch him.

Next to the tiny outpost was a multistory UN Refugee Welfare Association (UNRWA) warehouse that housed, among other things, pharmaceuticals and toxic chemicals. Youths stole into the warehouse and tossed bottles of acid and other harsh chemicals onto the outpost from the upper windows. Sweeping up the shards of glass became a daily chore. From the nearby orchards, youths darted out to toss firebombs over the outpost gate and then quickly took cover in the orchard. The firebombs would land on the tiny volleyball court in the outpost, exploding into flames on the asphalt.

Itamar warned the owners of the orchards. "Keep the teenagers out of there. If there are more firebombs, we'll have no choice but to remove the trees."

"Cut off my hands, just don't cut my trees," one of the old men said. The orchard had been in the family for over two hundred years. But the firebombings continued, and bulldozers arrived to clear the orchard back to beyond the distance from which a firebomb could be thrown. Two elderly women and one old man lay down in front of the bulldozers. The local youths looked on with contempt. Doron and his soldiers wept together with the old men and women. There was something about the destruction of an ancient orchard that tore deep into his soul. He felt a pervading sense of futility. They knew they were punishing the innocent. Doron tried to remind himself that it was self-defense, but it didn't change how he felt. Forty meters of trees were uprooted.

Back then it was firebombs. The firebombs could do serious damage, and more than one took a toll on Doron's soldiers. One soldier, Mario, suffered third degree burns on his hands when a firebomb exploded near him. But as bad as the firebombs were, it was an era of relative innocence. The use of rifles and grenades was extremely rare.

The soldiers learned to identify the 'sharks', the inciters who fomented the crowds. The sharks had subtle ways of working a crowd into a frenzy while at the same time using it for cover. They were often masked. After the sharks had gotten a crowd going, one of them would dart out in front, throw a firebomb, and then disappear within the throng.

"They're all going to be sorry they met me," averred Udi, the Lieutenant

Company Commander. "So will most of you." He took great pains to stake out his reputation as the toughest warrior in the Gaza Strip. He professed unbridled contempt for Doron's openly empathic nature. He called him *xnoon*. Wimp. "You're yellow. You'll see what your bleeding heart will get you."

But it didn't take long for the chinks to appear in Udi's gruff exterior. He had a way of making money mysteriously appear in the bank accounts of less fortunate soldiers. Doron would overhear conversations between Udi and the *Mashakit Tash*, the company personnel clerk. "Deposit this in Yakov's army bank account. He has a tough situation back home. Tell him it's a bonus from the army for soldiers serving in Gaza." Udi's father was a wealthy building contractor. Whenever a group of soldiers stopped anywhere for food, Udi always insisted on picking up the tab.

During one violent riot, Udi spotted what he was sure was the main inciter.

"*Wallah*, I caught the shark. Look at that guy. He's definitely the main one. I'm going after him." A tall, heavyset, bearded man, thirty five or forty, was by far the most animated of the rioters. He was holding a bicycle at arms' length above his head and was shaking it in the air. He seemed uncertain where to throw it. In the end he threw it on the rioters next to him.

"Are you sure about that one, Udi?" Doron asked him. Something looked wrong about him. The hatred in the eyes of the other rioters was unmistakable. But this man seemed randomly wild. His movements were frenzied and chaotic. He didn't seem to be focused on any one object in particular.

After Udi brought him in, it quickly became clear that the man, Abu Lutfi, was severely disturbed. At first he spat at the soldiers and tried to bite them. His body convulsed violently. After Udi gave him a cup of water, he calmed down.

Doron was amazed at Udi's tenderness with the prisoner. Udi even spoke a passable Arabic.

"Listen, Abu Lutfi," he explained to him slowly. "Whenever soldiers bring you in here, there are two words that I want you to say. '*Ayfo Udi*?' Where is Udi? Then the soldiers will come and get me and I'll explain to them that you're not dangerous. OK? Can you say those two words for me?"

"*Ayfo Udi*". Abu Lutfi grinned broadly.

"Excellent. You'll be fine." Udi sent Abu Lutfi on his way.

As far as Doron was concerned, Udi's cover was blown.

* * *

Near the end of his stay in Jebaliah, Doron and his patrol caught a hail of rocks from a group of stonethrowers. Doron, with his wiry build and long legs, quickly took the lead as they raced after the group. He zeroed in on the leader of the gang. The man sprinted towards an alley. It was now or never. Doron leaped and tackled him by the legs. As Doron struggled to keep hold of his quarry's legs, the man reached into his *jalabiyyah*, his flowing robe, and pulled out a kitchen knife. Doron grabbed his hand, keeping the knife at bay. The other soldiers, who had caught up by now, fired in the air. The man appeared to surrender, but then grabbed for Doron's rifle. Doron retained his grip. After the attacker was subdued, Doron's soldiers wanted to pummel him. Doron wouldn't hear of it.

"He's our responsibility now. You all know the rules."

"But he was going to kill you!" they protested. Doron began tying the prisoner's hands.

"Don't tie him!" One of the soldiers yelled. "We know you. Then you won't let us touch him at all."

Itamar had lectured them often on the subject of *Tohar Neshek*, the IDF Purity of Arms ethic. "Remember," he had stressed, "You have no right to *punish* with violence. Only to *defend*."

He had a saying, "Never forget what it means to be a Jewish soldier. The significance goes far beyond that of obeying orders. Our first obligation is to act like a Jewish army."

One of the soldiers objected. "Isn't it a bit bombastic to paint ourselves as morally superior to other soldiers?"

"Take it however you want," Itamar responded. "I put it to you as an obligation, not as a badge of superiority. If anything, it's about humility. Remember: we didn't choose this situation, but the obligation to conduct ourselves as Jews is no less compulsory."

It wasn't easy, thought Doron. Hands had a tendency to take on a life of their own.

They brought the prisoner to a tent. A group of non-combat personnel were assigned to guard him until the Military Police arrived. Doron brought the prisoner food and water. His hands were still bound, so Doron held the plastic cup to his mouth as he drank. *Allah yirda aleik,* said the prisoner. May Allah watch over you. He was sobbing now. My enemy's blessing, thought Doron. Perhaps this is what Jacob felt after wrestling with his angel.

Doron returned to the Company Command Post to fill out an incident report. He later found out that the soldiers placed in charge of the prisoner had beaten the man. Doron was angry and disgusted that it had happened on his watch. He had taken great precautions to treat his would-be killer with honor. Itamar brought all of the guards up on charges. Regulations on excessive use of force were stringent. If the Border Police received a prisoner who had been beaten, they would set him loose as a lesson to the arresting soldiers. "If you think you can take the law into your own hands, then he's free to go." As a result, prisoners were treated with kid gloves. This was an egregious exception. All for naught, thought Doron. His enemy's blessing had been undone.

* * *

Doron often found himself in the role of 'stopper', that of calming down soldiers who had suffered loss and were bent on revenge. But there were times when the opposite role was thrust upon him.

It was Id Al Fitr, the last day of Ramadan, in 1990. Doron and his squad patrolled the street in a crowd control vehicle. A mob was assembling. The driver of the vehicle was a new soldier, fresh out of boot camp. Doron was perched atop the vehicle. He felt the crowd about to boil over as the mosques disgorged throngs of worshippers into the streets. As they passed by a mosque, the mob enveloped the vehicle from all sides. Best to focus on getting back to the outpost now, he decided The crowd began to rock the vehicle back and forth. Doron heard a noise behind him. A bearded man climbed up the back of the vehicle and with a shout of *Allahu Akbar* lunged for Doron's rifle. Doron spun and saw him at the last moment. There was no time to raise his rifle and shoot. As he pushed the man off the vehicle with the butt of his rifle, a large rock slammed down on him from atop the wall surrounding the mosque. The impact knocked him over. He lost consciousness. As he lay on the roof of the vehicle, rocks rained down on him from the mosque wall. He awoke, perhaps a minute later, to find himself covered by rocks of all sizes. He felt a throbbing pain in his groin.

He couldn't understand why the vehicle wasn't moving. "Drive in reverse! Drive in reverse!" he shouted into his radio microphone. Then he noticed that the microphone cable had been severed by one of the rocks.

Doron could see the crowd behind the vehicle, refusing to disperse. They were shouting "*Allahu Akbar! Allah Yixdak !!* " Allah is Great. Allah will take you. It was a throbbing chant, like drumbeats. Frozen with shock, the driver was unable to bring himself to back up into the crowd. Rioters were climbing onto the vehicle from behind. In a matter of seconds, they would all be dead. Doron fired a couple of shots past the front cabin to snap the driver out of his shock. "Drive in reverse!!" he yelled again.

The decision to back up was the hardest that Doron had yet faced. There wasn't any time to consider the pros and cons. He would have to go on instinct. The only way to come out of that crowd alive was to back up now, and people would certainly be injured if not killed. The alternative was to stay put and be killed themselves.

The driver finally threw the vehicle into reverse. Doron heard wild screams as the crowd parted. He had felt the tremendous power in crowds before, but never like this. The destructive energy of a mob was a terrible thing to behold. In concert, these people seemed animated by a superhuman strength. But once separated from the mob, as his erstwhile attacker had been when he offered him a cup of water, they became sheepish, even affable.

Speeding in reverse towards the outpost, Doron looked back towards the mob. There was blood on the pavement. Two or three people were injured, but no one had been killed. The outpost gate was blocked by rioters. There was only one way back in -- through the fence. Crowds of rioters, armed with wirecutters, were continually trying to break through the perimeter fences. Now he was going to show them how it was done. His vehicle crashed through the perimeter fence, an 18 foot high outer fence meant to keep stones from being lobbed into the compound. Then they crashed through the inner fence, a 9-foot-high barbed wire fence.

That clash in 1990 was eventually called "The Events of Jebaliah." It left four dead and 120 injured. The Nahal outpost was at the epicenter of the attack. In all, Doron spent four months in that outpost. Then his army service was over.

*   *   *

After the army, Doron pursued a degree in Education. He and Itamar, his former Company Commander, studied together as *Hevruta*, one-on-one study partners. It was important to Doron to have Itamar, who was studying to be a rabbi, as his partner. They had both grappled with the same ethical issues as soldiers. Now, together, they were able to search for the answers in the scriptures. One of Judaism's greatest sages, the *Rambam* (Maimonides), wrote extensively over eight hundred years ago on how a soldier should conduct himself in battle. In *Hilchot M'lachim* (The Laws of Kings), the Rambam wrote : "And when a man goes to war he will rely upon the Hope and Redeemer of Israel in times of strife, and shall know that he is waging war for the glorification of his Name and will place his soul in His hands and he will not fear and will think neither of his wife nor of his children but will erase their memory from his heart and will turn from all things to the battle at hand."

"Is that realistic?" Doron asked Itamar. "Is it reasonable to expect that a soldier who goes to war could put his wife and children out of his mind?" It didn't seem human.

"When you think too much about your family, how much good are you to your buddies?" Itamar argued. "If a soldier is fighting for the entire People of Israel, he has to be at the top of his game."

To Doron, about to be married, the edict seemed severe. "If someone else had written this, I would have said the guy either had marital problems or had never gone to war, " he said to Itamar. But the Rambam's message was clear. "And anyone who ponders too much the dangers of war breaks this commandment, for the people of Israel depend upon their army."

Doron continued. "The Rambam may have known persecution in the twelfth century, but did he know war as we know it?. And besides, he was a physician. Did he ever go to war as a father and husband, like we do?"

"Maybe not," said Itamar. "But still, he has a point about not dwelling too much on the dangers of war."

"I guess." Doron could often feel such preoccupations distracting him in the army when he allowed his mind to roam free. But he doubted that he would ever be able to separate himself from thoughts of his family, once he had one. His parents had poured their entire lives into him and his siblings. He planned to do the same.

CHAPTER 3 The Pokemon Soldiers

After Doron and Liron were married, he accepted a position as resident counselor and teacher of Jewish Law at the Yemin Orde Youth Village, an idyllic community of some 500 teenagers and staff perched high atop Mount Carmel. The vast majority of his students were immigrants, primarily Ethiopian and Russian, who had either arrived without their parents or whose home situations were problematic. A handful were native *Tzabarim*.

The Ethiopians considered him one of their own. His humble, reserved nature fit the contours of their own culture. They felt that they could speak with him freely. Each year, in the Spring, Doron would hold a special class for his male high school seniors on the subject of their upcoming military service.

Meir was the undisputed leader of the Ethiopian upperclassmen. In the classroom, he worked hard to emulate the nonchalance of his flip *Tzabar* classmates. Now, in the Army Preparation Class, Meir played the contrarian. "Look, I'm not against being in a combat unit or contributing to the country," he said, "But I have nine brothers and sisters at home, and sick parents." Being a *jobnik*, a non-combat soldier, would allow him to work nights and help out his family. He didn't see how joining a combat unit, which would entail weeks away from home, was feasible for him..
"I just want you to know what options exist," said Doron.

That night, Meir stopped by Doron's house with Berhanu, another Ethiopian student. Despite the obstacles, they were giving serious thought to joining a combat unit. Doron was their idol, and they knew that he had been in the Nahal Brigade. Berhanu had other concerns. He was very religious, and was concerned that joining a combat unit might compromise his religious practices.

"My experience has been just the opposite," said Doron. "In civilian life, I usually pray alone. In the army, I always pray in a *minyan* when there is one. I just find myself needing that feeling of community. In civilian life, I usually pray quickly. In the army, I find myself praying much more slowly and thoroughly, dwelling on each word. Take *Slichot*, for example."

Slichot, penitential prayers, are recited during the month leading up to the Jewish New Year. The custom of religious Sephardi Jews is to arise in the middle of the night to do their accounting with G-d. In civilian life, Doron didn't always make it to synagogue in the early morning to pray *Slichot*. But when *Slichot* fell during his army service, he arose fastidiously every morning at 3:30 to pray.

"I think you just demand more from yourself in the army in all respects," he said to Berhanu. "It's just the mode you fall into. You demand more from yourself physically, so it just seems natural to demand more from yourself spiritually."

"I really would like to join a combat unit," said Meir. "What do you think I should do?"

"It's an important thing to take upon yourself if you're able," Doron told him. "I want you to feel that you're the equal of anyone in this country." He saw in Meir the potential for leadership. He wanted him to have the pride that comes from having given, and not just having received.

Doron's hunch proved correct. Meir and his Ethiopian classmates formed the first Ethiopian *gar'in* in the Nahal Brigade. Doron kept tabs on them through his army contacts. At each stage of their training, he received glowing reports from their commanding officers.

Each year, when Doron left for *Milu'im*, his annual month of reserve duty, his absence was felt far beyond his immediate family. He was deeply involved in all aspects of his students' lives. Some were battling addictions. Some were recovering from abuse. He had only one rule with his students. He agreed to share his innermost feelings with them, without embellishment, and in return expected them to do the same. All turned to Doron as a gentle but unwavering source of support.

He was called up for *Milu'im* in November, 2000. The peace talks had just collapsed. There was sporadic violence, but no clear sense of where things were headed. Doron was vague with his parents about this *Milu'im*. He told them that it was an infantry exercise in the south. To Liron, he was constitutionally incapable of lying. But he wasn't specific. "We'll be in the Jordan Valley, " he told her. He didn't tell her that he would be headed to Jericho.

The timing was bad. Doron and his students had spent months preparing a *Sigd* celebration, the traditional Ethiopian Fall gathering. They planned a procession, composed prayers for a special service, and even wrote a play. There would be a traditional Ethiopian meal and a recreated Ethiopian village in the gymnasium, complete with a *gojjo*, an Ethiopian hut, and a well at the center of the village. Amir Zohar, the Company Commander of Doron's reserve unit, granted Doron leave to attend the ceremony. He asked only that Doron come along for a quick walk-through so they could survey the situation together.

Doron was First Sergeant and Squad Leader in his unit and functioned as the lieutenant commander of his platoon. He always arrived one day before the rest of the troops, together with the other officers and squad leaders.

They assembled in Jerusalem. Amir suggested that they drive down to Jericho to get a feel for the terrain. He and Doron drove together. The Mountains of Edom rose like a dreamy watercolor sketch beyond the Dead Sea as they drove down the descent from Jerusalem into the serenity of the Judaean desert.

"I hope this doesn't end up being a *fadicha*," Amir said. An embarrassment. A non-combat assignment. "Looks like they're bringing us down here for a *Tiyyul Shabbat*." A leisurely Sabbath outing. The rest of the staff followed behind in their rented army vehicles.

"Would an *easy Milu'im* be such a bad thing?" Doron wondered aloud. "A little rest wouldn't kill us." The previous *Milu'im* had begun in Gaza and ended with long manhunts in Jenin. Amir requested the assignment in Jenin. He knew that's where the company would end up if war broke out. He stressed to the staff how important it was for them to get to know Jenin like the back of their hand. He took them on numerous patrols in Jenin, and they became acquainted with the name of every neighborhood and alleyway.

Amir's thoroughness was exasperating at first, but soon everyone grew to depend on it. Doron drew confidence from the certainty that Amir's analytic mind was constantly thinking around corners, searching out chinks in their defenses. Amir's slim build and gentle demeanor belied his true measure as a commander. He was bold, charismatic, and overflowing with optimism. Some considered him a paradox: he was both a brilliant military tactician and vocal advocate for peace. But Doron grasped Amir's essence. He understood the common thread that ran through all of Amir's varied endeavors. Whether he was bringing souls closer together or protecting them from one another, Amir simply didn't believe in leaving things to chance. He was as thorough and proactive about peace as he was about war.

Amir grew up on Kibbutz Gal-On, between Ashkelon and Jerusalem.

He had a great love of Nature, and spent much of his childhood hiking the goat trails and terraced hillsides of the area. After the army, he settled in Jerusalem. He built a dynamic housewares business, but felt the need for a challenge beyond economic success. At age 30, he sought his path in education, becoming the Director of a Community Center in Jerusalem's tough East Talpiyot neighborhood. He cultivated excellent relations with the *Muchtar* of Sur Baher, the neighboring Arab Village. He and the *Muchtar* focused on the practical rather than political details of coexistence. How can we organize a soccer match between the children of Sur Baher and those of Talpiyot? How can the children of Sur Baher participate in courses at the Community Center? They became fast friends. When the violence broke out in the Fall of 2000, Sur Baher remained peaceful. Both Amir and the *Muchtar* hoped that ultimately the storm would pass over the island of peace that they had created.

Amir always stayed on the sidelines of political discussions within the unit. He refereed many a debate, but never injected his own opinions. If someone voiced an extreme position, one way or the other, he always played devil's advocate. Everyone knew what his political orientation was, but he scrupulously kept it out of play.

The small motorcade arrived at a Border Police base outside of Jericho. Amir wanted to begin the assignment in daylight, but the orders kept on changing, based on ever-changing notifications from intelligence. Something was brewing in Jericho. Finally, in late afternoon, they set out for a tiny Nahal outpost called Elisha, a few miles north up the Jordan Valley road.

Outpost Elisha hadn't been 'civilianized'. Perhaps it never would be. Although it was in Area C, the Israeli-controlled section of the Jordan Valley, the outbreak of violence in November 2000 made it a hot target for attacks.

Elisha had a smattering of vegetable fields and a rudimentary military base. Someone had painted a bright welcome across the entrance to the base. "Nahal Elisha: The Gates of the Garden of Eden are Opening Before You." The humor didn't sit well with Amir. "What's that supposed to mean?" he asked.

"Come on, lighten up." Doron smiled at the double entendre. He pondered the change that had come over him now that he was a *Milu'imnik*, a reservist, with a family. We don't laugh at the same things any more, he thought. The morbid humor that kept them laughing as regular soldiers didn't strike them as funny any more. Even the smallest thing took on a new meaning now.

An unexpected reunion awaited Doron at the base. Meir and his classmates from the Youth Village, now a Nahal unit, were stationed at Elisha. They were headed out on foot patrol. They hugged and kissed Doron in the traditional Ethiopian manner, glancing their cheeks against his three times on each side. This was the first time that Doron had seen Meir and his classmates as soldiers. He brought them over to meet Amir.

"I've heard some great things about you guys," said Amir. There was no time for conversation. Darkness was approaching and Amir was in a hurry to survey the base. Doron arranged to meet his students later that night and catch up. They would be leaving for a new assignment the following day.

"Looks like you guys have yourselves a summer camp here!" Doron joked in parting. Meir immediately became serious, and warned Doron not to be lulled by the apparent calm. "Doron, you have to be really careful here," he said. "It's hot. *Real* hot."
How fast they've grown up, thought Doron. But they're still only boys.

The Outpost Commander was a young lieutenant, fresh out of Officer's Training School. He couldn't be more than twenty, thought Doron. Amir was surprised to find someone so young in command of the base. They quickly surveyed the base in the remaining light. Amir pointed out a gap in the sand embankment on the outskirts of the base. "See that point? The breach in the embankment? It's the only decent vantage point in this outpost. It's also the most dangerous. I'm going to get some bulldozers in here tomorrow to create some decent defensive positions." The gap had been put in place to allow a tank to maneuver out through the embankment. Because the embankment was five feet high, one could peer out at the breach point without lying down, getting a better view of the territory outside the base. But this was the danger. A well-aimed sniper bullet could find its way between the top of the embankment and one's helmet. The outpost had no real watch tower. The closest thing was the roof of the bomb shelter, but even there one had to lie down and the view wasn't very good.

Darkness. Amir left for the Border Police base with the Staff Sergeant to receive the operational instructions. He drove his army issue Peugot 205. It wasn't bulletproof.

All of a sudden, the outpost came under fire. Doron could see the tracer bullets coming at them from the direction of Jericho. Everyone ran to his position. Doron's heart skipped a beat as he saw Meir head straight for the breach point. He wished that Meir would be a little bit less courageous. Just enough to stay alive. Those who could, returned fire. Suddenly, Doron had a sinking feeling. "Who has Amir's cell phone number?" he called out. No one did. A minute later, Amir called. He spoke in a whisper. "We're OK. They might be aiming at us, I can't tell. We're under good cover though, don't worry."

A tank was stationed in the outpost. It rolled up its ramp to take aim at the source of fire, but the report from the Tank Commander was disappointing.

"They're holed up on the far side of a tiny hill. I don't have a straight shot on them." The parched, wrinkled earth surrounding Jericho allowed the enemy gunmen to get close to the base and still remain under cover. Extremely close, thought Doron. Close enough to lob a grenade.

The fire was unrelenting and precise. It wasn't the impulsive, random crackling of Kalashnikovs. These were the disciplined single shots of professional snipers. Throughout the firefight, the *Pal-Han* staff spread themselves around the base to best get a sense of its defenses. Asi, the Executive Officer, stayed in the Operations Room to monitor reports from the Observation Post high above them in the mountains overlooking the Jordan Valley. Doron stayed close to the Base Commander.

Around midnight, the shooting stopped. Amir drove back from the Border Police base. He was fuming. "We're sitting ducks here. This outpost is wide open. This base would have been fine ten years ago, pre-Oslo, but now the other side has rifles. The rules of the game are different." Before July 2000, the enemy had rarely used rifles in attacking Israeli targets. Now it was becoming commonplace.

" I'd probably have asked for an authorization to attack," said Amir. In this situation, he explained, the best course of action would be to have a tank attack straight on, and then flank the enemy with infantry. He dismissed such a plan as wishful thinking. In the uncertain geopolitics of November 2000, it would never have been approved.

"It would mean entering Area A. We're allowed hot pursuit into area A, but only with the authorization of a Regimental Commander. This probably wouldn't seem reason enough to stir up a political storm."

Tomorrow, he would begin his program of base improvements. "Best to just improve the fortifications and not be bothered by them," he said. Amir wanted a bulldozer to level the area around the base and to builder higher, stronger, positions to fire from. As it was right now, the only fortifications surrounding the outpost were a few sand hills.

"Still, I wish we could be more proactive here," he said. Amir felt strongly about taking control of situations. "The worst thing is to be passive. The worst thing is to wait." Amir congratulated the young lieutenant and his soldiers. They had acquitted themselves well under fire.

Doron made notes as to which paths in the outpost were vulnerable. He jotted down some reminders to himself to not let non-combat personnel near the vulnerable paths, and where to station troops in the event of another attack.

As he entered the Operations Room, a report was coming over the radio from the observation post. "There's a group of five uniformed gunmen headed your way. They've just left the Police Station. They're in the vineyard next to it. They fired at you before from behind the deserted white building next to the vineyard ….wait….OK….they're on the move again. They're roughly 150 yards away from you right now."

They waited until midnight, but the next attack never materialized. The *Pal-Han* staff decided to call it a night. They all slept in the same room. The showers were on the other side of the base, and they debated whether or not it was worth the trip.

"Forget it, let's get some sleep," said Amir. "Tomorrow the troops will be here. We'll need our rest."

Yair, the Lieutenant Company Commander, laughed. "If I know you, you'll be too busy to even take your shoes off tomorrow." It was true, Doron thought. Amir was the ultimate detail freak. They all took great comfort in that fact.

The conversation drifted on to children. Amir had four-year-old twins, a boy and a girl, and his oldest son had just celebrated his sixth birthday. Amir recounted with great satisfaction the birthday party that he had organized for his son and his friends. His wife Orly, a Nature Guide, shared his passion for hiking in the wild. For the birthday party, they took the group of children on a hike to the deserted village of Liftah, on the terraced hills sloping down from Jerusalem.

"So how many kids are you up to now?" Amir asked Doron. They were close friends in Milu'im but somehow never kept in close touch in their civilian lives. At that time Doron had two children, and Liron was pregnant with their third. But it was only one month into the pregnancy, and Doron hadn't even told his parents yet. He debated whether to say 'Two' or 'Two with one on the way'.

"Two."

"You're lagging behind a bit, aren't you?" Amir kidded. " Shouldn't a religious fellow your age have five or six already?"

"Don't worry, we're working on it."

Amir wasn't an outwardly religious man, but he related to Doron how excited he was that his son would be receiving his first Bible in school. He had deliberated for days on the inscription that he would write. "I pray you'll know how to extract from this book the values found within it," he finally wrote.

Doron and Amir awoke at 8:00 the next day. Midday by army standards. Doron went to pray in a small trailer that served as a chapel. A few soldiers were leaving as he arrived, their rifles and velvet prayer bags in hand. Facing the Judaean Hills to the west, he prayed *Shaharit*, the Morning Prayers.

His mind wandered back to the previous night. He had been a soldier for fifteen years now, but this was his first time under concentrated fire. He mused over Amir's words, *Tiyul Shabbat*. A cakewalk. No, it's definitely not what we thought it would be. But Amir had everything under control. Whatever it was that he, Doron, was feeling now, however tinged with adrenaline, it still wasn't fear.

Amir was leisurely waking up when Doron returned. He stretched. "*This* is how I like to start the day", he yawned. Then they were off on yet another tour of the base. They compiled more lists. Requests to make of Upper Command. Issues to bring up in the first company assembly later that day. Amir urged the squad leaders to be particularly thorough. "Don't be bashful, guys. We're going to be here for a month. I'll do my best to get everything you ask for."

By one o'clock, all of the troops had arrived. Some came on the military bus but most brought their own cars. Amir and Doron drove north a few miles to a roadblock at the entrance to Jericho. The roadblock was there to prevent unauthorized locals from entering Area C, which was under Israeli control, but also to prevent Israelis from entering area A, which was not. Not long before, two unsuspecting reservists had taken a wrong turn into the Area A town of Ramallah. They were surrounded by a mob and lynched. According to intelligence, any Israeli in Jericho could expect the same fate.

Doron couldn't fathom the notion of Israelis seeking to enter Area A. "Do you really think there are Israelis who want to enter Jericho?" he asked.

"Just because someone's an idiot doesn't mean he needs to die," said Amir. " If people are stupid enough to risk their lives over cheaper vegetables, then it's our job to protect them."

The roadblock was located at a dip in the road, vulnerable to fire from the surrounding hills. Far from ideal, thought Doron.

Amir arrived at the roadblock. He frowned as he took in the situation. He scanned the area with his binoculars for a few minutes, lingering particularly on the hostile Police Officers Training School, less than three hundred meters to the east, in Area A.

"That's not good. There are a few hundred officers in training there. If they attack the roadblock, it would take us at least five minutes to get here from the outpost, more if they send a second force to pin us down with fire."

Amir sank deep in thought. To avoid any doubt, Doron registered his opinion. "I feel pretty exposed here."

Amir had it worked out. "There's only one way this is going to work. I'm radioing Battalion Command for a jeep of spotters up on that hill." He pointed to the highest hill in Area C. "It's not ideal, the good hills are in Area A. But they'll be equipped with night vision, and at least they'll be able to see any force headed this way. Then we'll have an ambush in wait over there," he pointed to a spot closer to the Police Officers Training School. "If they get any ideas about attacking the roadblock, we'll be waiting."

Doron was visibly relieved.

"Just don't get complacent," said Amir. " There's an intelligence alert about a possible car bomb."

Amir assigned a detachment of seven soldiers to man the roadblock. Doron chose mainly "veterans", reservists in their mid-to-late thirties, for the assignment. He needed their level-headedness and maturity, both in dealing with the civilians at the roadblock as well as for whatever else might be in store that night.

Doron got in the jeep. *Lehitraot.* See you later. He was about to step on the gas when he realized that he had forgotten something major. He knew the radio frequency on which to contact Amir, but didn't know his code name.

"What am I supposed to call you on the radio?" he asked.

"I don't know, just make something up for now. Use *KodKod Panter* if you want." Head Panther.

Doron allowed himself a quiet laugh. Amir could certainly be as fierce in battle as any panther, but he lacked the bloodlust. He was sensitive and practical, a basketball coach and nature lover. There was power in his gaze, but it was a strength born of peace. In his smile, there was great serenity. He radiated calm and confidence to all around him. Perhaps a lion, thought Doron. Definitely not a panther.

"*Yihyeh B'Seder,*" said Amir. It'll be OK.

Words took on a different meaning when pronounced by Amir. Coming from most Israelis, the phrase *Yihyeh B'Seder* signified a polite form of dismissal: 'Enough already. Stop asking questions. ' Coming from Amir, it retained its original meaning. It meant that every possible detail had been taken care of and that the future could be approached with confidence. Coming from him, it was an insurance policy.

At 5:00 pm, Doron met with the four soldiers who would be lying in ambush. They were army regulars with fancy new equipment. Their sniper rifles were particularly impressive, with sophisticated sights. They worked out some common points of reference for radio communications, and agreed upon signals should they be required to approach each other in the dark. The Officers' Training School in Area A would be called the "White House". The main road would be the 12 o'clock reference point.

The spotters in the jeep arrived. They were from an Armored Recon unit. Giants, each one of them, thought Doron. He felt reassured. The security arrangements that Amir put in place gave him a sense of confidence. Things had been taken care of.

At 6:50 pm, an Israeli vehicle arrived from the North. There were journalists inside, Israeli employees of a foreign newspaper. The car bomb warning had the soldiers tense. They trained their rifles on the nervous passengers. They passengers stared back, irritated and hostile. The search of the car was particularly thorough. "Sorry", Doron told the driver. "No entry permits for Israelis right now into Jericho." An afterthought. "Just out of curiosity…why do you want to go into Jericho? What's going on?"

"We heard they're firing on Outpost Elisha."

Doron hadn't heard anything, nor had he seen any tracer bullets. He could see the outpost clearly from the roadblock. Nothing. He radioed the Operations Room, and asked if there had been any shots fired.

"Nope. All's quiet here."

Doron thought for a minute. He remembered well the "press invitations" of his days in Gaza. But things were infinitely more serious now. It wasn't teenagers with stones and molotov cocktails anymore. The enemy was now organized and well-armed.

"Get ready then," Doron advised. " They've already invited the press."

Doron turned back to the journalists in the car. "Where did you hear about the shooting?"

The passengers were impatient and angry. They bristled with contempt. "What do you mean where did we hear about it? We heard about it."

Doron turned them back. "It's for your own sakes."

They turned around, drove a few hundred yards, and then turned off the main road onto a dirt path through a field. Their headlights bobbed up and down as they sped over the bumpy path towards Jericho. It wasn't hard to circumvent the roadblock.

One of the soldiers pointed towards the car as it entered Jericho. "Look, Doron. We're just decoration here. Are we really supposed to believe that a terrorist would drive past this roadblock on his way out of Jericho? "

"It's their problem now." Doron responded. "They're adults. We've warned them. They're responsible for their own safety now."

Doron called Amir on one of his soldiers' cell phones. "Amir, the night vision goggles aren't working too well, I need better ones."

Amir was in the middle of briefing the new arrivals.. "I'm tied up right now. I'm handing you over to Yair. He'll see to the night vision and whatever else you need."

The observation post came on the radio. "Gunmen moving from the Police Station towards Elisha." Then the shooting began.

"Everyone stay down," Amir called as the new soldiers raced to take up positions. He ran straight to the breach point. He raised his head a few inches above the embankment to get a view.

Shots rang out. He ducked back down. "I'm hit," he said quietly. Then he collapsed onto his side. A bullet had passed through his shoulder but hadn't exited. Cries of "Medic!" rang out. Soldiers dragged him from the embankment onto a stretcher and carried him to a secure spot.

Yevgeni, one of the company sharpshooters, spotted the five gunmen who had been shooting at them. They were now escaping from a gully into an ambulance that had driven out into the field to collect them. The observation post confirmed his sighting.

"Correct, the gunmen are being picked up by an ambulance. None appear to be injured."

Yevgeni saw the gunmen getting into the ambulance. Yair, the Lieutenant Company Commander and now acting Company Commander, gave the order on the radio to both Yevgeni and the Tank Commander of the outpost's lone tank. "Fire on them."
Yevgeni fired. "I hit one of them in the hand," he reported back.

The tank commander was less certain. "Are you sure about this?" he queried Yair. It was a Tank Commander's nightmare. He imagined himself on the front pages of tomorrow's newspaper as the tank who fired on an ambulance. He hoped Yair would reconsider.

As often happened, the enemy's use of ambulances as personnel carriers created so much confusion that by the time decisions were made, the ambulance was far from the field of battle. It was a game. Ambulances were off limits. The observation post came on the radio again. "They're headed into Jericho now. Better make up your minds."

"I'm sure, " said Yair. "Fire. Fire already."

A voice came on the radio. "No one in my theater of operations fires on an ambulance. No one. Period. Over and out." No one was sure exactly who it was, but there was no doubt that the voice belonged to an authority much further up the chain of command. The Tank Commander backed down the ramp

From the roadblock, Doron heard the medic radioing for a doctor.

"There's a *flower* in the house, apparently *KodKod.*" "Flower" was the code word for "wounded". As the Magen David Adom ambulance sped towards the base, Doron heard the doctor ask the medic if a helicopter would be needed. He couldn't make out the response.

The observation post came on the radio again. "Nine gunmen headed towards the roadblock, in three groups of three. It looks like an exercise in squad formation. Very orderly."

Concentrate. Doron tried to focus on the immediate threat. Amir had seen to everything. Things would turn out all right. He and his detachment took up positions behind the cement blocks of the roadblock. "No one lifts his head above the blocks," he instructed. "Just eyes and helmet. Nothing more."

In spite of the force advancing in their direction, everyone's thoughts were on Amir. The soldiers listened intently to their radios for word from the outpost. Doron cautioned them to keep the noise level down. "If you're going to listen to the communications, use earphones." He listened together with Miki, the soldier next to him.

A few minutes later, he heard the doctor on the radio informing the Regiment Commander that he wouldn't need a helicopter.

"Yesh!" Miki whispered in a hushed cry of joy. "No helicopter. He's going to be all right."

In any other context, it would have seemed an oddly disconnected remark. But Miki, like everyone else in the company, was the product of Amir's pragmatic but fervent brand of optimism. Expect the best and prepare for the worst. Doron immediately sensed that there was no cause for celebration. A heaviness overtook him. He tried desperately to concentrate on the immediate threat, the nine gunmen headed towards the roadblock. Then a voice came over the radio. *"Kodkod harduff."* The *harduff*, Hebrew for Oleander. A flower prized for its beauty. Like most code words, it began with the same Hebrew letter as the word it denoted. *Harug* in Hebrew means "killed."

Put it aside. Concentrate. Doron felt himself falling into an abyss even as he strove to concentrate on the approaching gunmen. It was growing very cold. He passed from position to position, trying to bolster his soldiers. "It's true. Amir is dead. We just can't think about it now. Replacements won't be here for a while. We've got to stay alert. If you feel yourselves getting drowsy, move around."

He could see the tears streaming down their faces. "Try to save it for later. There's nothing to be done. We have to continue." He tried to look into the night goggles, but his eyes were burning and he couldn't see. He put the goggles down. Then he remembered. These were the only night goggles that worked. He raised them to his eyes again and forced himself to see out into the night.

Doron made frequent contact with the soldiers in the ambush and the spotters in the jeep, those that Amir had put in place. "You guys OK?" He found himself wanting to make contact with them every few minutes, just to check that they were still in place.

A flashing light identified the roadblock for the benefit of approaching motorists. A little too convenient for the gunmen, Doron thought. He moved the light a number of yards away in case enemy snipers were planning to use it as a point of reference. The road was illuminated by street lamps at thirty-meter intervals. One of the soldiers suggested shooting out the street lamps to make the roadblock less visible.

"If we can't turn those damn things off, let's shoot them out."

Doron looked up at the lamps. They seemed far enough away.

"No. There's no need to destroy property."

Doron tried again to make contact with the ambush team on the radio. No response. He hadn't heard shots, but he needed to know that they were out there. They were only 100 meters away. He crawled over to them, just to make sure. He gave the agreed upon signal, a tearing sound as he pulled the Velcro strap on his flak jacket. They signaled back. He wondered how far away the enemy gunmen were.

The spotters were parked in their jeep on a low hill over 200 meters from the roadblock. It was the best hill that Area C had to offer. The hills in Area A towered above them. The previous week, while Meir and the other students were manning the roadblock at night, eerie fireballs came rolling down at them. It was a terrifying sight. They turned out to be burning tires. The large tractor tires still lay partially burnt on the ground by the roadblock. The smaller tires had burned to shriveled crisps.

Replacements arrived at 3:00 am. Doron took his soldiers back to the outpost. He rolled up Amir's sleeping bag and collected his things. Out by the guard post, men were sitting on the ground, sobbing. Doron assigned guard duty in twos that night. No one wanted to be alone. The Regimental Commander went to inform Amir's family.

Amir had been intimately involved in the lives of all of the soldiers in the company. He was in constant touch with those going through difficult situations, even couples undergoing fertility treatments. Whatever anyone needed, he took care of.

At the funeral, Doron was approached by a close friend of Amir's who had been asked to give the eulogy. He didn't feel that he could bring himself to read the speech without breaking down. Could Doron read it in his place? Doron scanned his notes.

"I've lost my friend in a war over these accursed lands," it began.

Amir had always said this land was holy, thought Doron. Even if we end up having to give part of it up for peace. It's holy even if we have to bid it farewell.

"I can't read these words," Doron said. "It's not how Amir felt. I'd be honored to read the eulogy, but not those words."

Amir's brother spoke of Amir's legacy of optimism. "In your death, you have bequeathed unto us a will of unbridled optimism," he said.

The *Muchtar* of Sur Baher also spoke. "I promise you, Amir, to follow the path that we both began together. I promise you, no matter what. Without preconditions. " The *Muchtar* had never been much for the party line. A few months later, riddled with bullets, he was fighting for his life after an assassination attempt.

Many of Doron's students attended Amir's funeral. They hadn't known Amir, but knew how devastated Doron was, and were there for him.

At the *shivah*, the seven days of mourning, Doron was again asked to speak. He decided against reading Psalms 83, often read over a fallen soldier. It wasn't fitting for Amir, thought Doron. It spoke of the revenge that God would wreak upon the enemies of Israel. Vengeance had always been far from Amir's heart. Were he alive, thought Doron, he would still be seeking dialogue. He was a man of peace. Victory, yes. But never revenge.

Amir's parents were secular *kibbutzniks*. Doron took the Army Rabbi aside and gently asked that he honor the sensibilities of the parents. He didn't want them to feel that the Army Rabbinate was imposing any ritual upon them. But Amir's parents deferred to Doron's judgement. "Do whatever is customary," said Amir's father.

Doron explained the significance of the *kaddish* prayer. He wanted it to have meaning for them. This had always been his bond with Amir: their common passion for teaching, the burning desire to imbue everything with meaning . During one reserve duty that fell shortly before Passover, Amir asked him to lecture the troops on the meaning of Passover. Doron didn't feel comfortable with the idea. He didn't want to be perceived by the other soldiers as a proselytizer, an instrument of religious coercion. He begged off.

"I'm disappointed in you, Doron," said Amir. "The soldiers need to hear this. They should understand what this country is all about."

"But I'm not a missionary."

"This isn't proselytizing. It wasn't your idea. I'm the one who asked you to do it."

It was the only time that Amir had ever expressed disappointment in him. Doron knew that he had let him down. He had been unfaithful to the passion that they both shared.

Now it was time to close the circle. Doron chose Psalm 15, which speaks of closeness to G-d. It was the passage that he read at Saba Nissim's funeral. It spoke of ethical behavior rather than ritual. King David must have had men like Amir and Saba Nissim in mind when he wrote this Psalm, thought Doron. Men who reached a high level of righteousness without requiring the ladder of *Mitzvot*, the framework of traditional observance; men with an unerring moral compass. For most men, Psalms 15 was a road map, a wish list. For Amir and Saba Nissim, it was a curriculum vitae.

Lord, who shall sojourn in Thy tabernacle?
Who shall dwell upon Thy holy mountain?
He that walketh uprightly, and worketh righteousness,
And speaketh truth in his heart;

That hath no slander upon his tongue,
Nor doeth evil to his fellow,
Nor taketh up a reproach against his neighbor;
In whose eyes a vile person is despised,
But he honoreth them that fear the Lord;
He that sweareth to his own hurt, and changeth not;
He that putteth not out his money on interest,
Nor taketh a bribe against the innocent,
He that doeth these things shall never be moved.

After the funeral, Doron and his soldiers returned to the outpost. Their stint of reserve duty became a month of mourning which took place informally, in small groups, in between patrols. For Doron, characteristically reserved, speaking of Amir opened up unaccustomed channels of communication with his men. It was a rare opportunity to probe the prickly issues of secularity and religiosity without defensiveness. Some of the secular soldiers asked him to expound to them his views on G-d and religion.

"Do you think you're more righteous because you're religious?"

"I don't look at it that way," Doron explained. "Some men are better than me without ever keeping the commandments. Like Amir."

"So you mean Amir wasn't required to keep the commandments? He was off the hook?"

"No. The commandments always uplift. That's how I see it. The commandments elevate absolutely. But they elevate me relative to myself, not relative to anyone else."

The night after the funeral they returned to their routine. Yair, now acting Company Commander, asked Doron to take a detachment out to the roadblock again.

"Do you feel up to it?" he asked Doron.

"Sure. I'll do it." But he didn't feel that he could. He was coming apart. In between bouts of vomiting and diarrhea, his body was racked by sobs. He asked Leo, one of the other squad leaders, if he could replace him.

"Of course," said Leo. "What a question."

Yair had also been very close to Amir. They had planned to move into houses next door to each other in a newly constructed neighborhood.

"Go ahead, spill it," Yair said to Doron. "Tell me what you're thinking."

"I don't know what I'm crying over," said Doron. "I don't know if I'm crying for Amir or for myself. I keep on thinking about my own children. What it would be like for them if they lose me now."

"Tell me what you want to do. Do you want to go home? You're not even supposed to be here right now. You're supposed to be with your students at Yemin Orde."
Doron was silent.

"Do you want my personal opinion?" Yair asked him. He continued without waiting for a response. "Don't go home broken. We need you here. You're the dominant force for the morale of the company. You're in the middle between the older soldiers and the new kids. We need you as a bridge."

"I'm with you." Doron answered. He felt his resolve returning, but another wave of nausea was coming on. "I think I just need one night's sleep."

The rest of the month dragged on. The firefights continued. One of the casualties on the other side was the Commander of the Police Station in Area A.

The day after the Station Commander's death, a cordon of seventy enemy 'policemen' escorted his corpse to the Adam bridge for burial in Jordan, where his family lived. An ambulance carried the body and the police guard marched behind it. Doron was in charge of a small detachment of four soldiers manning the outpost next to the Adam Bridge crossing. They checked the ambulance and sent it through.

A crowd was gathering in the distance. Doron sensed there would be trouble. He instructed his soldiers to close the gates leading to the bridge. Seventy or so youths approached the outpost. They began throwing stones. The crackle of kalashnikov fire was drawing closer. Bullets began whistling overhead.

Doron's squad took up positions near the low sandbag walls of the tiny outpost. Someone's cell phone rang. It was Big Zvikah, the machine gunner. In the confusion, he hadn't had time to turn it off. It was his six-year old son.

"*Abba,* what's going on? Are those gunshots?"

"No, *caparah.*" No, my soul. "We're playing Pokemon War. You know, like the video game you play all the time. Listen." He held up the phone.

All of the soldiers in the tiny outpost had heard the conversation. They all had young children , and knew the sounds that emanated from their children's Pokemon video games.

"Pikachu lightning!" Doron called out.

"Pepper Strike! Digimon Strike!" called out another soldier.

Doron drew his fingers across his throat in a signal to Big Zvikah. End the conversation. Enough is enough. Big Zvikah's wife came on the line.

"What's going on, Zvikah?"

"Nothing serious. We're just dispersing a demonstration. We're firing some warning shots, that's all." He hung up. Soon it was dark, and the crowd dispersed. The gunfire died down, and Doron and his men returned to Elisha.

When Doron returned from *Milu'im*, he wept as he hugged Liron. It was the first time that his children had seen him cry.

"*Ima,* why is *Abba* crying," asked Shoham, his five-year old son.

"A friend of *Abba*'s was killed," said Liron.

"Oh." Shoham was silent.

CHAPTER 4   The Tightening Circle

Wednesday, March 27, 2002. Doron felt it was important to maintain a routine in the Youth Village, but it was getting harder. Tonight would be the first night of Passover. He wondered how to prepare his students for travel outside the village without scaring them. They needed to be aware of the dangers. There had been over one hundred terror victims in the previous month, the bloodiest that Israel had ever known. In the end, it turned out to be moot. For the first time ever, most of the students wanted to stay in the Youth Village for the holiday.

Doron and his family had lived at the Youth Village for six years now. Soon, he would be completing his doctorate in Jewish Philosophy.

There were far fewer school trips this year. Only the most important ones were left on the calendar, and with twice as many security guards. The Jerusalem trip was still very important, particularly for new *Olim,* new immigrants to Israel. It was in walking the streets of Jerusalem that the new *Olim* were introduced to the full spectrum of Israeli society. The annual Jerusalem Walk would weave through Jerusalem's neighborhoods, from Meah Shearim to the Old City, culminating at the Wailing Wall. This year, they covered the streets in a bulletproof bus.

The atmosphere was one of war. Doron hadn't remembered such a feeling since the Gulf War, when the scud missiles were falling and everyone was making sure that his gas mask fit snugly. In smaller towns like nearby Haderah, the streets were empty in the evenings. Cars had to pass through a checkpoint to enter the town.

Everyone felt the circle tightening. Every day, one or two killed. We don't even count the wounded any more, thought Doron. If there are none killed in an attack, we say *Baruch HaShem*. Praise G-d. Itai, a youth counselor in the village, had just arisen from the week of mourning for his brother, killed in the Gaza strip. The brother had been on final furlough from his regular army service, awaiting his release. Trouble broke out in Gaza and he was called back. He was killed by friendly fire. It was the first casualty directly connected to someone in the village. Everyone in the Youth Village, both students and staff, wanted to travel to the funeral. But the funeral was in Ofrah, an area where busloads of children had been the targets of previous terror attacks. In the end, the bus went directly to Har Herzl, the military cemetery in Jerusalem.

Two weeks later, Itai met his brother at a Jerusalem café to plan their fallen brother's thirty day commemoration ceremony. As he waited by the cash register to pay his bill, a monstrous blast tore through Café Moment. Itai landed a number of meters away, in the middle of the street. Someone found his wallet and called a social worker in the village. The stranger didn't know what had become of Itai. The Youth Village was seized by panic. Finally, Itai called. He had awoken in the emergency room, bruised but without major injury.

With his own three children, Doron was finding it harder and harder to allow them to watch TV unsupervised. Children's programs were interrupted with the news of a terrorist attack, complete with graphic footage. Just last week, Doron's five-year old son, Shoham, called to him, "*Abba*, there's a *pigua*." A terror attack. "With pictures."

The graphic pictures began roughly six months ago. Before then, there were only announcements. People became complacent, even to the point of morbid humor. The pictures put an end to all that.

Doron and Liron worked hard to get their small house koshered and clean for Passover, removing all traces of *hametz*, or leaven. Liron was already well along with their fourth child. Doron got down on hands and knees to scrub the corners. The arduous preparations for the holiday were a long-standing joke: to celebrate our freedom, once again we become slaves!! Taking all traces of *hametz* that had been collected the night before, Doron's children helped him burn the crumbs on the walkway outside.

At 3:00 pm, the family piled into the car for the ride to Doron's parents' house where they would spend Passover Night. Doron and Liron assigned each child a role in the Seder. They practiced all of the songs in the car. Doron's five year old son, Shoham, could barely contain his excitement. This year, for the first time, he would ask the Four Questions.

Sundown was nearing when they reached Bat Yam. Doron's younger sister was already there with her family. The house was joyous and full of children. The men of the family had already gone to Evening Prayers at the small neighborhood synagogue. Doron rushed to join them.

* * *

Gadi Ezra spent the afternoon with his girlfriend Galit, rushing around Bat Yam in search of presents for his nieces and nephews. When they arrived home, he headed straight for the kitchen, already redolent with the aroma of his mother's famous legume soup. For Galit, of Ashkenazi descent, legumes were not considered kosher for Passover. For Gadi's family, of Sephardic lineage, they were. He called to Galit excitedly.

"Galit! Come here! Inhale. Just think. This time next year you'll be able to have as much of my mother's soup as you want." Gadi and Galit had only known each other for three months, but everyone could feel that a wedding was imminent. Two months, three months tops, guessed Yossi, his older brother.

"Next year, you'll be one of us," Gadi joked.

This year, however, she would spend the Seder with her family and Gadi with his, as was considered proper in religious circles. Gadi was concerned that it might seem improper if he were seen walking with Galit in the neighborhood before their betrothal was announced. As always, he consulted his childhood friend, Kobi Danieli, on the matter. Kobi was generally the more stringent of the two, but in this case he laughed off Gadi's concerns.

"So what's the big deal?" Kobi shrugged. "When you get to the neighborhood, you go one way and she goes the other. Then you meet up at the house."

"Vito, I need to get a haircut and take Galit home," Gadi called to his older sister Vittoria. Every year, before Passover, Gadi made the rounds distributing bouquets of flowers to all of his aunts and uncles in Bat Yam.

"Don't worry, I'll deliver the flowers," said Vittoria. "You have more important things to take care of," she winked. It was almost sundown when he returned from Petah Tikvah, where Galit lived. He rushed to get ready for *Ma'ariv*, the Evening Prayers.

"Stay, relax for once, " said his older brother Yossi. One of these days, he would get his baby brother to lighten up a bit. Gadi and Yakov, the eldest Ezra brother, were highly driven, each in his own way. Yossi, the middle brother, held more to a philosophy of moderation in all things. Even where religion was concerned. Things weren't meant to be overdone. A Biology teacher, he found himself less drawn to things ethereal and metaphysical. He liked things with moving parts.

Yossi could feel the strain that his little brother was under. Gadi was a squad leader in the Golani Infantry Brigade, nearing the end of his regular army service. His unit had been moving from operation to operation with little rest in between. The last operation hadn't gone well. One of the Company Commanders in Gadi's Battalion had been severely wounded and a new commander, Avihu Yaakov, had been brought in to replace him.

Yossi, of medium height and square build, had the wide shoulders and rough hands of a man of the land. A religious man, he gave heaven its due, but believed in staying state-of-the-art when it came to soldiering.

"So tell me ... do you have a ceramic flak jacket yet?" He asked Gadi. The new generation of bulletproof vests, made of a composite ceramic material, were more lightweight but not yet standard army issue. Yossi was savvy in the ways of the army. He knew where to procure things. He wished his baby brother would lean on him every once in a while.

"Not yet."

"I'll get one for you."

"But none of the other guys have them."

"Gadi – you don't always have to be first in the charge. Sometimes it's OK to be number three."

"Gotta go. I'm late." Gadi insisted on rushing to Evening Prayers at the small neighborhood synagogue. It was the synagogue where their grandfather, Saba Yossef used to pray.

* * *

By the time Doron was finished praying, there was only one worshiper left in the synagogue, deep in silent prayer. It was Gadi Ezra, his friend Yossi's younger brother. Gadi was always thorough in his prayers. Doron waited until he was through.

Gadi gave Doron a powerful hug. Gadi was tall and bear-like, and his hugs were an envelopment of warmth. "One second," he said, as they turned to leave. Gadi went over to the *gabai*, the synagogue caretaker, and apologized for having kept him so long on *Erev Pessach*, the first night of Passover.

"You're almost through with the army now, aren't you Gadi?" Doron asked him.

"Couple more months."

"Have you thought about what you'll do afterwards?"

"They've asked me to be the Director at the *Kav LaHayim* camp this summer. After that, I want to work with youth. But not the cream of society. Youth at risk. Tough kids, like the raw recruits we get in Golani."

Doron took in the changes in Gadi. It had been two years since he had last seen him. Gadi had lost much of his pudginess, and now looked the part of a Golani squad leader. Two years ago, on Gadi's first week-long furlough from his regular army service, he had spent the week at Yemin Orde where a *Kav LaHayim* (Life Line) summer camp was being held. Gadi had been active in Kav LaHayim, a program for terminally ill and severely impaired children, since his yeshivah days. Doron was thrilled to see Gadi at the Youth Village. He invited him to stop by his house for coffee. Gadi stopped by, but only for a quick minute to apologize that he had no time for coffee. He only had one week to spend with the children, and there were so many of them. Every minute was for the children.

* * *

The "Big Passover" came once every two years for the Ezra family. Each of the married Ezra couples alternated years, one year in Bat Yam with the Ezra family, one year with the spouse's family. This year was the year for Bat Yam.

Gadi was extremely particular when it came to conducting the Seder. He had his own annotated *Haggadah* full of commentary from the *G'marah*, the Oral Tradition, and loved to engage his brothers in passionate debate on the most minute details. His older brother, Yakov, now a neurologist in Jerusalem, was the same way. The debates threatened to last all night.

Yossi's wife elbowed him as he groaned. At least Yakov has a wife to shut him up, thought Yossi. Next year, G-d willing, Gadi will too.

Gadi and Yakov dwelled at length on the story of Bnei Brak, the city where the Jews reconstructed their institutions of learning after fleeing Jerusalem. Yossi yawned loudly, but Gadi and Yakov remained impervious, in their own world. The story told of a certain Seder Night in Bnei Brak when all of the great sages of the age were gathered: Rabbi Akiva, Ben Zoma, Rabbi Yehoshua, Rabbi Eliezer, and Rabban Gamliel. They studied all night. It was one of the worst periods in Jewish history. Akiva, the youngest of the sages, was not yet as highly revered as the more senior sages. But that night he showed his greatness. He alone was able to celebrate the Exodus from Egypt and the redemption that it symbolized with true joy. He alone was possessed of great enough faith to know with certainty that it would happen again. Only he could see the light at the end of the tunnel with razor sharp clarity.

By 3:00 am, the Ezra household had barely fallen asleep. The ring of the telephone shattered the silence. Religious households don't answer the phone on Shabbat or the Jewish holidays. Most unplug them. But Yakov was a doctor, Yossi was a reservist in a combat unit, and Gadi was still in his regular army service. The phone had to be left connected. It could only be one of two things – a wrong number, or a dire emergency.

It was Leibovich, Gadi's platoon commander in the Auxiliary Company of Golani Battalion 51. There had been a major terrorist attack in Netanyah. A Passover Seder at the Park Hotel, an entire banquet hall, blown to bits. Over twenty-five killed, scores wounded. Leibovich himself lived in Netanyah, and heard the ambulances at 8 pm.

"First of all, *Hag Sameach*," said Leibovich. Happy Passover.

"What's going on? Are we headed back?"

"Yes."

Leibovich knew where they would be headed. He decided not to share all of the details. With Gadi, there was never any of the ordinary grumbling. "No problem. When?"

"As soon as possible. Do you have any way to get to the military transport at the train station?"
"It's not a problem. My dad can bring me."

"Call me when you get to the train station. Tell me which soldiers have arrived. Get the bus driver to stop in Netanyah, and I'll be waiting there."

Gadi arose and began calling the soldiers in his squad. He packed only those objects that he was permitted to carry on the holiday according to Jewish Law. At 7:00 am, Yossi and his father were in the kitchen as he made ready to leave. He had a long tear in his army pants.

"When you come back, Mom will sew it, " said Yossi.

CHAPTER 5 The Dance of the Valkiris

Rafi Laderman had no doubt as to where he wanted to spend the first night of Passover. Even though he wasn't on reserve duty, he wanted to be with his regiment.

Two weeks earlier, Rafi had been promoted to Staff Operations Officer for Regiment 5, his reserve duty regiment. After fourteen years as Regimental Intelligence Officer, this would be a welcome change of pace. He would be the Regiment Commander's right hand man, responsible for all logistic, personnel, and inter-unit liaison matters. And the evacuation of the wounded.

Rafi had always felt there was something special about Regiment 5. Something unspoiled. The spirit of common sacrifice remained undiluted. These were good men. Moreover, everyone in the Regiment's Upper Command was new. Col. Didi Yedidiah, the Regiment Commander, had only been appointed three weeks before. The Lieutenant Regiment Commander had been appointed a scant two days earlier.

Rafi decided to spend the holiday with Battalion 8111, stationed near the community of Morag in southern Gaza. Rafi felt that his presence would uplift the soldiers' spirits on the first night of the Seder. The clashes in Gaza were growing more intense, and they all knew that this would not be an easy *Milu'im*. He would stay a few nights in Gaza, he figured, and then head home to Kfar Saba.

Rafi and his ex-wife shared joint custody of their five-year old daughter, Ma'yan. She stayed with Rafi every other weekend and a few nights each week. This Passover, she would be spending the holiday with her mother. He called to wish her a Happy Passover.

"Where are you going to be, *Abba*?"

"I'm going to *Milu'im* to be with some other soldiers."

"When can I be a soldier?"

"You already are. Your job is to take care of *Ima*. You'll be Private Ma'ayan."

Darkness fell, ushering in the holiday. Because of the high alert, fifteen additional soldiers showed up unexpectedly that night. The cooks scrambled to prepare enough for all. One of the religious soldiers conducted the Seder, explaining every detail. Not far away, a barrage of gun and mortar fire erupted. The soldiers tentatively proceeded with the ceremony.

The battalion shared the base with a Bedouin tracking unit. Rafi sat next to Ahmed, a tracker. As the Seder progressed, Ahmed asked Rafi about the significance of each ritual.
"What about the egg?" he asked Rafi. Rafi explained to him that it represented the Passover sacrifice performed in the days of the Great Temple.

"So why four cups of wine?" Ahmed, a devout Muslim, did not imbibe alcohol. "And the crackers you call *Matzot* – why do they taste like cardboard?"

In the midst of singing *V'hee She'amdah*, "And in every generation there will be those who try to destroy us…", a mortar shell exploded near the mess hall. The Seder was put on hold. Everyone scrambled to take up positions. The outpost remained under fire the entire night. They never returned to the table. At 4:00 am, Rafi decided to grab a few hours' sleep.

The ominous tones of Wagner entered his dreams. The Dance of the Valkiris. Over and over, the haunting opening strain. It refused to stop. Rafi awoke. The Dance of the Valkiris was the tune that he had programmed into his cell phone to identify calls from the army.

It was Sarit, the Regimental Personnel Officer. "Didi wants you to come to Ashkelon." Ashkelon was the Divisional HQ. It was then that he learned of the attack in Netanyah. By 6:00 am, he was in Ashkelon.

Regiment 5 would be headed for Jenin. Rafi's first task would be to get everyone to El-Yakim , the training base, then on to Giv'at Oz, a kibbutz one kilometer inside the 'green line' which would serve as the regimental gathering point. All supplies would flow through Giv'at Oz. The regimental command post, Ginat, would be set up on a hill to the west of the Jenin refugee camp.

A decision was taken not to use heavy force. There would be no artillery or planes. Those were the parameters. The soldiers would just have to work as carefully as possible.

Rafi was intimately familiar with Jenin. As the Intelligence Officer of the regiment, he spent long hours canvassing the streets and alleyways of the town, often with Amir Zohar, the former C.C. of the Regiment's Engineering Recon Company. They steered clear of the refugee camp. "You'd have to be crazy to go in there," said Amir. Rafi was quick to agree.

CHAPTER 6 The Callup

Thursday, March 28, 2002. For Doron and his family, the night of the Seder passed in peace. Religious families spend their holidays beyond the reach of the electronic media, so Doron's family was spared the news of the attack in Netanyah. That afternoon, relatives arrived and relayed the news.

The conversation quickly turned to the feeling that something finally had to be done. Israel was suffering more casualties than in any war since the War of Independence. Even in the Lebanon war, there hadn't been this many casualties. And these were civilians. People were afraid to leave their homes.

Events were gathering speed. Doron decided it would be best to return to Yemin Orde to prepare his gear in case of a callup. They drove north, stopping at Liron's parents' house in Haderah. Friday morning, Doron continued on to the Youth Village. He listened to the messages on his answering machine. Nothing about a callup. Still unsatisfied, he called Asi, the new Company Commander, to see if he had any news. "Right now, the officers are arriving," said Asi. "You squad leaders can take your time, but be sure to be here by tonight. We're definitely going to be called up."

Doron wanted to be there already. He decided to return to Haderah and hitch a ride with some friends rather than take the army transport, which was slow and circuitous.

This callup would be difficult for Shoham and Adi, Doron's seven-year-old daughter. Usually, he had ample time to prepare them before leaving on reserve duty. This time, he would be leaving without preparation. It would be difficult for him as well. It hadn't been the same since Amir's death.

Doron returned to Haderah to say goodbye to Liron and the children. He was in uniform, but without his rifle. Shoham was deep in thought. Doron could tell he was trying to figure something out.

"Daddy, are you going to war? Are you going to kill the bad people?"

"Well, actually I'm going to try to protect the good people."

Doron could tell that the answer didn't yet satisfy his son. A piece was missing.
Adi was concerned with less abstract matters. "When are you going to be back, Daddy?"

The sun had already set, ushering in the Sabbath, by the time Doron's reservist friends arrived. "Doron, aren't you religious? " asked Shimi, who was driving. "I thought you couldn't drive on Shabbat?"

"This is *Pikuach Nefesh*. The saving of lives. It takes precedence."

They arrived at the Emergency Supply Depot to gather their equipment and ready their vehicles. No orders had come through yet. They knew they would be headed for Jenin. The question was when.

They were all there, and the official callup hadn't even begun yet. Some had even flown in from abroad without having received a callup notice. Itzik, who had opened a restaurant in London a few months earlier, was there already. He heard from a friend that the *Pal-Han* was being called up, and booked the first available flight to Israel.

*   *   *

Rafi Laderman shivered. It was a wintry Passover; it felt more like December. The official callups would begin that night. There were intermittent blackouts. Kosher for Passover food, always a problem in the army, would now be a serious issue. Soldiers in the Emergency Supply Depot began pulling back the tarpaulins covering the Armored Personnel Carriers.

Rafi had been to the Emergency Supply Depot many times, but had never seen anything unpacked. The depot hadn't seen action since the Lebanon War. The APCs were old, but well maintained. Everything had always been neatly wrapped. Now, there was a metamorphosis taking place. Hundreds of growling steel machines angrily stirred to life from their cocoons.

"What should we do with all the *hametz* in the APCs?" one religious soldier asked. They put it in a separate room and locked the door. At least some of the food in the APCs was kosher for Passover.

Rafi had a thousand things to check on, but a voice inside made him stop for a second and take notice of what was happening. "Forget about the little things. Look around you." People were streaming in. It was far to early for them to have received callup notices. They just came.

*   *   *

Dr. Yakov Ezra, Gadi's older brother, was called up on Friday. He was the Chief Medical Officer for the Regiment assigned to Ramallah. On the way to Ramallah, in Bet-El, he saw an APC with the insignia of Golani Battalion 51, Gadi's Battalion.

"Do any of you guys know Gadi Ezra?"

"What do you mean? Everyone knows Gadi."

"Where are you guys headed?"
"Inside."

Golani Battalion 51 had received its orders. Their mission would be to take the *Mukat'ah*, the British Mandate era fortress that now served as the epicenter of the enemy's security apparatus. Yakov tried Gadi's cell phone. Gadi answered in a whisper.

"Gadi, where are you?"

"I'm in the Mukatt'ah. We're inside. "

"I'm here too, right outside. Take care of yourself."

When Yakov thought of his little brother, the character of Rabbi Akiva always came to mind. Legend had it that Akiva, who became a renowned scholar only in his forties, had resisted the call to scholarship. He feared that becoming overly learned would make him arrogant. He wanted to remain simple and pure of heart.

He and Gadi had a favorite story from the *Gmarah*, one that purportedly involved Rabbi Akiva. A poor laborer came to collect his week's wage from his wealthy employer.

"I'm sorry, I can't pay you today," said the employer. "I have no money."

"Very well, " said the employee. "Perhaps you could give me something in kind."

"I'm sorry," said the employer, "I have nothing to give you."

"Very well," said the employee, and wished his employer well.

Two weeks later, the employer sought out the employee. He brought him his wages, and additional gifts to compensate him for the wait.

"Why didn't you protest when I told you I had no money?" asked the employer. "Didn't you wonder how it could be that a wealthy man lacked the wherewithal to pay wages to his workers?"

"Well, I assumed your money was temporarily tied up in a transaction," said the worker. Indeed, it had been. "And what did you think when I said I couldn't part with anything in kind?" asked the employer.

"Well, I figured perhaps there was a lien on your assets, and that you would pay me when you could." Indeed, such had been the case. The employer was dumbfounded by the degree to which the employee had given him the benefit of the doubt. According to legend, the employer was Rabbi Eliezer and the employee was none other than Rabbi Akiva.

Yakov always enjoyed that same simplicity, that willingness to give the benefit of the doubt, in Gadi. Gadi was always so grateful for everything, especially these past three months with Galit. Finally, all of his loves were connected: his love for his People, his love for G-d, his love for his family, his love for his friends, and now his love for Galit. "Our love has brought me to entirely new heights," Gadi confided to him. It reminded Yakov of Saba Yossef's teachings regarding the spiritual significance of loving a woman. To reach true love of G-d, one needs the love of a woman. The essence of love, Saba Yossef taught, is proximity. "When the feeling of proximity is great enough, you let go of the feeling of 'me'. Only then, when you feel yourself totally connected, do you feel love. When you love a woman deeply, you can love G-d best."

The rabbis once debated whether or not the Song of Songs should be included in the scriptures. It was, after all, a love song. It was Rabbi Akiva who prevailed in the debate. According to Rabbi Akiva, so important was its message that mere inclusion would not suffice. It should be the holiest book in the scriptures.

Nothing would happen to Gadi, thought Yakov. He was too pure.

CHAPTER 7 The Safe Side of the Green Line

Nahum, not quite thirty, had last been on reserve duty in August. He served as the combat medic in his unit. On the last day of *Milu'im*, the men threw a farewell party. They barbecued steaks on an open fire and passed around bottles of beer. The Regiment Commander stopped by to commend them on a job well done. An alert came in. A group of tanks had fallen under heavy fire in a village outside of Ramallah.

Shay was Nahum's Company Commander. He, Daniel, Eran, and Nahum operated together as the C.C. squad. They were like four limbs of the same body, thought Nahum. Everything had become second nature. They jumped into the C.C. jeep and sped towards the village. On the outskirts of the village they fell under a barrage of withering fire from both sides of the road. Their attackers lobbed grenades and raked the jeep with gunfire. Daniel managed to throw the vehicle into reverse as the others returned fire. They returned shaken but unscathed. It was Nahum's first time under fire as a reservist. It felt different now. Ravit, his wife, was four months pregnant with their first child. Nahum had to hear her voice. It was 11:20 pm.

"Nahum? Is everything OK?" He couldn't bring himself to tell her what had happened.

"I was just lonely, that's all."

She knew something was wrong. Nahum was usually full of jokes.

When he arrived home the next day, he told her what happened.

"That's it," she pronounced with finality. "You're going to be a father now. Enough. "

As her pregnancy progressed, so did the intensity of her campaign for Nahum to seek a non-combat posting. It became a constant barrage. When Nahum received his next callup notice in January, the intensity increased.

"Make sure to marry a *Polani*," Ravit's mother had always advised her. A Polish Jew. "They take the best care of their wives." Ravit's parents were of Turkish descent. Her mother had turned out to be only half right. "A Polish *jobnik*, mother. A non-combat soldier. That's what you should have told me," Ravit would joke when Nahum was in reserve duty. And besides, Nahum was only half Polish.

The callup notice was for April 28th. Nahum tried in vain to convince Ravit that his being in Ramallah was the only way to guarantee her safety in Tel Aviv. Still, he felt guilty. In Ramallah, in the company of Shay, Daniel, and Eran, he felt totally safe. Even under fire. While in Milu'im, he couldn't escape the feeling that he was infinitely safer than his wife and son in Tel Aviv.

"I'm going to give Shay a piece of my mind. You're not going anymore. I forbid it. I'll take our son and leave. We'll leave Israel," said Ravit.

"But I'm doing this for our son. For our son and for you. I'd rather die in Milu'im than have something happen to you here. This is the front line now. " Nahum's rebuttals fell on deaf ears. Ravit was resolute.
"You're not going and that's it. I'll tie you to a chair if I have to. No one ever asks us what it's like. What it's like to hear the knock on the door,

to look through the eyehole and see three officers with a notice."

Nahum insisted that someone was watching over him. But she knew him. There was nothing that he wouldn't do for his buddies. She was certain he would tempt fate.

Ron, their son, was born in March. Then came the Netanyah attack, which changed everything Ravit was stoically silent in the face of the inevitable. It was clear that the situation couldn't continue. *O l'can, o l'can,* Nahum thought. One way, or the other, something has to happen now. The phone rang. It was Shay.

"Eran and I are on the way to the Emergency Supply Depot. Keep your cell phone on."

Nahum called his father to tell him that Ravit and Ron would be coming over to stay while he was in *Milu'im.*

"*Shmor al atzmecha*," his father said. Watch yourself. Conversations were never prolonged when Nahum went off to the army. The unspoken seemed to drown out anything that could be said.

Nahum arrived at the depot Friday afternoon. The essentials were there, but they lacked amenities. The combat vests were old and musty. He couldn't find the combat medic's vest that he had grown accustomed to. They would be well armed, but uncomfortable.

Danny, a Jerusalem attorney in his fifties, was one of the first to arrive. He had been released from reserve duty when he turned 45 but kept on showing up for operations. There was some awkwardness in the beginning. Nahum was there to replace him as company medic.

"Danny, how much longer are you going to keep coming?" Nahum asked him.

"Every year, I tell myself that this is my last time. But when everyone else receives a *Tzav*, I can't keep away."

Secretly, Nahum hoped that he would stop coming. Danny was devoted, fearless, and in remarkably good physical condition for his age. But Nahum wanted a buddy his own age beside him in combat.

They found a gymnasium in a nearby moshav, and the entire company slept there Friday night. Over one hundred men, they covered the entire gym floor with their sleeping bags.

Before going to sleep, Nahum called Ravit.

"You can relax, baby. I'm on the safe side of the green line."

"Really?" she answered. "Which side is that?"

CHAPTER 8 Shneor

In Jerusalem, news of the Netanyah attack spread quickly. Shneor Alfasi and his family were spending the Seder at his in-laws. He phoned some friends in his reserve unit to find out what was going on. No one knew. He called a clerk in the battalion administrative office. Still, the response was sketchy. Half an hour later, the phone rang. It was Dror Bar, his platoon commander.

"Come now, Shneor."

Inwardly, Shneor hoped that Dror would tell him to go home to collect his gear first. He, his wife Orah, and their three children lived in Gush Qatif, in the Gaza strip. It didn't feel right, leaving for battle without consulting Rav Noach, his spiritual mentor. He had a thousand questions he wanted to ask him. Should he carry his *tfillin* bag in his ordinance vest? Was he allowed to eat non-kosher food if there was no choice? Rav Noach had a knack for offering up words of wisdom that infused their precarious Gush Qatif existence with meaning. "Don't forget," he would say. "You are the envoys of the People Israel. Don't forget."

"All my stuff is in Gush Qatif," he said to Dror. "Shouldn't I go there first?"

"You'd better come straight to the Supply Depot," said Dror.

Shneor had finished his annual stint of reserve duty only one month earlier. Orah was in her ninth month, due any day now. Still, there was no pleading. As he hugged her goodbye, Shneor tried to calm her with an image of divine providence.

"Remember the deer," he said. "We're looking at it from afar, running over the hills. All we see is a tiny speck, disappearing into a valley and reemerging at the top of a new hill. What we can't see is that it's running forward. All the time forward." Orah nodded. Shneor's implacable inner calm never failed to soothe her nervous energy. She tried to push her fears aside and share Shneor's image of the deer.

Hanoch, a friend from Shneor's unit who lived nearby, arrived with a spare uniform. To Dvir, Shneor's seven-year old son, Hanoch and the uniform seemed out of place.

"*Abba*, where are you going? It's Passover," asked Dvir.

Shneor and Ora believed in direct answers. "There was an attack, people were killed."

For Shneor, reserve duty was a passage from one family to another. He always looked forward to rejoining his brothers in arms. The force that bound him to them was as strong as any he had known. He particularly looked forward to seeing Dror again.

Dror arrived in the platoon five years ago. Things were chaotic. Most of the soldiers were new, and the unit hadn't yet come together as a family. Dror quickly unified them. Shneor remembered the moment when he first learned to appreciate his new platoon commander's human qualities. The unit was stationed in an outpost on Mount Hermon. Dror happened to pass by a group of soldiers who were using a dilapidated shack as a makeshift chapel. He made some calls, and before long an orderly chapel was built for the outpost. It was typical of Dror. Although he was secular, he went to great lengths to make sure the special needs of the religious soldiers were attended to. He often asked the soldiers if they needed anything. "What's wrong?" he would inquire, even if a soldier hadn't voiced a complaint. He read their faces, he saw what they were feeling in their eyes.

In civilian life, Dror was a computer trainer. It fits him, thought Shneor. Dror was the most patient man he had ever met. He had all the time in the world for anyone who felt the need for more details after one of his briefings, even after a sleepless night. He was known for his modesty. He had no problem saying, "I don't know." He insisted on being in the KP rotation and performing guard duty with his troops. It was unheard of. Some of the soldiers suggested that he save his strength for more important tasks, but he refused. He was tall, pure, and direct. And never without that unique smile.

At Giv'at Zeev, north of Jerusalem, Shneor and Hanoch linked up with some of the other soldiers in the unit. Shneor's cell phone rang. It was Dror, checking to see who had arrived. Almost everyone was at the Emergency Supply Depot already. There was going to be a serious shortage of equipment. The following day, Shneor was sent home to fetch his rifle from Gush Qatif.

CHAPTER 9 The Pathfinder

This year, Hanoch and Efrat hosted the family Seder. Two of Hanoch's brothers had just arrived from abroad. His third brother, Haim, a policeman, was now on the phone. "Turn on the TV," he said. "Then call me back."

The attack in Netanyah was all over the news. The Seder was effectively over. He called Haim back and they discussed the situation. They both agreed that this latest attack in Netanyah was in a 'new league'. There had been a constant increase in terror over the past year, but no one seemed to know where the breaking point would be. No one seemed to know what it would take to provoke the army out of its self-imposed restraint.

Ela, Hanoch's five-year old daughter, already knew what a terror attack meant. "Mommy, there was a *pigua. Saba* won't be coming tonight." Her grandfather, Hanoch's father-in-law, was a well-known news correspondent on Israeli TV.

He looked out at the vineyard behind his house and tried to commit each of its details to memory. It was a sight that always gave him peace. Wherever the coming days were about to take him, he would try to take the vineyard with him in his mind.

Hanoch was the Pathfinder of the *Pal-Sar*, the Recon company of Regiment 5. Their role was to go in before the main force and reconnoiter the territory. Like any other elite IDF reserve unit, most of the men were in the middle of their university studies. Hanoch, at 33, was already one of the "old men" in the unit. His tools of the trade were compasses, a GPS device, and his beloved maps. He was never without maps. In planning where to establish his household, he had surveyed an aerial map of Jerusalem. He chose a moshav that was just the right distance from the center of town. In pencil, he traced the route that he would take every morning to the offices of the internet company where he worked. He had purposely chosen a position that worked with the western hemisphere. Arising early in the morning to work with his American clients, he was able to cut out in the middle of the day to pick up his children from school and spend time with them at home. Then he could head back in the late afternoon to finish up the day's paperwork. And it afforded him the opportunity to travel.

Efrat, his wife, shared his passion for travel. Before settling down, they had covered much of the world, crowding onto overloaded passenger trains in China and trekking throughout the wilds of Malawi and the jungles of the Philippines. But his most memorable trip was the time he accompanied his father to visit his father's childhood home in Kiev. At age fourteen, his father had escaped the Chernowitz ghetto, arriving in Israel in 1950 after sojourning in Turkey for a number of years. In the Ukraine, Hanoch and his father rented a house from an old woman who cooked for them as well. The woman never ate in their presence, but sat at the table with them, catering to their every whim. Hanoch had no common language with the woman. His father slurped her borscht with gusto, but Hanoch had no stomach for the sour purple soup. He dutifully downed spoonful after spoonful as the woman sat and watched him. He couldn't help but wonder what role the old woman and her people had played in the extermination of his father's family. Still, sitting across from her, he couldn't bring himself to hurt her feelings.

Hanoch's father, an academic, had been at work for years now on the biography of an obscure nineteenth-century intellectual. Hanoch didn't like to become mired in the random details of people's lives. As in all things, he liked to take the aerial view, following trends and movements in broad strokes. He was particularly fascinated by two periods of Israeli history: the destruction of the Second Temple, and the twelve-year period leading up to the birth of the state of Israel. They were periods of the few against the many, periods when individual acts of bravery could have historic consequences.

Everyone in Hanoch's unit was already at the depot when he arrived. No one had yet been officially called up. Some who arrived had even 'graduated' from reserve duty over five years ago. Everyone had lived through the past year and half of terror. Everyone wanted in .

Oren, the Company Commander, assembled them for an informal briefing. He wanted only those who were in top shape. Those who hadn't been training regularly with one of the squads were thanked and sent home.

Hanoch hadn't known how much to pack – he hadn't even received an official callup notice yet. Perhaps he would be back for the weekend. Much of his time at work was spent dealing with current events. He couldn't help feeling that once again the army would just go through the motions, an enormous bluff. The powers that be would enforce an agreement and it would be over.

They had all been about to embark on Passover vacations with their families. Now, instead of soft hotel beds, they spread out their sleeping bags on the concrete floor of a hangar. Hanoch still had a thousand niggling concerns on his mind. No one at work knew that he was in *Milu'im*. He had forty or so American clients that didn't know how to reach him. He hadn't had time to train anyone at work to fill in for him. But there was nothing to be done now. Don't sweat the small stuff, he told himself.

CHAPTER 10 STU

For Stu and Judy, Passover was truly the holiday of emancipation. Over a decade earlier, each had set out from America to build a life in Israel. Now, every Passover, their respective families would fly in from the States to gather in their small apartment in Bet Shemesh for the Seder dinner. With grandparents to care for their four small children, this would be their one opportunity each year to slip away for a two day vacation. For two days, Stu and Judy would have the unaccustomed luxury of a hotel room, and some time, to themselves.

Not that there was a single thing about their rigorous daily routines that either one of them would change. Stu arose every morning at 5:00 for his *Daf Yomi* session, his daily session of Talmud with a study partner. After prayers, he would get the kids ready as Judy prepared to rush off to her job as a textile buyer in Tel Aviv. When the children were sick, it would usually fall to Stu to stay at home with them. He worked in Jerusalem for the Jewish Agency, and had an easier time managing things by phone.

Stu grew up in a 'Modern Orthodox' home in New Jersey. In those years, everyone seemed to be growing apart. As his parents grew less observant, he became more fervent in his faith. Then his parents divorced. In Jerusalem, where he spent a year in yeshivah after high school, things always seemed to be growing together. There was a magical, centripetal magnetism about the city that seemed to draw people inward. When he was 18, Stu participated in a Jerusalem Day celebration at the *Mercaz HaRav* yeshivah in Jerusalem. He danced all the way from the yeshivah to the Wailing Wall. The dancing lasted all night. It was a coming together. People of all colors and hues danced wildly in small circles. Praying at the wall, he felt a power he had never felt before. He had never known such pure joy.

He spent the next four years back in America, studying European Literature at a liberal arts college. He tried to emulate the intellectualism of his professors, but it felt cold and sterile. Like those of no particular bent, it was assumed that he would become a lawyer. Often he found himself thinking back to that one night in Jerusalem, of the wild dancing until dawn. It gave him chills. As a graduation gift, his father gave him a plane ticket to Israel. He never used the return half.

Stu and Judy often thought of themselves as a single person. It went beyond completing each other's sentences; they had a sixth sense for knowing what the other was feeling. Stu once read aloud to Judy a story from the biography of Rav Aryeh Levin, a revered scholar and mystic whose powers of empathy were legendary. The rabbi and his wife went to visit a doctor for the wife's foot ailment.

"Doctor, my wife's foot is hurting us," said the rabbi.

"Hey, I thought that was *our* line," said Judy.

Many of their friends were Jerusalemites. They were caught up in the same web of daily apprehension, one degree removed. Each day, before driving to work, Stu would find himself thinking, 'What next?' In March alone, 126 people were killed in terror attacks. He couldn't even remember specific events any more. There was the explosion that killed the couple going for their ultrasound appointment. Stu's friend Michael had a bookstore next door. He'd been unable to get him on the phone. He didn't know whether to call Michael's wife or not. He decided to call another mutual friend first to see if he knew anything. Michael, it turned out, had been twenty meters away from the blast. Things just kept on getting worse.

Stu thought back to the beginning of the violence. The bomb on the No. 18 bus in Jerusalem. The bomb on the No. 5 bus in Tel Aviv. We've become too well-drilled at dealing with the aftermath, he thought. Back then we weren't so good. Back then, each explosion brought life to a standstill. After the bombing on the No. 18 bus, he and Judy went to make out a will. They didn't have any possessions of significance, but wanted to square away the issue of custody for their children in case they were killed together. One had to think about everything now.

Last year, for religious reasons, it would have been unthinkable for anyone to bring a cell phone to prayers. Now, for security reasons, the Chief Rabbinate had decreed it mandatory to have a working cell phone available at all times. Now, they even locked the doors before praying.

This year's getaway to Tiberias had been months in planning. Friday morning, as they were about to leave, the phone rang. It was Adi, the Company Commander of Stu's Armored Corps reserve unit.

"Stu, get ready. I'm not sure when we'll be called, but make sure your bag's ready." Stu threw his duffel bag in the car. When they arrived at the hotel in Tiberias, he still hadn't heard back from Adi. "This really isn't right," he said to Judy. "Maybe they've been trying to get hold of me and haven't been able to get through. I can't be *Rosh Katan.*" A smallhead. "I have to call in." Smallheads were soldiers who needed to have everything spelled out for them. Bigheads connected the dots for themselves.

Judy felt her long anticipated getaway about to evaporate. "Are you sure not calling means being *Rosh Katan?*"

Stu could feel it in his bones: his buddies were already assembling. It wasn't right, heading off on a vacation that he knew would never come to fruition.

He reached Adi. There was no longer any doubt. "Come."

A tearful farewell in Tiberias. His friend Danny, who had come from the States for the holiday, hugged him. "You're doing this for all of us." Tears were streaming down his face. It was commonplace for the children to see women crying, but Stu worried that seeing a man cry would alarm them. Benny, his two year old son, was already fully bilingual but didn't understand what the 'marmy' was. He understood that Mommy was sad.

It was almost Shabbat. Stu deliberated whether or not it would be appropriate to call his rabbi, Rav David. He tried to think of a specific question to ask him, but his mind was blank. He decided to call anyway.

A *Rav* isn't someone you call to shoot the breeze with, Stu reflected. The rabbi-student relationship went beyond friendship. It was more structured, less casual. Stu often pondered that sentence from Ethics of the Fathers, "Find yourself a Rabbi and acquire yourself a friend." What's was the implied difference between 'find' and 'acquire'? 'Making' was a more active verb. It required more on one's part. Implicit in the verb was a certain measure of *kni'ah*, willful submission, to the Rabbi's authority. One was willfully submitting himself to his rabbi's judgement. Stu found it liberating. It rid one of ego. It made people come together. He had placed a measure of distance between his new life and his former life, the life in which acrimony mushroomed as people grew apart. The life where everyone knew the answer. Humility wasn't such a bad thing. He found tremendous freedom in humility.

"Rav David, I just got called up. What can you tell me?"

"Just try to do as little *chilul shabbat* as possible." Desecration of the Sabbath. Driving. Working. Handling money. The kindling of a flame.

"Just try to minimize the problems that will arise." Near Jerusalem, Shabbat fell twenty minutes before sunset. "Use those twenty minutes," Rav David advised him. "Make it as late as possible when you bring in Shabbat."

Stu considered Rav David a righteous man. His *t'filah*, his prayer, had great weight in Stu's eyes. He always prayed for the safety of Israel's soldiers.

"Don't forget me in your prayers, Rav David."

After he hung up, he was glad that he had called Rav David. He had needed to hear his voice.

On his way to the gathering point, Stu stopped to pick up his *kibbutznik* friend Oded. Oded's wife was crying. This was something different for their generation. For those under thirty, there had never been a callup like this. Stu remembered his first day in the *bakum*, the army intake base, when his teeth were photographed. His *Tzabar* friends thought it was funny. That's how out of touch we were back then, Stu thought to himself.

CHAPTER 11 Lists

Saturday, March 30. Doron awoke early Saturday morning and searched for a place to pray. A small ordinance shack had been converted into a makeshift chapel, and he joined the soldiers who were gathered there for Sabbath prayers. It was an abbreviated service, only an hour. There was no Torah scroll, so they skipped over the Torah reading.

Doron's squad gathered at their APC and began loading it with the tools of urban warfare: mortar rounds, explosive bricks, and explosive "fingers" -- elongated bags of plastique used for opening doors. In spite of the Sabbath, there was unavoidable writing to be done. Equipment forms had to be filled out, and "Next of Kin" forms had to be signed. Doron had filled out such forms many times before without giving it a second thought. This time, it felt different. His hand trembled as he wrote his wife's name.

Since Amir's death, the company had already gone through three company commanders. The last Company Commander, Eli, had recently taken a leave of absence to care for his ailing father, and Asi, the Executive Officer, had been asked to fill in temporarily. Now he was the full time C.C..

When Asi joined the company eight years earlier as X. O., there were quite a few skeptics. He loved to sing, and was never without his guitar. He was particularly well-versed in Beatles tunes, of which his favorite was "Imagine". But Asi soon proved himself gifted in other critical areas as well. He was an amazing navigator, able to orient himself in the field unlike anyone Doron had ever met. He was practical, concise, and calm under fire. In civilian life, he was a Marine Biologist.

At 2:00 in the afternoon, Asi summoned all of the officers and commanders to a staff meeting. He began by requesting a status report.

"Whose APC isn't ready yet?" No one raised a hand.

"Let's hurry up. Get your personal equipment ready. We need to be ready for every possible scenario. We may not need the APCs in the end, but we have to be ready."
Silence. "OK guys. Everyone take a close look at your neighbor…"

He struggled for a second, as if trying to decide whether or not to stick to his rehearsed speech. Then he changed direction.

"Look, our arrival isn't going to surprise anybody. They're waiting for us. I know most of you want to enter fast before they can prepare a nice welcome for us, but we're going to have to train first."

Now came the hard part. No one wanted to be left out of this operation, but the soldiers far outnumbered the weapons and vehicles.

"We have many more men than APCs. We'll figure out afterwards who will stay and who will go. In the meantime, I want each platoon commander to compile his own selection list." He turned quickly and left the room.

The platoon and squad leaders debated which criteria made sense for the selection. Eyyal, the leader of Platoon 2, decided to base it on family status.

"Bachelors in and family men out. The fighting is going to be fierce. I don't want to be responsible for any more widows or orphans."

Doron objected. "That doesn't make sense. The main criterion should be skill. It usually comes out the same anyway – the younger soldiers are in better shape, and have had more advanced training." But there were exceptions – veteran soldiers who added wisdom and depth to the younger soldiers' fighting skills. And Doron himself, now one of the more veteran soldiers, certainly didn't plan on staying behind.

In the end everyone agreed with Doron. They began compiling their lists.

Each APC was only meant to carry ten soldiers. Ten lean, wiry regular soldiers, not ten ample, well-fed reservists. But everyone wanted in, and soldiers insisted on not being left behind even after the APCs were filled. Some APCs ended with as many as twelve soldiers. It was going to be a tight squeeze.

After Doron had compiled his list, Amzaleg, one of the older soldiers, pulled him aside. "Listen, Doron, I got a call from Uzi's wife. She made me swear that I would keep an eye on him. We've been together since our regular service. We've always looked out for each other. I promised her."

Doron suppressed a smile. The two were inseparable. Both Amzaleg and Uzi had come to the *Pal-Han* from Golani. Uzi was an irrigation engineer and worked for a landscaping company. He loved politics and had run for public office. When he first joined the company nine years ago, he had just returned from a long trip in the Far East and sported an earring and ponytail. But he quickly distinguished himself as an outstanding soldier. He was a systematic, strategic thinker and would often take the younger soldiers under his wing, coaching them and keeping them from acting impulsively.

Amzaleg, on the other hand, never made it to most of the reserve duties. He wasn't particularly big on training exercises. "Look, guys, if it's something serious – you always know you can count on me." In this operation, he had proved true to his word. He was among the first to report for duty, even though his wife was in her seventh month of a difficult pregnancy.

Doron approved Amzaleg's request and transferred him to Uzi's APC.

Some of the older soldiers who were to be left behind protested strenuously. "Doron, how could you do this to us?"

"Don't take offense. It's about who can best carry out the mission. "

The older soldiers stood their ground for some time before conceding. Big Zvikah, who at 39 was one of the oldest in the company, made a last ditch attempt. "True, there are probably guys in better shape than us. But we still want in!"

Doron had his doubts about Big Zvikah. He was tall, portly, and strong as an ox, but had long been plagued by a bad back and was forbidden to lift heavy things. Many times in training exercises Doron had ordered him to leave his flak jacket behind.

"Zvikah, I admire your strong will. But it won't help you if your back goes out."

Zvikah paused to consider his situation. "All right. But I'm going to be right at the camp exit waiting with all of the APCs. If anything happens, you call me and I'll be there right away."

Doron decided that the best way to handle the rest of them was to let them argue among themselves. "Listen", he told them. "I have two places left in the Lieutenant Company Commander's APC, but I want you to really think about this. Decide among yourselves."

The steel walls of the APCs were vulnerable to the enemy's large caliber Kalashnikov bullets. They had to line them with sandbags. The driving rain turned the mounds of sand to mud, and the sandbags were excruciatingly heavy. It was hard work, but everyone ran around offering to help. Doron had never seen such a high level of motivation. It was the culmination of a year of pent-up frustration. A year of terror.

By Saturday Night, the *Pal-Han* was ready to move on to El-Yakim, their training base closer to Jenin. On the way to the new base, Doron, Shimi, and Maor stopped off in Haderah to check on Liron and the children. Doron called ahead to tell her that they would be passing through, and asked if she could round up some leftovers, as there had been no Kosher-for-Passover food in the Emergency Supply Depot. He was ravenous.

A sumptuous feast awaited them. The dining room table was festooned with every conceivable delicacy: lamb, goulash, and myriad salads. Shimi and Maor were in heaven.

It was 11:00 pm, but the children were still waiting up. This time Doron had his rifle with him, and Shoham instantly brightened. He seemed confused when Doron left in uniform on Friday without his rifle. Now, he seemed reassured. The missing piece was in place.

Adi threw her arms around Doron and wouldn't let go. By the time he and his friends left, it was after midnight.

*   *   *

Sabbath bore no resemblance to any Sabbath that Stu had ever known. He and his company spent the day preparing the tanks. As he slid the shells in place, he thought of where they'd be headed. These were the wrong shells. They wouldn't be needing armor-piercing shells. This wouldn't be the battle they had always prepared for, on wide plains, at great distances, against other armored forces. This would be point blank, against who knows what. Stu rummaged through all of the shell crates but found only a few shells that made sense for urban warfare. He hefted them into his favorite spot, where he could reach them with his eyes shut.

*   *   *

Saturday night. Yakov Ezra still hadn't been able to make contact with his brother Gadi. It was freezing cold in the hills surrounding Ramallah. He had already treated one soldier for hypothermia. Gadi and his unit were operating around the clock in the *Mukatt'ah*. Finally, despairing of locating his baby brother that night, he took shelter from the cold in a small barracks and took a nap. Perhaps by morning Golani would complete their mission and he'd be able to catch up with Gadi.

*   *   *

"Where were you? They were looking for you." Mulu's mother was afraid. In Ethiopia, the army often arrived unexpectedly in the villages to press young men into service. They came looking for Mulu's brother when he was fifteen. He was tall and muscular for his age, and had caught the attention of the recruiters. Somehow, he managed to evade them.

Mulu, twenty eight, had finished his stint of reserve duty as an APC technician only two weeks ago. In civilian life, he taught part-time as he studied towards his Master's degree.

To the older Ethiopians, war was like any other natural disaster, horrific in scope and random in its choice of victims. Mulu and his generation saw things differently. They were defending their own homes. It was their choice. In Ethiopia, the army did not bother to inform the villagers what the fighting was about when they came in search of young conscripts. People didn't see their sons for years. The only way home was in a coffin or as a pensioner. Here, thought Mulu, you're never more than an hour or two from home. And never more than a phone call away.

"So what do we do? What if they come back?" His mother was still trembling. How could he explain to her that this was different, thought Mulu. This is *our* army. *Our* country.

"It's OK. Don't worry."

"Maybe you should sleep at your sister's apartment. Perhaps if you stay away for a few days, they'll forget about you."

Mulu called the base. "When can you be here?" asked the personnel clerk.

"In two hours," answered Mulu.

"Yehonaw hono, majjamariya attehun," Mulu's mother pleaded with him in Amharic as he prepared to leave. "Promise me you won't try to be first this time. Just promise me that." Mulu had always been first. He was the youngest of the children, but the first to attend college. He was the most Israeli in the family. That's what scared her the most.

CHAPTER 12 Cover Fire

Sunday, March 31. The attack had gone like clockwork so far, thought Gadi. The Auxiliary Company of Golani Battalion 51 began in the building next to the *Mukatt'ah* which housed the local police. Initially there was sporadic fire from some of the buildings in the compound, but the tank shells put an end to that. Now Duchan, Gadi's company commander, arrived with new orders. They were headed inside the compound to sweep for snipers and collect material for Intelligence.

Leibovich's squad of four would lead. Gadi's squad would bring up the rear, providing cover fire and making sure that no one was left behind.

Over the past year, Gadi and Leibovich had become the 'parents' of Platoon 5. Leibovich, although not an officer, had been appointed acting platoon commander almost a year ago. The appointment was supposed to have been temporary, but Battalion 51 kept on moving from one operation to another and Leibovich was a natural leader. Platoon 5, the recon platoon, was always out in front. Gadi, a squad leader in the platoon, was his second in command. Gadi was the platoon's 'kind father'. Leibovich, whose first name was Itzik but whom everyone called Leibovich, was known for his tough love. Together, they made things happen.

Gadi's squad was known for its high level of motivation. When they were called back from lookouts, the response was always the same:

"We're OK. We can stay a bit longer." Roman, the machine gunner in Leibovich's squad, was particularly driven to excel. "Let's train more," he would spur his fellow soldiers on. " It'll be better in the long run." Roman was tall and winsome with blond hair and blue eyes. His good nature was contagious. Gadi saw in him kindred spirit, and often asked Leibovich to loan him to his squad on missions. If it was a special mission, one that involved only a select few from the platoon, Leibovich invariably agreed. But if it was a mission that involved the entire platoon, as in the attack on the *Mukatt'ah*, Roman stayed put. Roman was the machine gunner that Leibovich wanted covering his back.

David Zinni, Leibovich's official replacement as platoon commander, arrived that day. There wasn't enough time to bring him up to speed, so he tagged along as a soldier in Leibovich's squad.

An external staircase led to a metal door on the second floor of the first building inside the compound. Leibovich explained to the soldiers how they were going to take the building. He stressed caution, but tried not to appear overly worried.

"*Yallah.* Let's go. Let's get our equipment on." Roman sensed the hoarseness in his voice. "Leibovich! " Roman called too him. "What are you worried about? You know I've got your ass covered."

"Fire on the door, " Leibovich instructed Roman at the top of the staircase. Roman loosed a machine gun burst and Leibovich kicked the door open. Inside was a long hallway, a series of offices on either side. With the exception of one heavily metal door at the end of the hall, all of the doors were wooden. One by one, they fired into the offices and made their way down the hallway. Soldiers came up from below to occupy the offices that had been secured. The offices had been occupied until extremely recently. There were rifles on the floor and full magazines. In one office there was a stove, still warm.

Roman tried to open the steel door at the end of the hall. Locked. Leibovich motioned for silence as they listened for sounds from within the room. Nothing. They decided to take the office across the hall from the locked room, and then have a go at the fortified steel door. Roman crouched with his back to the steel door, covering Leibovich. Leibovich swung at the wooden door with a sledge hammer. There was a knocking sound, steel on steel, from within the locked room.

Leibovich was dimly aware of hands pulling him back towards a secured room. Roman was being dragged too. Duchan, the C.C., was speaking into the radio, "I have two wounded. Bad. I need an immediate evacuation."

The bullets, large caliber Kalashnikov rounds, had come through the steel door. Roman had been caught square from behind. He had taken two bullets in the chest, one in the stomach. Leibovich was hit in an arm and a leg.

The steel door burst open and enemy gunmen opened fire. Kalashnikovs angled around the doorjambs, spewing fire down the hallway.

Gadi fought his way towards the room into which the wounded had been dragged. The medic applied a tourniquet to Leibovich's leg and went to work on Roman. Gadi pulled out his green tourniquet and applied it to Leibovich's arm. Leibovich faded in and out of consciousness.

Two soldiers carried Leibovich down the external staircase. Before being evacuated to the hospital, Leibovich awoke to find Ido, the Battalion Medical Officer, working on his arm.

"Roman," he murmured. "Take care of Roman."

"Don't worry."

Gadi hurled grenade after grenade into the room with the steel door and then stormed it. The building caught on fire, and the soldiers fell back to the police building where they had holed up.

*   *   *

Gadi accompanied Roman's body on its final journey. Roman, an immigrant from the former Soviet Union, hadn't been recognized as Jewish by the religious establishment. Gadi made the identification at the Army Rabbinate, and gave the rabbinate officials careful instructions as to how the body of his friend was to be cared for. He brought Roman's uniform together with the body. The official from the *Hevreh Kadishah*, the Volunteer Burial Society, assured Gadi that his wishes would be carried out.

The Army Rabbi was amazed at Gadi's command of the ritual relating to the death of a soldier. In high school, Gadi had studied under Rav Ruja, one of the authorities on the subject. There was an ancient ritual that a soldier or murder victim was to be buried in the clothes in which they were killed, in order that their blood cry out for revenge. Gadi reminded the officials of the Army Rabbinate of the ritual. "If this happens to me, I want to be buried in my uniform." Gadi requested. "Remember. No autopsy. No clean clothes."

Back in Ramallah, he searched for his older brother Yakov. Troops were still arriving. Amid the chaos, no one seemed to know where he was. He desperately wanted to find him. There were certain conversations that he could only have with Yakov. He wanted to tell him about Roman. Of all of the Ezra children, Gadi and Yakov had been most deeply connected to Saba Yossef. Now, in much the same way, they were connected to each other. Yakov, like Saba Yossef, was a healer and student of the soul. Gadi desperately hoped that he would catch up with him before his Battalion moved on to Jenin.

*   *   *

Saba Yossef, Gadi's maternal grandfather, was only sixteen when he underwent his training as a *Mohel*, a ritual circumciser, in Algeria. He went on to study medicine in Toulouse, France in the late 1930s. He then returned to Algeria to practice as an eye specialist.

With the expulsion of Algeria's Jews in 1962, Saba Yossef brought his family to France where he established a homeopathy clinic in Montpelier. Gadi's parents met in France, where both were studying pharmacy. Gadi's four older siblings were born in France. In the late 1960s, Gadi's family made *Aliyah* to Israel.

When it was announced that their mother was pregnant, the four Ezra children were overjoyed. Around the kitchen table, they tried to think up a short, monosyllabic name befitting the family's first *Tzabar*. The first native Israeli. Dan, perhaps, if it's a boy. Their mother cast a veto. The tribe of Dan bore a snake as its insignia. How about "Gad"? Although those outside the family called him "Gadi", to his family he was always "Gad". His birth was emblematic of his family's journey from old to new. The first Ezra child to be born in Israel, he was the last child to be circumcised by Saba Yossef.

Gadi had many 'little parents'. Yakov would sneak out of his yeshivah at lunchtime to enjoy a few minutes of playtime with Gadi at his preschool. Vittoria would proudly take him for walks through the neighborhood. She delighted when strangers would mistake her for little Gadi's mother. Vivian, only eight years old when Gadi was born, doted endlessly on her little brother. She took him everywhere, even wangling special permission to bring him on her school trips. She was his "little mother".

Saba Yossef, already 75 years old, opened a small homeopathy clinic in Bat Yam. When Yakov became a neurologist, he worked in Saba

Yossef's small clinic a few days a week to observe his remarkable clinical skills. For Saba Yossef was not only a student of medicine. He was a student of the human soul in all of its aspects. In the Ezra family, spirituality and science blended naturally into one another.

By the time Gadi was four, the older children had all left the house. With his parents both busy in their pharmacy, Gadi spent much of the day with his grandparents. He developed a deep connection to Saba Yossef. He felt as comfortable in Saba Yossef's world as he did in the other worlds that he straddled. With Saba Yossef, he studied the Zohar, the central text of Jewish Mysticism, and learned to chant the Torah reading in Saba Yossef's North African melody.

Gadi was a tireless builder of bridges. To unite all of the many worlds in which he found himself, he had to learn the peculiarities of each. After learning Saba Yossef's North African Torah melodies, he enlarged his repertoire, adding the Jerusalemite melody (the Sephardic tradition), and the Ashkenazi melody. Even at age two he was already creating linguistic bridges. Family members spoke to him in French, and he would translate to his babysitter in rapid-fire Hebrew.

He beheld the world in wonderment. Strolling home from school, he would trace the movements of the clouds as he hummed to himself. It wasn't uncommon for a tree or a lamppost to shake him out of his reverie. "Don't ever buy that child a bicycle," one of the neighbors warned his mother.

When a new child from France arrived in his first grade class, Gadi immediately adopted him. Every afternoon, he brought the boy home and helped him with his homework until his Hebrew became fluent.

Gadi's parents lived a largely secular life in France. In Israel, the children were enrolled in religious schools and gradually the family adopted a religious lifestyle. Still, there remained a certain heterogeneity within the family with regard to observance. There was no shortage of debates on the subject of religion, and Gadi was the classic mediator. He asked endless questions of all sides in mediating a conflict; he needed to know everything before attempting a resolution. He was a deep listener, able to give each side the feeling of being totally understood. He energetically promoted tolerance within the family while at the same time not negating his own religious principles.

He drew inspiration from the teachings of Rav Kook, first Chief Rabbi of the Jewish Community in the period leading up to the establishment of the State of Israel. In his shirt pocket, he always kept a book of Rav Kook's teachings, *Orot Tshuvah*. Rav Kook had been fascinated by the paradox of Jewish secularity. Not content to dismiss the abandonment of tradition as a failing, he took a more deterministic view of secularization. Perhaps it was a process that needed to be traversed, he posited. A road that needed to be crossed to get to the other side. Perhaps people became secular not out of pathology, but out of the expansiveness of their souls. Not out of smallness, but out of greatness. Rav Kook was particularly enamored of the kibbutzniks, whose role in the creation of the Jewish State struck him as holy albeit not in the traditional sense. Gadi delighted in the working of Rav Kook's mind. Here was a true builder of bridges. A truly righteous man.

Yossi and Yakov, Gadi's older brothers, gained endless amusement at the transformation that Gadi had worked on their once strict father. They had been brought up with an iron hand. But no one could resist Gadi's charms. Now they laughed at the escapades that never would have been tolerated in their own childhood, especially Gadi's habit of adopting people and bringing them home. Many a morning Solly Ezra, Gadi's father would discover a complete stranger asleep on the couch.

"Gadiiiii…..."

"Oh, don't worry, *Abba*. It's Shmulik. He had a falling out with his parents."

Gadi was pure. It was impossible to be angry with him.

Gadi had a soothing influence on all around him. His father was unable to fall into a deep sleep until Gadi was home safe at night. He would lie half-awake, dimly awaiting the sound of Gadi's key in the door.

"Gadiiiiii…"

No matter how silent Gadi was, his father would snap awake at the sound of that telltale 'click', as if that turn of the key was transmitted to his father on their own special frequency, their own special connection. "It's me Dad, you can go to sleep now."

Gadi was a charismatic group leader and gifted organizer in the *Bnei Akiva* youth movement. He couldn't stand for anyone in his immediate circle to be unhappy. At the *Kav LaHayim* camp, the circumstances were often grim and the volunteers became depressed when not in the presence of the children. Gadi wouldn't stand for it. "I'm not leaving until there's a smile on your face," he once said to a particularly inconsolable volunteer. By the time the meeting was over he had her in stitches.

As a teenager, Gadi was already becoming known as a gifted poet and orator. From high school onward, he gave the eulogies at family funerals. Some in the family tried to convince him to harness his impassioned oratory as an attorney, but he knew that his calling was that of an educator.

After high school, he studied for two years at the Or Etzion yeshivah. A leading student, he never radiated superiority. He radiated simplicity and humility. Whenever his friends came back to the yeshivah from vacation, they would seek Gadi out for his famous bear hugs.

Study alone was not enough for him. He became moody when

immersed in his studies for too long. He needed to help. He needed to be connected to the lives of others. He needed to always be giving.

In his first year at Or Etzion, the *Kav LaHayim* program fell early, while the yeshivah school year was still in session. One of the older students who was involved in the camp went to the head of the yeshivah to get permission forsome students take time off from studies for the camp.

"OK, but only the older students. No first year students."

"Well, there's one exception. I need Gadi Ezra."

"Of course, that goes without saying," the head of the yeshivah said without hesitation. "No first year students other than Gadi Ezra."

Rav Ruja, his high school principal, had a phrase for him: *maskil el dal*. He who knows how to approach the less fortunate. Some try to help the less fortunate and end up smothering them with their good intentions. Not Gadi. From Saba Yossef, he learned to study a man's soul before attempting to help him. Gadi knew how to give sustenance without smothering.

Gadi opted not to combine his yeshivah studies and army service into the joint four year *hesder* program. Instead, he pursued a full two years of yeshivah studies at Or Etzion followed by a full three year army stint in the Golani Infantry Brigade, known as the ultimate cross-section of Israeli society. He would have more to contribute as a commander in Golani, he felt, than among his highly motivated peers.

Gadi was invited to join a special unit of the Golani Brigade. Project *Reshit* was a one-year variation on boot camp that paired inspirational, highly motivated recruits such as Gadi with potentially problematic recruits from troubled backgrounds. The results were extraordinary. Never much of an athlete, Gadi was not the typical infantryman. In boot camp, his feet were so swollen that it was difficult to lace his boots to the top, lending him a disheveled appearance. But he poured his heart and soul into each mission. He proved how far an abundance of love could go in surmounting physical challenges. His love was always overflowing. He loved every minute of that first year, even when they ran him ragged. When at first he floundered on the climbing wall, he took the Athletic Director aside. "We have to try this wall again. We're going to make this happen." Eventually, he succeeded.

He loved the esprit de corps of the Golani Brigade, but there was one thing that made him uneasy: the profanity. He never cursed. As always, he worked out his own solution. He sang the off-color Golani songs with gusto – but only after replacing the profane words with less objectionable ones.

He developed strong bonds with every level of command, from the lowliest cook to the Battalion Commander. He went out of his way to give encouragement to the support personnel. The other soldiers knew that there was only one way to get food out of the kitchen during off hours. When approached directly, the irascible cooks would always show them the door. But they all loved Gadi. Gadi would never come back from the kitchen empty handed.

When his unit was stationed in an outpost on the Lebanese border, he called his mother to get her recipe for baking *chalot*. He baked *chalot* for the entire unit. On those Passovers that he spent on base, it would fall to Gadi to conduct the Seder. More than anything else, he loved dancing ecstatically on Simchat Torah.

Gadi was chosen for Officer's Training School. The educational aspect of an Officer's commission appealed to him, but it soon became painfully clear that he didn't have the athletic ability to become a combat infantry officer. The obstacle course was a near disaster, but it was the orienteering test that finally proved his undoing. The only option for an "athletically challenged" officer was a commission as a non-combat instructor. Gadi desperately wanted to remain in a combat unit. In the end, he didn't complete the Officer's course. As was his attitude in everything else, he was certain it was for the best.

Back in a combat unit, he became a squad leader and jeep commander in the Recon platoon of Battalion 51's Auxiliary Company. For non-commissioned army personnel, it was the pinnacle of achievement. As a commander, he was demanding and encouraging in equal measure. He was an idealist, but not an overly serious one. He loved life, food, and laughter. It was no wonder that every soldier wanted to be in Gadi's squad.

Gadi met Galit three months before Passover, at her cousin's wedding. She was his first girlfriend. Yossi heard tell of the blossoming relationship and was dying for Gadi to volunteer some tidbits. Finally, at a family *briss* (circumcision ceremony), Gadi opened up.

"I'm starting to see someone." He was blushing.

Yossi tried not to laugh. He knew what an innocent Gadi was. He had always imagined that Gadi would fall in love with the first girl who was friendly to him. In fact, it had taken quite a number of phone calls on Gadi's part to finally get Galit to agree to meet with him. What a pair, thought Yossi. They were both 'crazy' in the same way. Galit, like Gadi, was devoted to the less fortunate. She understood completely when Gadi spent his entire leave visiting wounded fellow soldiers instead of spending time with her.

And that obsession with the Book of Psalms, thought Yossi. Galit even more than Gadi. Two months ago, Galit came to visit Gadi on his base. The Friday afternoon bus came too late for her to leave without travelling on the Sabbath, leaving her stranded on the base. What did they spend their time doing? A nature walk? Relaxing with friends? No.

They read the Book of Psalms. No doubt about it, thought Yossi. Those two were meant for each other.

After a recent difficult operation, Gadi called Galit from his base. The fighting had left him shaken. "Galit, I've written you a letter in case anything should happen to me."

"I don't want to hear about it."

"Then I'll leave it somewhere for you."

"Tear it up. Or better yet, bury it. We'll laugh over it when we're sixty."

CHAPTER 13 Cops and Robbers in the Rain

Hanoch and the *Pal-Sar*, the Regimental Recon Company, began training Sunday morning. Their orders for the *Pal-Sar* kept on changing. With each change, Hanoch, as Pathfinder, had to familiarize himself with a new set of aerial maps. He was becoming frustrated. Even worse, the aerial maps were woefully out of date. Refugee camps are dynamic, growing organisms. The low, cinderblock houses sprouted additions in all directions. Neighborhoods mushroomed randomly. Hanoch's job was to continually translate the minute details of the aerial maps into simple road maps for the Company Commander. He had been in refugee camps before – Jebaliah, Dehaisheh – but never in battle. And never in Jenin.

"These aerial maps are from 1997," Hanoch complained to Oren.

"They're too old. I don't feel comfortable with them." Oren promised to request some newer ones.

After studying the maps for a few hours, Hanoch realized the true magnitude of the operation. The entire Jenin refugee camp was no more than a quarter square mile. All of the forces would be converging on the same central point. Keeping all of the converging units aware of each other would be a virtual impossibility, thought Hanoch. Throughout the battle, it would fall to him to keep track of where each unit was positioned and to cross off the houses that had been secured. Maybe going in slowly, house by house, wasn't such a bad idea.

*   *   *

Doron's company began training Sunday morning. Target practice first, then urban warfare drills. They all knew how to storm an uninhabited building: toss a grenade, spray the room with fire, everyone grab his corner. But what was the drill in buildings that were inhabited by civilians and gunmen together? Asi, the Company Commander, had gone on to Jenin already, so Yossi and Big Zvikah, veteran soldiers who had tasted urban warfare in the first wave of violence over a decade earlier, lead the drills. Maor, the Lieutenant Company Commander, assigned a family role to each.

"OK, Zvikah – you be the father. Yossi – you're the mother. Sami – show us what we can expect from a 14-year-old youth." It was like drama class at the Youth Village, thought Doron. Maor brought one of the younger soldiers over to the building's entrance.

"OK, let's drill the entry. You announce, no one answers. What do you do?"

"I open the door by shooting out the lock."

"That only works in the movies," said Doron. "In reality, you shoot at a lock and it can become permanently stuck. Think about your other tools. You have a ten-pound sledgehammer and an explosive brick."

The young soldier opted for the sledge hammer. He swung it, pretending to break open the door. As he rested it by the doorjamb, Yossi, the 'mother', ran to the door and pushed him backwards. The young soldier raised his hand to strike.

"Nope," said Maor. "She's a woman. You can't touch her. Think."

"And by the way," said Zvikah, the 'father'. "You've been dead for around ten seconds now. I have a revolver."

Doron demonstrated the entry technique, keeping his body out of the doorway until he had scanned the entire room with his rifle sight.

"Keep close watch," said Maor. "This protects you and the civilians as well."

In another "scene", a soldier pretended to blow open the door with an explosive brick, then angled his rifle on the doorjamb as Doron had done. But he allowed his rifle to protrude inwards too far and Sami, the "youth", grabbed the barrel and pulled it into the room. The soldier fell into the waiting arms of Yossi, who stabbed him repeatedly with a make-believe knife.

"These are all things we've seen," said Yossi.

"But wait." The young soldier was confused now. "If we can't do this, and we can't do that, then what *can* we do? You're telling us to avoid killing innocent people, and to avoid being killed. How do you do both in a split second?"

"We want thinking soldiers, not machines," Maor replied. "Intelligence has advised us that the camp is still full of civilians. Some have no where to go. Others still don't believe that we'll dare enter the refugee camp. So you're just going to have to think every situation through." The younger soldiers appeared dissatisfied but no one pressed the point in the freezing rain. They wanted directives, concrete rules. All Maor could give them was conflicting principles, arguments that would need to be weighed and resolved in an instant once the time came. He gave them the old speech about asking the right questions. "Remember. Question marks are more important than exclamation points." Still, they kept on asking the same question. "But what *exactly* do we do?"

"What you do, is you look at everyone through your sights," said Itzik, one of the other squad leaders in Doron's platoon. "No matter how hard it is. Women included. You don't fire unless fired upon, but you're always looking through the cross hairs." Doron envied Itzik's amazing instincts. He always knew exactly what to do. Doron was senior to him, but he always thought of Itzik as more of a well-tuned fighting machine. Being next to him made Doron feel safe.

"A lot of things won't be clear until we're there," Maor continued. "Remember, finger on the trigger every second. I want everyone's back covered by someone else's rifle. If a commander lowers his weapon to check an ID, whoever's covering him doesn't waver for an instant. Above all else – avoid the streets."

At the end of the day, they came out of the drills feeling strengthened, feeling that each of them could rely totally on his buddy. Doron called Liron.

"You can relax, I have a bodyguard now." He thought the attempt at humor would calm her down. It made her more nervous.

"That's not a good sign."

"It's OK, you can count on him. He's from Golani like your brother."

Although they hadn't discussed it since he was called up, she knew that Doron's unit would be headed for Jenin if war broke out. He told her that they'd have a one hour break Monday night.

"Can we come to see you before you leave, then?"

"Sure. That would be great."

"What are you doing now?"

"Still drills."

"When are you going in?"

"Can't talk about it."

"What did you do today?"

"We played cops and robbers in the rain."

CHAPTER 14 Departure

Monday, April 1. Hanoch still felt that he was in the dark. On the key details, he was still drawing blanks. In the briefings, they had been continually warned against *mit'anim*, the makeshift bombs and booby traps. But what did a *mit'an* look like? Never one for abstract concepts, Hanoch needed to see one with his own eyes. He asked Oren if he had any photographs to show them. There were none. "Look, they're usually explosive bricks attached to propane tanks. If you see a propane tank with lots of wires coming out of it, that's a *mit'an*. Of course, then there's the soda cans. They can have explosives in them. Or the burning tires. Or regular tires. Or anything, basically. The tiniest thing can be booby-trapped. Anything can be a *mit'an*."

Hanoch called his father-in-law, the TV news correspondent. He had been in Jenin two weeks earlier with the Golani troops. He had seen *mit'anim* from up close. Hanoch asked if he could come talk to them about what he had seen there. He met them at a park near the base. Hanoch brought Hemi, the X.O. and Ofer, the Lieutenant C.C. with him. Over a picnic table, they spent five hours going over what they might expect to find. His father-in-law described in great detail what a booby-trapped window looked like, and what form a tiny makeshift bomb could take. He warned them to stay away from the garbage cans, and to be particularly circumspect in houses with posters of suicide bombers plastered all over the walls.

Until that evening, Hanoch had assumed that he would be stationed in a lookout on the southern hill overlooking the refugee camp. That was how it had always been in training exercises. But here, lookouts were ineffective – there were too many small, low houses, separated only by narrow alleyways. Even from the surrounding hills, one couldn't see between the houses. They would all be going in together.

The Regimental command post, code named Ginat, was set up to the west of the refugee camp. To the east of the camp, on the seam between the Jenin refugee camp and the city of Jenin, the Naval Commando took up positions. Golani Battalion 51 would be entering the camp from the south. Battalion 7020 would be surrounding the camp. Hanoch and the *Pal-Sar* would be entering from the north. Each company would receive an attachment of two tanks.

*   *   *

For Doron and the *Pal-Han*, Monday was another day of drills. Liron and the children arrived at nine o'clock p.m. They sat in the parking lot and hugged and kissed. When the children weren't looking, Liron wiped away a tear.

"*Abba*, can I touch your rifle?" asked Shoham. Doron and Liron never allowed him toy weapons. Objects of violence were anathema, even in play. Shoham had put up such a fuss that they finally gave in and bought him a squirtgun.

Shoham's eyes were huge. "Where do the bombs come out from, *Abba*?"

"They're bullets, not bombs. Let's talk about something else." Doron couldn't bring himself to forbid his son from touching the weapon, but he didn't want Shoham to become acquainted with such things at his tender age. Shoham stroked the barrel lightly. "Now I know how you're going to beat the bad people, *Abba*. With your rifle. Before, I couldn't figure out how you were going to beat them."

Doron changed the subject. "So what did you do today?"

"We went to see Peter Pan!" said Shoham.

"We were the only people in the theater," Adi chimed in. It was true. Doron's mother had pleaded with Liron not to go. The danger of a bombing was too great. But Liron had promised the children a movie, and she felt obliged. Doron agreed, it was better that way. It was a philosophy he and Liron both shared. They didn't believe in tempting fate, but didn't want their children to miss their childhood either. Wherever possible, they wanted to maintain a sense of normalcy for the children. Taking them to a movie was an acceptable risk.

Adi told the story of Peter Pan in great detail. Shoham related the part that he understood. "And the good people beat the bad people!! *Abba*, are you going to beat the bad people?"

"Of course."

"And when will you come home?"

"When we've beaten all the bad people."

"Do you want them all to die?"

"I'd rather that they stopped being bad. I don't want anyone to die."

Orly, Amir's widow, came with her three children to see the troops off. She was still very much a part of the company. The men had set up a rotation, and every week a few of the soldiers spent an afternoon with Amir's children. Doron felt guilty that he hadn't stayed in closer contact with Orly and the children, but he couldn't shake the dread that filled him whenever he saw them. Seeing Orly always brought him face to face with his own mortality. Particularly when he saw the children. He too had two sons and a daughter. Looking at Amir's children, he couldn't keep his mind from forming the unbearable parallel: that's what my children will look like without their father.

After the families went home, Asi held another staff meeting at 11:00 p.m. He had more specifics now. "It's not just Jenin. We're going into the refugee camp. We're going to be the first company going in. We'll be coming in from the south, and together with Golani Battalion 51, we'll be in charge of taking the east side. Another battalion from the north will take the west side, and a third will hold the perimeter." It's tomorrow, thought Doron. The drills had been tough, but he was still abuzz with adrenaline. He forced himself to sleep. He would need all of his strength tomorrow.

CHAPTER 15 Point Blank Range

Tuesday, April 2. The morning of final adjustments. They were in the Valley of Dotan, just south of Jenin. Doron and his men checked their equipment one last time. Helmet snug. Bulletproof vest comfortable. A truck arrived with new optical gear and boots. They had never received such amenities before. Usually it was make do with what you have. It made them even more nervous.

Doron still couldn't shake the feeling that had taken hold of him the previous night when Orly and her children appeared. It seemed so clear: this is the final farewell. The scriptures say that thirty days prior to a man's death, he has a premonition. Doron had always steered clear of mysticism. He considered himself more of the Rambam's school, a rational man of faith. But still.

He ran into Hezi, an intelligence officer who had been one of his soldiers in the Nahal Brigade. Hezi was the younger brother of Doron's best friend, and had assumed that their informal relationship would continue into the army. He insisted on calling him Doron, instead of *hamfaked*, Commander. Doron pulled him aside one day and laid down the law. "Listen, Hezi, I don't know you and you don't know me. Understand? If I hear you calling me 'Doron' one more time there are going to be consequences." Hezi got the point. Now Doron found himself hoping that Hezi had forgiven him.

"Hezi, can you tell me anything?"

"Well, *hamfaked*, I can tell you this: the other side is ready. We know they have at least two large caliber machine guns, RPGs, LAU missiles, and hundreds of kilograms of explosives. What unit are you in now?"

"The *Pal-Han*."

"Oh wow," Hezi blurted out. A moment of silence. He wished he hadn't said anything. "You guys are going in first. You'd better be real careful."

The tables had been turned on Itzik, Doron's fellow squad leader, as well. Maor, the *Pal-Han*'s Lieutenant Company Commander, was a soldier in Itzik's squad during their regular service. Now Maor was Itzik's Platoon Commander. "Remember how you used to make me run, Itzik? Do you remember how many soldiers you abused?" They laughed. Itzik had been tough, but fair. Now Maor treated him with the same respect.

Col. Didi Yedidiah, the Regiment Commander, addressed them. He tried to lighten things up with some humor but then quickly turned serious. "Don't leave any stone unturned. Remember that you'll be preventing future attacks." An armored regiment would be entering the city, an infantry regiment would be entering the refugee camp.

It was Asi's turn to go over last minute instructions. He opened up the maps. "Not a word on casualties over the radio. Only on cell phones. Those fighting need to keep their concentration."

Doron's company broke up into platoons. Maor, his Platoon Commander, went over the chain of command in case of injury. "If I'm taken out, then Doron's in command. Then Itzik, then Basher." He stopped there. "We should go all the way down the line," said Doron. "If things get bad, better that everything be mapped out beforehand." Maor stopped to consider who would take over from Basher.

Back in the tent, Itzik sat down next to Doron. "Let's face it. We won't be coming back the same number of people."

Doron was uncharacteristically irritable. "How's that supposed to help, Itzik? Some things are better left unsaid." The briefings had affected them all. Soldiers removed any non-essentials from their vests and added a few more grenades.

At 3:00 p.m they took a bus to the Saalem interchange where their APCs were unloaded. Sandbags were missing from many of the APCs; either they had fallen off en route or had been appropriated. "Quit deliberating," said Maor. "There's plenty of sand here, and there's a shovel. Start filling." New rifles arrived. The soldiers had to decide between the newer, more convenient short M-16s, and the longer, bulkier M-16s that they had thoroughly calibrated during their two days of drilling.

Asi left the decision up to each individual. "Decide for yourselves. If you're comfortable with a new weapon that hasn't been fired, take it. If not, keep your long M-16." Most of them opted for the shorter weapons with fancy telescopic lenses. Some of the soldiers seemed unable to decide.

"What's the big debate? " asked Itzik. "At point blank range, I wouldn't be that worried about calibration."

CHAPTER 16 Only People

Leibovich awoke in the intensive care unit. He was connected to a battery of monitors. Duchan, the Company Commander, was by his bed.

"What about Roman?" asked Leibovich.

"Dead." Leibovich was silent. The monitors attached to him began to beep.

Leibovich received a visit from a family whose son had been a soldier in Platoon 5 and had fallen. They had remained very much a part of the platoon over the years, and always came to its gatherings. They brought pictures from a recent platoon reunion. One of the pictures was of Gadi and Galit.

After Roman's funeral, the platoon came to the hospital to visit Leibovich. Gadi arrived with Galit. It was the first time that Leibovich had met her.

"Remember Leibovich, you owe me a green tourniquet," said Gadi. It was their private joke. The black, standard-issue army tourniquets were considered inferior to the green, non-military tourniquets. Gadi had managed to procure a green one. It was Gadi's coveted green tourniquet that he had tied onto Leibovich's arm.

A few minutes after they left, Leibovich noticed that Gadi had forgotten the picture. He called Gadi on his cell phone.

"You forgot your picture."

"Don't worry. I'll pick it up next time I see you." Gadi and Galit had other things on their mind. Gadi was only one month away from the end of his army service, and they were headed to a jewelry store to look at rings.

*   *   *

Battalion 51 had finished the capture of the *Mukatt'ah*. Now they were moving north with a short rest stop in Netanyah. Gadi Ezra called his parents.

"*Ima*, I'm in Netanyah for a little bit. You and *Abba* can come and meet me."

His parents rushed up to Netanyah. They brought dairy food. Gadi had just eaten meat, so he gave the food to his friends. They sat for a while and talked in the car. He was deeply shaken by the Roman's death, but was determined not to show it. "If I let it break me, they've won," he said to his friend Kobi. On the way back to Bat Yam, Gadi's parents received another call. It was Gadi. He had forgotten his cell phone in their car. They made a U-Turn and zoomed back to catch him before the bus left for Jenin. One last time, they hugged goodbye.

The Auxiliary Company of Battalion 51 was sent up to man an outpost on Har Dov, near the Lebanese border. All except for the hard hit Platoon 5. They would be attached to the Rifleman Company under the command of Avihu Yaakov, and would continue on to Jenin. They would keep on fighting.

Gadi was pleased. He preferred the adrenaline of an operation to the long, empty hours of manning an outpost. And besides, he would be fighting under Avihu. Among the tight community of Or Etzion graduates, Avihu Yaakov was nothing short of a legend.

* * *

"The orange bomb of energy," Avihu's friends called him, referring to his shock of red hair. He had a compact frame of tightly wound steel and had about him the crackling voltage of an electric current. Every morning he awoke recharged, ready to electrify all those around him. His greatest joy lay in pushing himself and his soldiers beyond what they thought were their limits. As a cadet in the Naval Commando, he was just as likely to walk the twenty miles home from the base as he was to hitch a ride.

Avihu and Gadi were bound by a common life philosophy: *Rak B'Simchah*. In all things, only joy. Their favorite holidays were Purim and Simhat Torah, those of unbridled joy. Even as he climbed the ladder of command, Avihu always insisted on celebrating on Purim in costume. He injected joyous spirituality into the macho Golani culture.

Avihu, like Gadi, came to the Golani Brigade out of a sense of social purpose. His defining moment came after Officer Training School, when he chose to take a commission in the Golani Brigade rather than return to the elite Naval Commando. Golani drew from all levels of society; it was the antithesis of an elite unit. Soldiers didn't volunteer for Golani – they were assigned. Avihu sought an educational challenge of the highest magnitude.

"What's the challenge of being a company commander in the naval commando?" he said to his commando friends. "Anyone can build an elite fighting force with those soldiers. I'm going to show that it can be done with Golani soldiers. "

*   *   *

Avihu's father, Gadi Yaakov, chose a similar path as a youth. Kalonymos Yaakov, Avihu's grandfather, departed Nazi Germany in 1933 and settled in Haifa. A man of deep religiosity and an all-embracing social vision, he worked all of his days in the Ata textile plant. When it came time for high school, Gadi Yaakov chose to study in the local *ma'abarah*, the refugee camp for new arrivals to Israel, rather than at the prestigious *Reali* high school nearby.

In the army, Gadi Yaakov's Nahal unit was attached to Kibbutz Shluchot in the Bet Shean Valley. It was there that he met Beri, Avihu's mother. She arrived on Kibbutz Shluchot with a group of volunteers after the Six-Day war. She was the "adopted sister" in the kibbutz family that also hosted the burly Nahal soldier from Haifa. No one imagined that anything could possibly develop between the refined South African immigrant and the rowdy, impulsive *Tzabar*.

Gadi and Beri had six children. They named their first son Amir, and then continued on according to the Hebrew alphabet. Bet and Gimel were already taken care of : Beri and Gadi. For the next letter, Dalet, a son Da-El was born. Then came another son, Hadas. When Beri was pregnant with their fourth child, they realized they would be stumped if it were a boy. There was no male Hebrew name that began with the Hebrew letter Vov. Gadi's friend Zvi had an idea. The weekly Torah portion told the story of Nadav and Avihu, the two sons of the High Priest Aaron. In Hebrew 'and Avihu' is *v'Avihu*.

"So there's your Vov," said Zvi.

After Avihu came two daughters, Zohar and Chen.

The Yaakov family settled in Kfar Hassidim, a farming village founded in 1925 by a group of Zionist Chassidim from the Poland. Gadi planted a variety of vegetables on his 100-dunam lot: pumpkins, artichokes, and many varieties of squash. The village felt like one extended family. Everyone cared for everyone else. Neighbors volunteered their own cars whenever they saw Gadi and his children piling into his rickety Ford station wagon. "Gadi, for G-d's sake. Take my car, I don't need it right now." Gadi became the mainstay of the village *Hevrah Kadishah*, the Volunteer Burial Society. When there were graves to be dug, his powerful sons were conscripted for the task. As with everything else, it quickly became a contest. The object was to see who could dig himself up to his shoulders the quickest. Avihu, the youngest, invariably won. He was the smallest, but more than made up for it in raw strength.

"Hey, it's no fair," Avihu's brothers kidded him as dirt flew in the air. "You're shorter than we are."

Avihu took his school assignments seriously. In researching an assignment on Trumpeldor, an early Israeli pioneer, he insisted that his father take him to visit the kibbutz where Trumpeldor had lived. He was drawn to animals, particularly those that he felt were unduly scorned. He became a passionate defender of the much-maligned goat, to which he dedicated his eighth-grade science project.

"People think that goats do damage," he wrote. "I disagree. I find that goats are extremely helpful to humans. People don't like the fact that they nibble low-hanging branches, but when forest fires break out in the forests of the Carmel, it is the 'damage' done by goats that keep the fires from spreading." He detailed every aspect of caring for goats, down to the most minute, unsavory details of fertility treatments and deliveries. His project won top honors.

As a teenager, Avihu desperately wanted to attend Or Etzion yeshivah, a much sought after religious boarding school. As part of the entrance exam , he was asked to draw a person, a house, and a tree. He sketched a tiny house, an equally minute tree, and filled the rest of the page with an extremely detailed drawing of a human being. When the examiner asked why the images were so disproportionate, Avihu laughed. It seemed obvious. "People are important," he answered. "Things aren't."

He failed the exam, and enrolled in the local high school. But he didn't give up. Over the next two months, he flooded the head of the yeshivah with correspondence. Finally, the principal gave in. Avihu was allowed to enroll mid-term.

Avihu always found a middle ground between his high standards for himself and his empathy for those less fortunate. To copy from other students was unthinkable, but he debated whether or not concealing his own notebook from others constituted a lack of altruism. In the end, he decided that they were responsible for their own actions, and kept his notebook open.

In high school, he and a group of his friends were accused of having similar results on a math final. The others agreed to redo the test, but Avihu steadfastly refused. His were the only results that were ultimately recognized. A stubborn *gingey* (redhead), his father laughed, recognizing his wife's hair color but his own stubbornness. Stubborn as a mule.

Gadi Yaakov's humility was extreme to the point of secretiveness when it came to his sons' military exploits. Amir, the eldest son, volunteered for *Sayeret Matcal*, the super-elite commando unit best known for the raid on Entebbe. Gadi was characteristically tight-lipped about his son's service.

Moshe, Gadi's neighbor, was dying of curiosity.

"What's Amir up to in the army? You never talk about him much."

"He works in the PX." Moshe nodded politely and changed the subject.

Six months later, Moshe found out the truth.

"How could you have told me such a lie!!" he confronted Gadi. "I asked you what your son did in the army, and you told me he worked in the PX. Now I come to find out that he's in *Sayeret Matcal*!! Why would you have told such a ridiculous lie??"

"So now you know what he does." Gadi shrugged. "You've known Amir all his life. Now that you know that he's in *Sayyeret Matcal*, does that change your opinion of him?"

The other Yaakov sons also served in elite units. Avihu was the first to join the Naval Commando.

Avihu inherited his father's humility. He seldom donned his ceremonial Navy whites, his *alef* uniform. His father once joked to him that it would be nice to see him in *alef*, with all of his medals, for a change. "Do I look like a bulletin board?" he replied. His father chuckled. Typical. He only felt at home in his *bet* garb, his work clothes.

Most of Avihu's platoon buddies in the Naval Commando were secular, but he wanted them to share his love of Judaism. On Purim, he brought his entire platoon to listen to the reading of the Scroll of Esther at Kfar Hassidim. He gave them all a copy of *Pirke Avot*, The Ethics of the Fathers, the collection of rabbinical wisdom that contained his favorite sayings. On Passover, he took them to the ancient city of Safed where he taught them all to bake *matzot*.

His unit was sent to perform patrols in Hebron. It was routine, tedious work: not the ordinary fare of an elite unit. The soldiers, accustomed to more daring missions, and protested the assignment of a crack unit to such drudgery. Avihu decried the aristocratic attitude of his fellow elite soldiers. "You guys are nothing but a bunch of little princes," he chided them. The nickname caught on. When the unit's tour of duty ended, they printed up T-Shirts as mementos. On the front was a picture of Saint Exupery's Little Prince.

As a Naval Commando, Avihu went on many missions in Lebanon. No matter what the assignment, he believed that everything should be done with joy. The philosophy carried through when he became a commander. He spent every free minute planning parties and events for his soldiers. He didn't believe in the philosophy of breaking a soldier down in order to build him back stronger. He drove his soldiers hard, but showered them with encouragement and support.

Avihu met Sivan in the Commando. He was immediately drawn to the serious, kind-hearted young woman who served as the *mashakit tash*, the Battalion personnel clerk. He asked her if she needed a ride home to Haifa. As it turned out, there were no spare vehicles in the motor pool. They hitched home together.

Sivan put on her best dress for their first date. She was hoping he would show up in his Naval Commando whites. She was certain her parents would be impressed. A horn honked down below. She went downstairs. He was in "be'": army work pants, sandals, and a T-shirt. He hadn't shaved. Sivan hesitated for a few moments - perhaps he would come around to open the door.

"Don't look for anything hidden. What you see is what you get," he said.

He was an innocent. He came into the relationship determined not to lose his independence. "I'll never tell a woman that I love her. That would mean I'd need to call her every day. No woman will ever make me do that." But Sivan only had to hint once that she wasn't hearing from him enough. From then on, he called her every night when he wasn't on an operation.

Avihu was chosen for Officer Training that year. He continued to take great pleasure in organizing parties for his fellow cadets. When he and Sivan were together, he would often be lost in thought, and then suddenly grow excited. "Man!! I just thought of the most amazing idea!!" Sivan always hoped that the new idea would be something romantic, something having to do with the two of them, but she knew better. It was always about the army.

Family ties were of utmost importance to Avihu. He wrote long, encouraging letters to family members in trying situations. To his sister Zohar, struggling to adjust to dormitory life away from home, he wrote:

> *"Don't criticize people. Say something good about someone whenever possible. Whatever you say always becomes known. Take everything in a good spirit. One even laughs about the worst things once enough time has past. It's OK to be lonely and cry. But by yourself, at night, into your pillow. Remember: even life's worst hour is only sixty minutes. In the end, everything passes. And so do we. But strive to leave a mark. Strive to leave every place better than when you found it."*

Sivan once asked him, "How do you keep in touch with everyone?" It seemed like he was constantly in touch with the entire world. He especially loved spending time with all of his nieces and nephews. He loved to hide little treasures for them and help them in their search.

He always had little mints in his pockets. Amir's two-year old daughter was convinced that mints grew from her ears – whenever Avihu came to visit he would pull one out for her.

"Avihu, you've convinced her of this foolishness, " Michal, Amir's wife, once complained to him laughingly. " Now she's always asking me to pull mints out of her ears. Do me a favor. Teach her where mints really come from."

He taught another nephew the secret of financial success. They planted some coins in the ground and covered them up with dirt. They watered the new seedling daily and waited for the "money tree" to grow. With each niece and nephew he had similar "special secrets". Whenever he was on leave they would all report to him on their progress.

He began making waves the moment he arrived in Golani. He took exception to the educational methods. He disagreed with the harsh treatment to which every crop of new recruits was subjected. He didn't like the sharp distinction that was drawn between the *vatikim*, the veterans, and the *tzeirim*, the newbies. He didn't believe that this was the way to instill true cohesiveness in a unit.

Avihu had admired his commanders in the Naval Commando for their authenticity and courage. They were men of deeds. They exemplified his favorite saying from *Pirke Avot* : "Say little and do much, and greet all men with equanimity." He appreciated the freedom of self-expression that they fostered among their charges. That was the culture that he would transplant into Golani, he resolved

In Golani, his first assignment was in the *Bakum*, the intake base for raw recruits. Being from the commando, Avihu could have begun as a company commander had he chosen to do so. But he wanted to learn the Golani culture from the ground up, from as close to the simple soldier as possible. He had himself assigned as Lieutenant Company Commander under Hanan, an old friend from boarding school. The phenomena he encountered were alien to him. Particularly shocking was the new recruit who refused to sign off on his rifle.

"Look, it's not as bad as it seems," he calmed the nervous recruit. "You won't need to shoot the rifle for a while. And we'll make sure you're totally comfortable with it first."

"I'm not signing off on this rifle."

"Well, I understand your how you feel. How about this – you sign off on the rifle, but not the bullets, OK? That way, it won't be dangerous for anyone."

The soldier agreed.

Avihu loved taking long marches with his unit, and made a point of staying in the base on Shabbat when the soldiers stayed. On the twenty-mile "Beret March", six soldiers fainted. He finished the march with the rest of the soldiers, and then went back to attend to the six. He talked with them late into the night, explaining, cajoling, reassuring. The next morning at dawn, he and the six redid the twenty mile march. None of them wanted to let him down. Together, they all made it to the finish line. "I didn't want them to see themselves as failures," he explained to Sivan.

He took up collections for soldiers who had fallen on hard times. He learned that one of his charges, an Ethiopian soldier, had plans to attend university but would have to postpone his studies by a year because of his untimely release date. Without even informing the soldier, he secured an early release from the Battalion Commander. When the soldier was summoned to the Battalion Commander's Office he didn't know what to expect. He was speechless with joy when he found out.

Whenever there were exotic vegetables to be found in the Yaakov family fields, Avihu loaded up a crate for the cooks. On their birthdays, each of his trainees would find a personally inscribed book on his pillow. It was a copy of *Fire in Galilee*, the chronicle of the Golani Brigade.

In November, he received the challenge he had been waiting for. He was put in charge of a company of *tironim*, or raw recruits. He attacked his educational mission with gusto. As Company Commander, Avihu became personally involved in the case of any soldier who had gone AWOL. Previously, the protocol had been to send the staff sergeant out to chase these men down and administer the consequences. He saw these cases as an opportunity to bring not only these soldiers but their families closer to the army. Many of the soldiers' parents had deep misgivings about their sons serving in a combat unit. He would sit down with the mothers over coffee at their kitchen table.

"I know every mother worries," he would begin. And then he would go on to tell them how much their country needed their sons, and swear to them that he would guarantee their welfare to the best of his ability. He knew how to touch everyone's heart. A mother who had met him had no problem releasing her son back into his care. No soldier in the company ever went AWOL twice.

Sivan and he would often debate the need for "distance" between soldiers and their commanders. Sivan felt strongly that it was necessary for discipline. Avihu disliked anything that interfered with direct, honest communications between two human beings. He felt uncomfortable being saluted, or when everyone rose in the middle of a meal when he entered the dining room. He didn't like the fact that no one was allowed to use his first name. But he found ways to stay directly connected to the simple soldiers. He went out of his way to clean his weapon at the cleaning station together with the soldiers, and always passed among the soldiers at night during guard duty.

He detested meting out punishments. Once, a soldier began to cry in his office. The soldier had been brought up on a minor infraction for which the punishment was the loss of his Shabbat leave. Avihu asked the staff sergeant to leave the room. He calmed the soldier down and told him not to worry, that it wasn't a serious incident. He allowed him to stay in his office until he had finished crying and wiped away the tears.

In one Battalion staff meeting, the Battalion Commander called on squad leaders, had them stand, and reprimanded them for minor infractions. When he arrived at a squad leader from Avihu's company, the young man stood.

"Sit down!" Avihu commanded the young sergeant. Everyone turned to Avihu, stunned. Avihu turned to the Battalion Commander.

"If you have any complaints with anything in my company, I'm the address. Not my squad leaders. If anyone is to reprimanded, it's me."

He loved the army's emphasis on professionalism, mutual respect, and physical conditioning. He hated it when Golani *vatikim*, the veteran soldiers, made the *tze'irim*, the newbies work at menial tasks. When a truck arrived and the veteran soldiers ordered the newbies to unload it, he joined in with the *tze'irim*, hefting crates of supplies to the kitchen. The shamed *vatikim* inevitably joined in.

Relations between staff and soldiers at times became strained. When the atmosphere in the company grew particularly overcast, he would declare a special "Squad Leader" day. Each squad leader would take a hike with his squad; Avihu prepared a special discussion for each stop along the way. At one stop, they would discuss what the soldiers would like to see changed. At another stop, the squad leaders would solicit the soldiers' ideas on how to improve the atmosphere.

In March, on Purim, Avihu dreamed up the idea of a Purim Carnival for his company, complete with a full menu of events: balloon shaving, shooting targets for prizes, and soldiers dressed up as chefs serving gourmet food. He and Sivan had their usual debate on "distance."

"Sure, 'distance' is important ," he conceded. "But Purim only comes once a year. Isn't it even more important to do things with joy?"

"But they're your soldiers. They need to respect you."

"Then how about if I go in disguise? I'll dress up like a private."

"That's ridiculous."

"I'll circulate among them as a simple soldier to get to know them better."

The idea of Avihu passing unrecognized among his own men made her laugh. He was 5 foot 7 and solid muscle. No costume would ever disguise him. They compromised. He would dress up as a sergeant. He felt that only by coming in costume could he impart the true lesson of Purim to his men: that no matter what one's age or rank, the power of innocent joy is always redemptive.

After the carnival, he gathered the soldiers who had dressed up as chefs and congratulated them on a job well done. He gave them a day's leave for their troubles. He never forgot anyone.

In March, the news came that Roi Greenwald, a company commander in Golani Battalion 51, had been injured during an operation. Avihu didn't know him well, but rushed to the hospital.

" What will you do if they ask you to replace Roi?" Sivan asked him before he left.

He felt torn. "I want to finish the course with my trainees. But if Roi is injured seriously, they'll need me more in Battalion 51."

It was in Roi Greenwald's hospital room that he first met Ofek Bukhris, the Commander of Golani Battalion 51. There would soon be an operation in Tul Karem. Avihu begged Ofek to take him along. It didn't matter that there were no slots for an officer. "I'll tag along as your radio man," he offered. Ofek had a reputation as a particularly unsentimental and exacting Battallion Commander. Sivan was sure that he and Avihu would get along just fine.

Avihu was invited to fill the wounded Roi Greenwald's slot. He was so excited to be back in action that he didn't even make it back to the training base to collect his personal belongings. He spent a few weeks without his wallet. He had little use for money anyway, unless he was buying gifts for others. Only people mattered.

*   *   *

Avihu's stuffed his ordinance vest with candies as he prepared to depart for Jenin.

"Avihu you're too much," said Michal, his brother Amir's wife. "So now the children of Jenin are going to think that candies grow out of their ears?"

CHAPTER 17 Prayer Before Going to War

Tuesday night was a holiday again, the last night of Passover. Doron prayed *Arvit*, the Evening Prayer. He searched for a bottle of wine with which to make the holiday *kiddush*, the blessing over the wine. There was none to be found.

Eli, their former Company Commander appeared with a bottle of wine. Officially, he was still on leave of absence. There was no available officer's slot, so he would be fighting as a simple soldier. Earlier that day, he had given the troops an excellent lesson in explosives, his specialty. Everyone was glad to have him along. He had a sixth sense when it came to booby traps.

Over forty soldiers gathered around Doron in the APC parking lot, wanting to hear *kiddush*. Someone found some *Matzot*. Doron ended up reciting the *kiddush* numerous times. Each time he would finish, new soldiers arrived, asking to hear it again. "Please, please! One more time."

"You can all make *kiddush*," he told them. "Believe me, right now G-d is open to prayers from anyone."

Nissan and Tzafi, soldiers from Doron's platoon, called for him to say something. A benediction. Some words of wisdom. Doron thought of Nahshon Ben Aminadav, the first Israelite to jump into the Red Sea before the waters parted.

"Tonight is the seventh night of Passover. On this night, the children of Israel stood before the Red Sea with the Egyptians chasing after them. Everyone was afraid to enter the sea. Then Nahshon Ben Aminadav jumped into the waters, and G-d saw his great faith and parted the waters for the rest of Israel. Tonight, *we* are Nachshon. We're going in first. And perhaps tonight, too, the Almighty will split this sea of terror in two and all of the forces will follow us in safety. And in the end, G-d willing, we will sing the 'Song of the Sea', a song of Thanks to G-d."

One of the soldiers asked Doron to read the formal Prayer Before Going to War. He looked in his prayerbook. It wasn't there. Another soldier passed him an army prayerbook that contained the ancient prayer. More soldiers gathered around. The APCs were gathered in a circle, their lights turned on. A chapel of steel. He read the prayer, which calls upon the soldier not to fear, and had the group call out the refrain. "Save us O Lord. Bring us success." They called it out again and again, louder and louder. But something was still missing for Doron. He felt the need to say something in his own words. Perhaps, he thought, the prayer hadn't been written with reservists in mind. He recalled the words that had always meant the most to him in the Traveller's Prayer. "And, Dear Lord, please return us home to our families in peace." It felt good, leading the men in prayer, leading them in words that came directly from his heart.

Doron's voice was hoarse with tears. "Return us to our homes in peace," he shouted. Refrains of *Amen*. He felt very close to G-d at that moment. He had felt the closeness before, but never like this. He imagined that this is what the High Priest must have felt like when he led the People Israel in prayer on the High Holidays. This was *Am Yisrael*. The people of Israel. The simple folk. Some religious, some not, but all pure of heart.

They scattered to their APCs.

*   *   *

For David Zangen, Chief Medical Officer of Regiment 5, there was nothing more stirring then watching all of the men who had arrived without being called up, arguing with the officers of the regiment to let them participate. None was more adamant than Kobi Azoulay, a policeman in civilian life and officer in an infantry reserve unit. He insisted on volunteering. There was no refusing him. He was put in charge of the evacuation unit for Battalion 7020, the "Nachshon" battalion.

*   *   *

Doron had checked on everyone in his squad, but had neglected to check his own equipment. He didn't have a flashlight. He sat for a few minutes with Rami, one of the older soldiers who wouldn't be going in, in the cab of Rami's Toyota truck . Rami was a landscaper, and had done the landscaping of Amir's grave at kibbutz Gal-On. He would be staying behind at the command post. They listened to classical music. Rami was a devout atheist, but believed that G-d was definitely one of man's better inventions. Doron liked Rami immensely. They hugged goodbye. The time had come.

All of the men who would be staying behind in the command post came to shake the hands of those going in. Each was damaged in his own way. Rami had lost two fingers. Ohad had suffered a heart attack (He was too avid of a soccer fan, and collapsed when HaPoel Tel Aviv lost in the finals. He was only thirty-five). None of these men were obliged to continue reporting to *Milu'im*, but all chose to remain with the unit in whatever capacity possible.

Doron called Liron shortly before sunset. "I'll call when the holiday ends, G-d willing. Tell the children *Hag Sameach*." Happy Holiday. Upon hanging up, he was suddenly confronted by a vision of his own funeral. His students were there. The Ethiopian students were huddled together, too shy to approach Liron. He thought about his students who were in the middle of difficult struggles, those whom he was helping to overcome addictions. They would be angry at him for abandoning them.

He could feel thoughts of his family taking hold of him, contracting his entire body. He tried to invoke the Rambam's edict, to put them out of his mind. But he couldn't do it. They were as much a part of him as his arms or his legs. He couldn't separate from them.

It was 1:00 am when the APCs left Saalem Junction in a procession towards Jenin. From previous assignments, Doron knew every village along the route. He even remembered the major potholes. They passed the high schools where they were pelted with stones on their previous reserve duty. Hebrew signs still dotted the sides of the road, mementos of better times. The large electric signs, still illuminated, touted everything that would have been of interest to an Israeli consumer in the days of optimism: masonry, mosaics, porcelain fixtures, woodworking shops.

They passed what had once been Zaki's Gas Station. Zaki was no more, and the station was now called something else. Zaki was accused of being a collaborator with Israel. Zaki was no collaborator, but his gas station was highly popular with Israeli motorists. After his murder, one of his competitors took over the station.

* * *

Tuesday evening, Stu and his tank unit reached the main staging area. Night fell, and the religious soldiers in the company stood by the tank and prayed. Asher, one of the tank commanders, read the Prayer Before Going to War.

Asher, the commander of Stu's tank, asked Adi, the C.C., for permission to read the Prayer Before Going to War for the entire company over the external frequency of the tank radios. It was dark, and they were too close to hostile territory to turn on the lights in the tank. According to the order of the tanks, each of the seven tanks answered a staticky "Amen" over the radio.

The prayer was longer than Stu had remembered. To himself, Stu completed the prayer with his own addendum. "G-d, let's do this right. And let's all come back."

*   *   *

Hanoch and the *Pal-Sar* gathered in the APC staging ground. The rain came down in torrents. His brother arrived with some food, including an oversized bag of M&Ms that Hanoch had picked up at CostCo in the States. "You never know when you might need these. There are lots of kids in there." In Hanoch's mind, he was already "inside". Over and over again, he tried to visualize what the booby-trapped doors and windows would look like. He apologized to his brother for being so distracted.

"Don't worry about it. Just watch yourself. Call when you can," said his brother.

*   *   *

Shneor Alfasi had long been fascinated with the character of Nachshon Ben Aminadav. A single individual whose actions spurred on thousands. Tonight, everything seemed to be converging on Nachshon. It was the last day of Passover, the day in history when Nachshon made his leap of faith. And Battalion 7020, Shneor's battalion, was named the "Nachshon" battalion. It was all coming together. Soon, they would be entering the Jenin refugee camp. The hornet's nest, the source of an unending barrage of terror attacks. For years, no one had dared enter this camp.

They moved in a procession of APCs, tanks, and infantry towards the city. The tanks up on the hill provided scant reassurance. It was impossible to see down into the narrow alleyways between the low, flat houses. The entry into the camp was jarring. "Here we are," someone said. The back hatch of Shneor's APC swung open. They all jumped out and sprinted for the first house. Like a birth, thought Shneor, as he dove for cover, breathless. An emergence from a safe womb into a new and hostile world. Like parachuting. But with more adrenaline than he had ever experienced. The soldiers started working like clockwork. Everyone warned everyone else about booby traps. The narrow alleyways and poster-lined walls of the refugee camp reminded Shneor of the ultraorthodox Meah Shearim neighborhood in Jerusalem. The posters in Meah Shearim were exhortations to religiosity: "Read more Psalms. Our Neighborhood must improve its modesty." Here the posters commemorated suicide bombers.

They entered the camp from "antenna hill", to the south. That first night, their mission was to encircle the camp. It was freezing and wet. They hadn't planned for the cold. They had left their coats behind in order to reduce their load. It was a slippery march through knee-deep mud. Eyyal Azuri, the machine gunner, kept on slipping in the mud with the heavy gun. He wouldn't allow anyone to spell him. Another soldier succumbed to hypothermia. Shneor, one of two medics in his platoon, gave him some candy to stimulate his metabolism. Slowly, the soldier's color returned.

The "clerks' houses" were a partially built complex of apartment buildings on the outskirts of Jenin, skeletons of cement and rebar. The five snipers in the platoon, under the command of Avihai, bounded up the partially finished stairways while the other soldiers huddled together in the sand and concrete beneath the building. Many had already succumbed to hypothermia, and their lips were blue and trembling. Shneor hugged them for warmth. They lit a tiny fire in the middle. From the ground floor they watched as tracer bullets shot up from the low houses of the camp, seeking the snipers on the upper floor. The bullets smacked into the ceiling of the upper floors, showering the snipers with cement dust. Dogs barked in the distance, announcing the unit's arrival.

Dror and the other officers were red-eyed from lack of sleep. Shneor wished there were something he could do. He wished he could kiss their red eyes in the same way that he kissed his children's eyes when he put them to sleep. But the officers never slept, it seemed to Shneor. While others slept, they poured over maps.

Shneor worshipped them. They always placed themselves at greater risk than the other soldiers. Not only that, but they needed to get approval from above on even the smallest things. When would they ever find time to sleep?

"OK, now I'm going to rest," said Dror. But it never seemed to happen. The shooting resumed and he ran to a lookout point to identify the source. This army is the greatest gift our people has ever received, Shneor thought to himself. Certainly there was no greater honor than being called upon to bear arms for the Jewish People.

CHAPTER 18 The Second Temple

The Prayer Before Going to War filled Rafi with emotion. Somehow, it seemed a very 'biblical' prayer to him. He assembled all of the soldiers in his APC, and asked their permission to read the prayer over the internal radio after they passed the Saalem roadblock. Everyone agreed. Rafi's voice trembled as he read the words. It was a long prayer. Was it wise to switch from external to internal frequency for three minutes? He felt it was important for his soldiers. After the prayer, there was silence.

In of all his years in the army, it was the first time that he had prayed that prayer.

For each major event in his life, Rafi had no problem identifying the historic parallel. Without a doubt, this past year was the Destruction of the Second Temple. For the second time in his life, things were veering wildly out of control.

The first such cataclysm took place when he was eight years old. His family took a vote on whether to stay in America or make *Aliyah* to Israel. Rafi was outvoted four to one. "But it's too dangerous there," Rafi protested. "I don't want to go."

"There's really nothing to worry about," his parents reassured him. It was August, 1973.

Rafi's paternal grandfather, his "American" grandfather, was an Orthodox Rabbi as was Rafi's father. His mother grew up in Jerusalem and Rafi's maternal grandparents, his "Jewish" grandparents, still lived there. At the age of eight, it seemed that everything he had heard about Judaism had to do with war and suffering. Rafi considered himself very much an American.

When the decision was made final, Rafi's parents offered to buy him whatever he wanted to make up for it.

"I want a ten year diary." Inwardly, Rafi gloated. He knew they'd never be able to find one.

"That's an interesting choice," said his mother. "Any particular reason?"

"I'm eight. By the time I finish the diary, I'll be eighteen and I'll be able to come back to the States."

"Bye San Francisco," Rafi whispered as the plane took off. "I'll see you in ten years."

Two months after they arrived in Jerusalem, the air raid sirens went off. It was the Yom Kippur War. Rafi marched into his parents' bedroom. "I told you so," he said. But he was more frightened than angry. War was Rafi's worst nightmare. Throughout the Yom Kippur War, he slept with his clothes on, including his shoes. He was prepared at any moment to run down to the bomb shelter.

There were shortages of everything, especially able-bodied men. His father became a volunteer baker. Every night, he stoked the ovens at *Maafiyat Angel*, the main bakery in Jerusalem.

Before long, Rafi was completely immersed in his new life. As a teenager in the *Bnei Akiva* youth movement, he was known as a patient, caring counselor. He had other loves. Music filled his soul with joy, and secretly he nursed a passion for dance. He played the French horn in the Jerusalem Youth Orchestra and in the National Youth Band. For the most part, he was too busy for school.

In the summer of his eighteenth birthday, Rafi's family travelled to the States for a few weeks. Rafi opted to stay in Israel with his friends. Soon they would be in the army. They all wanted to join elite units. Each one devised his own grueling training regimen. Rafi, a longtime admirer of the Kenyan marathon runners, took to running barefoot from one end of Jerusalem to the other. America would have to wait.

In the army, he entered an intelligence unit. The emphasis was on working alone. It ran counter to his Israeli upbringing, but there was something about this approach that resonated with him. If he could become totally self-reliant, he figured, things could not veer out of control.

In his second year he was chosen for Officers' Training School, and became the Intelligence Officer of the Jordan Valley Regiment. He learned that he could get by with very little sleep. At night, although not required of his position, he lay in ambush with the soldiers.

Near the end of his service a surprise party was planned for him. His family was invited to his base in the Jordan Valley. Rafi's unit had been tracking a local gang that was throwing firebombs on the Jordan Valley road. That night, the gang attacked a civilian bus on the Jordan Valley road. The attack quickly became a worst-case scenario. One of the firebombs caught an open window and exploded within, turning the interior of the bus into an inferno. A young mother and her three children were burned beyond recognition. Thinking of that night would give shivers for many years to come. Rafi's family was in one of the first cars to reach the bus from the southern side of the scene. From their end, they helped the wounded. Rafi was stuck on the northern side of the bus. Civilians were asked to leave the area. His family never made it to the base that night.

He met his wife in college. One night, unexpectedly, she called and asked him out. Rafi prided himself on his analytic nature. Decisions weighed on him greatly; things needed to be resolved quickly before they clogged his thinking. Where was this leading? Rafi tried to place himself in the position of the man he would be years in the future. Would he still be enthralled by this woman? Would he still delight in her impetuousness? Would their conversations still last late into the night? It took him two weeks to exhaust all of the permutations, an eternity for his mathematical mind. Yes, apparently she was the one. His future wife's decision took a month longer. His reasoning was sound, she knew, but what was he feeling? She had to be sure.

Fatherhood pulled together all of the disparate threads of his life. It was the thing with which he found himself most at peace. There was nothing in the universe more fascinating to him than his daughter Ma'ayan. Rafi reveled in her freedom, the abandon with which she immersed herself in the passions that he only permitted himself to dabble in. She indulged a fluid, natural dance ability; and already, at age five, music was her mother tongue. She easily identified composers without a second thought, as if stating the obvious. In her natural, intuitive vocabulary, Vivaldi's Four Seasons was 'the quick music'. She allowed her moods to respond to the music without the mediation of intellect. She most loved Vivaldi's Spring, she told Rafi. It gave her joy. When he needed her to rush through her morning routine without the usual dawdling, Vivaldi always did the trick.

Seven years later, again unexpectedly, his wife announced that she wanted a divorce.

After a year of counseling, Rafi realized that the marriage was beyond saving.

Once again, he turned to history. He found comfort in the figure of Rabbi Yohanan Ben Zakkai, the ancient sage who moved the seat of Jewish learning to Yavneh when Jerusalem's demise became inevitable. He chose to build something new rather than struggle to preserve the ruins of the past. Ben Zakai reconciled himself to the destruction of the Second Temple, and as a result Judaism underwent a transformation that allowed for continued growth. The *G'marah*, Judaism's compendium of Oral Law, compared divorce to the destruction of the Holy Temple in Jerusalem, thought Rafi. By no means a dead end, it was a passage that had to be traversed. He would do as Ben Zakai had done.

But the blows kept on coming. Rafi's job dematerialized when his company was bought out by a foreign conglomerate with their own Product Development Manager. And what was happening to the country? Each national setback sent him on a tailspin, with none worse than the death of Madhat Youssef.

Madhat Youssef was a Border Policeman assigned as part of a small detail to guard Joseph's Tomb, a Jewish holy site located in the heart of Nablus. When riots broke out, Madhat Youssef was shot and lay bleeding. For four excruciating hours, the army debated whether or not to risk a larger conflagration by sending in a rescue force or to rely upon the good offices of the opposing "preventive security" forces to evacuate the dying soldier. It was early Fall 2000. The peace takls had just collapsed. The two sides still weren't sure whether they were locked in a struggle to the death or simply working through a bad marriage. It still wasn't clear whether violence would become the rule or the exception. In the end, the path of accommodation was chosen. When an ambulance finally arrived to collect Madhat Youssef, the popular young soldier was long dead.

Rafi agonized over the implications of the Madhat Youssef incident for the army. What would happen to the creed that this was an army that never left a soldier behind? What would keep a disaster like this from eating away at the core of the army's morale? After this, how could officers like himself continue to inspire blind faith in their troops? This was indeed the second destruction, thought Rafi. Only it refused to be over.

In moments of despair, Rafi took refuge in his music. In another life, he reflected, he would devote himself solely to music, his truest language. He would feed his frustrated love for dance; he would disconnect himself from the troubles of the world and submerge himself wholly in Dvorak's *New World Symphony*. His French horn was central in that piece. Its passage sounded an uplifting brass rallying cry. We are entering a new world, it seemed to say. But when?

CHAPTER 19 The First House

Wednesday, April 3. Eleven soldiers squeezed into Doron's APC but it was still freezing. At the "green line", the invisible dividing line between pre- and post-1967 Israel, a clerk collected passenger lists from each of the squads. The boundary wasn't marked in any other way, but the act of submitting a passenger list made it a passageway between safety and danger. Doron's APC was next to last. On the outskirts of Jenin, there was a sharp, muddy turn in the road. Gears gnashed; the APC refused to move. They were stuck. Asi came on the radio and asked Doron what was going on.

"The half-track is stuck."

"Try again." They tried to get the gears to engage. Nothing.

"Can we get a tow from the vehicle in front of us?"

"Negative, the incline ahead is too steep. Another APC wouldn't be strong enough to tow you."

They were stuck in the worst possible place. They were at the bottom of a gully, vulnerable from both sides. The sky was beginning to turn orange violet.

"I guess we thought of everything but this," said Asi. "See if you can find a higher place to stay put, OK?" Doron sensed a tenuous tone in his voice. It was more of a question than an order. Doron felt the ground disintegrating beneath his feet. He was falling, hurtling into an abyss of insecurity. He thought of all those he missed, his students and his family. A new thought occurred to him, something he had never considered before. Perhaps he was getting old. Maybe if he came through this unharmed, it would be time to put in for a non-combat position. He was transported back to the night of Amir's funeral, the night when his body was too convulsed to function. The night he couldn't stop vomiting. Once again, he was soaked to the core with sweat, and he could feel his stomach beginning to turn.

"Will we be staying here alone?"

Yoav poked his head out of his APC. Yoav who visits Amir's children every week, thought Doron. Doron signaled to him with his hands, "Is this it? Are we going to be left behind?" He was twenty or so meters away. He can make out my gestures, thought Doron, but is he close enough to read my facial expressions. Yoav signaled for Doron to wait a second.

Doron heard him on the radio with Asi. "Listen, it's low ground, and we're in hostile territory already. I should wait here with them." Doron felt a warm flood of relief. His greatest fear had always been that of becoming separated from the main force. To be in command of a squad, alone, in enemy territory.

It was time to leave the APC. Doron opened the hatch and began to climb out, but his legs failed him. He always popped out of the hatch and onto the roof in a single jump, but now his legs were leaden and weak. He could barely stand. Eyyal, always most attuned to the mental states of those around him, sensed Doron's paralysis.

"Here, come on out the back door," he said as he caught hold of him.

Doron was on solid ground now, but still needed to lean on the APC for support.

He couldn't tell how much time had passed. Everyone had taken up positions, and he was still in a dream-like state, moving in slow motion. He surveyed the houses on either side of the gully, and pointed out the one that seemed like the best starting point. Yoav passed in front of him in his APC.

"Doron! Doron!" He heard Yoav's voice as if from a distance. "Are you with me?"

"Sure."

"You know the drill. I'll secure the APCs, you occupy that house. " He pointed to a house a few doors down from the one Doron had chosen.

"No. It's not the right one."

"Why not?"

"Too many people. It has three floors. That one over there is better. It's only half built, there won't be as many people inside. We're only eleven, a full house will be a distraction."

"Makes sense. *Kadimah*." Onwards.

Eyyal slapped Doron's shoulder to shake him out of his reverie. Yoav came on the radio again.

"Doron! Preventive fire!" He felt stupid. Their presence was no longer a secret. They should have been firing at possible sniper positions. If this had been a training exercise, he would have failed already. Eyyal was the only one at full speed right now. He echoed Yoav. "Preventive fire, Doron! Preventive Fire!" Doron fired some shots from his rifle. A switch flipped. The rifle reports instantly brought him back to his efficient commander self as if they had been a hypnotist's predetermined signal. He started giving orders as they surrounded the first house. Yoav knocked on the door. *Iftach, Jeesh,* he called in Arabic. Open up, army. He spoke softly, as if delivering room service to a hotel room. There was no answer.

They tried a sledge hammer on the door. It didn't budge. The house, although half built, was on its way to becoming a stately villa. The door was thick steel. Yoav attached an explosive finger to the lock of the door. The blast was louder than they had expected. The door blew in, as did all of the windows.

Doron spotted a cave a bit further into the gully and sent Amzaleg and Uzi to check it out. They disappeared into the cave. Bursts of gunfire, then silence. The troops waited in tense silence for almost a minute. No one ventured a word as they trained their rifle sights on the cave entrance. Finally, Jackie and Amzaleg emerged nonchalantly. "Nothing," said Amzaleg with a shrug.

Yoav entered the house first and rolled up all the carpets. Everyone's boots were covered with mud. They split into two groups, first floor and second floor. Two snipers took up positions on the second floor. By 8:00 am, they had searched the entire house. It was empty.

Doron made the rounds of the younger soldiers and asked them how they were doing. They seemed OK. One of the younger soldiers, Roni, seemed a bit nervous. He had just finished his regular service.

"I'm dying to get married. I have a girlfriend, you know. I'm going to propose as soon as I get home."

"How long have you been thinking about proposing?" Doron asked.

"Ever since we got here. For about an hour now. Look at you. You have a wife and family. Even if you die, you've done something with your life. I want to do something with my life too."

Shots rang out from the direction of the kitchen. Amzaleg had tried to shoot out the lock on the back door. He seemed puzzled. Doron had no patience for Amzaleg's antics right now. "I told you that wouldn't work," he said to him. Now the door was firmly stuck. Amzaleg scratched his head. Doron tried using an explosive fuse on the lock, but to no avail. Eyyal brought a crowbar. "Here, watch this." He pried the door open with brute strength.

Asi and the main force moved into the refugee camp. At 11:00 am, Doron heard shots from the direction of the camp. It was Kalashnikov fire, and getting closer. Roni went into shock. He began shouting, crying, and vomiting. Two soldiers brought him upstairs to a bedroom. Danny, the medic, also in his first stint of Milu'im, attended to him. He asked Roni's friends if it had ever happened to him before. Yes, once before. Did he take any special medicine? No, it passes after a while. Yoav radioed for a doctor.

They didn't have much food. There had been a bit in the APC, but was it safe to go out there? It was broad daylight now. Ample time for an ambush to have been put in place around the vehicles. Shimi offered Doron his cell phone. "This is ridiculous," he said. "Call your mother-in-law. We're going back there."

They had been up the entire night and had no coffee. Amzaleg rummaged around the kitchen for anything with caffeine. "Look! Here's the real stuff. Fresh Turkish coffee with cardamom. I can get high just smelling this stuff."

"Don't even think about it, Amzaleg." Doron ordered him to put the coffee back. He wasn't going to tolerate any abuse of property in any of the houses that they occupied.

"Come on, Doron. We haven't slept all night."

"Absolutely not. If you want coffee so bad, I'll go out to the APC and get you a packet of coffee and the propane burner."

"You'd risk your life to avoid taking a few spoonfuls of coffee from this house?"

"If it's that important to you then yes."

"Forget it." Amzaleg fumed in silence.

Doron ascended to the roof, mulling over the ethical issues. Maybe it's permissible for Amzaleg to take some coffee, he thought to himself, if it affects his state of alertness. It could be life or death. But only as long as he washes the dishes. He thought of his father and mother, drowsy and irritable before their morning coffee. He had learned at an early age not to attempt conversation with them before their first cup. Doron had never been a coffee drinker himself. Perhaps he wasn't being sensitive enough to Amzaleg's needs, he castigated himself. Perhaps he ought to be more flexible with Amzaleg.

The aroma of cardamom filled the house as Doron descended. Uzi and Amzaleg were sipping tiny cups of the concentrated brew.

"What's this supposed to be?" Doron asked Uzi, ignoring Amzaleg.

Uzi remained silent. It was Amzaleg who responded. "Doron, forgive me, *caparah*. I couldn't go on without it. I wouldn't be able to function." He excused himself and went out back.

"What's with him?" Doron asked Jackie. "Is he normal?"

"Don't worry, Doron. When things get tough, I promise that he won't disappoint you."

Doron decided to let it go. According to *Halachah*, Jewish Law, taking food for sustenance from a captured house was not considered looting. What would the sages have considered a tablespoon of coffee? Sustenance, or pleasure? If it was for operational needs, he supposed, it could be justified. He thought of asking Amzaleg to clean up after himself in the kitchen, but thought better of it. It would be easier to do it himself. He washed the coffeepot and wiped the countertop clean.

At the Youth Village, Doron was never one to ask his students to sweep a dirty classroom. He would always take up the broom himself, like his grandfather Saba David who swept the streets of Bat Yam. In the upper grades, his veteran students wouldn't let him push a broom, and would immediately begin sweeping themselves. The newer students hadn't caught on yet. Neither, apparently, had Amzaleg.

Doron allowed himself a final jab as Amzaleg entered the kitchen.

"This is great, Amzaleg. Not only do I not get to enjoy the coffee, but I also get to clean up after you. Just great."

Doron pushed the refrigerator door shut, but it bounced back open. Some of Amzaleg's earlier shots had passed through the back door, puncturing the refrigerator door and preventing it from closing.

"See, you're wrong Doron," said Amzaleg. "Bullets *can* open a door."

Nissan was an industrial engineer whose daily bread was cost/benefit analysis. He seemed obsessed with calculating the damage caused to the absent homeowners by the squad's visit. Let's see, that would be $400 for the door. $200 for the windows. 500$ for the refrigerator. When he finished his calculations, Nissan admitted that he felt bad for the owner of the house. "What's he going to think when he comes home to all this damage?"

"He's going to think, Thank G-d I wasn't here," said Doron.

Nonetheless, Nissan left a note. "Thank you for the hospitality. We apologize for the damage."

From the minaret in the center of town came the muffled bleating of a muezzin. "Soldiers, go home," the muezzin blared out in Hebrew. "Your mothers await you. Here, only surprises and martyrs await you. Go home to your mothers. There's nothing here for you but booby traps."

"Don't worry about me!" Amzaleg shouted back.

Effy Cohen, one of the younger soldiers, was working on his matriculation exam in Bible. Doron coached him in their spare minutes.

"Does that remind you of anything?" He asked him of the muezzin's call.

"Not really."

He told him the story of Sennaherib, the Assyrian king, who tried to conquer Jerusalem in the time of King Hezekiah. Sennaherib sent his envoy Rab-shakeh to wage psychological warfare on the Judaeans. He shouted to the guards at the gates of Jerusalem that there was no point in fighting. If they surrendered, they would be exiled but their lives would be spared. Shebna, the Judaean scribe, asked him why he was speaking Hebrew, since the Assyrians spoke Aramaic.

"We understand Aramaic. Speak Aramaic," said Shebna.

"I speak Hebrew for the benefit of the simple folk," replied Rabshakeh.

"Remember that for the test," Doron said to Effy.

"Fine. But who won in the end?"

" The Judaeans."

"That's good," said Effy. " You speak Arabic, don't you? Tell the muezzin he can keep on shouting."

The partially built house already had an opulent interior, full of mirrors and gold-plated fixtures. There were no posters of suicide bombers on the walls. Doron felt uneasy searching the house. Judging by the pictures, the family consisted of a couple with a young daughter. He didn't like the feeling of being in someone else's bedroom without permission. He felt like a voyeur searching through people's personal possessions. As necessary as it was, it didn't feel right. It continued to weigh on him.

Doron debated whether or not to enter the room where Danny was attending to Roni. He decided it was best for no one to see Roni in this state. For them and for him. From the hallway, he could hear him sobbing.

*   *   *

Hanoch's APC, the first in the Regiment, arrived at sunrise. Distant automatic weapons fire was already piercing the dawn like background static. Hanoch chose as an entry point a house with a large door on the ground floor where they could park their six APCs. They backed up the APCs and spilled out into the house. The houses on the outskirts of the camp were larger and more ornate than those further in. They were all empty. Their inhabitants all had better places to be.

Hanoch was as tense as a wound spring. He expected to encounter a sniper or booby trap at any instant. Amos, the machine gunner, thought he saw a sniper on a rooftop. The deafening cackle of 9 mm fire shattered the silence. For Hanoch, there was something official about the earsplitting reports. This was now war.

7:00 a.m. They passed through an olive grove on their way to the first house. It was still raining hard as they trudged through the mud. They split up. Half of the soldiers remained in the olive grove, half came inside with Hanoch. There were ten people in the house: a husband, a wife, an old man, and seven children. They moved them into a bedroom and assembled in the living room. Oren rolled up the carpets in order not to muddy them.

Hanoch asked the husband, a 40-year old man, to accompany him to the next house. "Don't worry, I just need you to knock on the door to notify your neighbors to come out." He seemed to understand. They went next door and he called to his neighbors. No one answered from within the house, but snipers immediately began firing on them from the surrounding rooftops. The gunfire became increasingly concentrated on the troops in the olive grove.

When they figured out which building was the source of the sniper fire, they surrounded it and called in a tank. The tank fired a shell, but a barrage of precise fire continued to pour down on the detachment in the olive grove.

Shouts of "Medic! Medic" rang out among the olive trees. A sniper bullet had caught Ofer, the Lieutenant Company Commander, in the leg. He was one of the younger officers in the company and had only recently assumed the position of Lieutenant C.C. He was still a student at the Shenkar Textile Institute. This was the young medic's first combat exposure. He froze.

A sudden thought ran through Hanoch's mind. He wished he had a wedding ring. He couldn't explain it . Neither he nor Efrat attached much importance to ornaments; they had grown up in the earthy *HaTzofim* youth movement. They were connected to Nature, to places, to people. Not to things. When they were married, they spent five dollars on a pair of plastic wedding rings for the ceremony so that they would have money left over for travel afterwards.

Now, Hanoch couldn't stop touching his finger, wishing a ring were there. He had often noticed that his friend Hemi, the Executive Officer, wore a wedding band. He would take on a far off look whenever he touched his ring, as if touching it transported him to his family. Hanoch felt isolated and insecure, his return to his family uncertain. He longed to have some secret portal on his person through which he could connect to them.

Shlomo, only one week before his wedding, took a bullet through the earlobe. He was otherwise unharmed. A tank rolled into the muddy olive grove and evacuated Ofer. Everyone was shaken. Oren, the C.C., snapped them back from their reverie. "We have to move forward. I'm going first." He looked at Hanoch. "You're coming after me."

They reached an open field. Hanoch arranged for a tank to provide cover fire as they ran across. On the other side of the field, they encountered the wall of a back yard. No doors. Moving through the alleyways to the other side of the houses would expose them to sniper fire from the rooftops. There was only one way forward: through the wall. Hanoch affixed an explosive brick, stepped back and to the side, and fired at it. Nothing. His last training with live explosive bricks had been fourteen years ago. He fired again. Nothing. He had the squad mortar specialist fire an M-209 shell at the recalcitrant brick. Then a LAU missile. Still the stubborn brick refused to explode. It was too damp.

"Hey, how about this?" Someone had found a step ladder. One by one, as Oren coordinated the covering fire, they clambered over the wall.

The first night was extremely cold. Hanoch and his fellow soldiers didn't have any blankets. They decided to huddle together, preferring not to use the blankets in the house. By the second night they covered themselves with blankets they found in the houses. In the morning they folded them and put them back in the cabinets. No one slept on any of the beds, only on the floor.

*   *   *

Somehow, one of the soldiers in Gadi Ezra's squad managed to have a cake spirited in to the house they were occupying, in celebration of Passover's end. But the house was also inhabited by a couple with five small children. Gadi and his squad decided to forfeit the long awaited baked goods to the terrified children. He brought the cake upstairs and divided it among the children.

*   *   *

The sun rose, and Stu looked out from his promontory on the south side of the camp. The high ground didn't afford as good a view as one might have hoped; the buildings were so flat and closely spaced that one couldn't see down between them. It was like looking at a tile floor. Pretty boring, he thought. Not much to do. From inside the tank, they heard some distant shots.

Fifteen minutes into the Operation, they heard over the radio that Moshe Gerstner, a Company Commander in Battalion 8110, had been killed. Their spirits fell. They weren't even an hour into it. The commander of Stu's tank ran behind the tank to get some supplies. Lying on their backs in the treads a few meters behind the tanks, two Golani soldiers were catching a smoke. Stu heard him address the driver over the infantry telephone on the back of the tank.

"Do me a favor. Don't back up."

By the following evening it was clear that there wasn't much for the tanks to do up on the hills of the south side. Four tanks were left there, attached to the local infantry units. Stu's tank and two others drove down to join the infantry forces that had entered on the north side.

*   *   *

No, thought David Zangen , Chief Medical Officer of Regiment 5, when the first casualty arrived. Not "Moshik". He had had sat though many a regimental meeting with Moshe Gerstner, a Company Commander in Battalion 8110. "Moshik" had taken a bullet to the head. There was nothing to be done. David hadn't prepared himself for this. Losing a patient was hard, but this was different. This was a close friend.

Not being able to talk openly on the radio made it doubly difficult. All of the casualties passed through his hands. Every second made a difference in saving a life. In certain cases, he overruled commanders who didn't think that a helicopter evacuation was necessary. Dori, a soldier in Battalion 7020, had taken a bullet to the stomach while running between houses. He seemed stable. The doctor in the field was in favor of evacuating the soldier via ambulance. David disagreed. He knew that such situations were capable of changing in seconds. In spite of the risks of landing in hostile territory, he overruled in favor of a helicopter.

*   *   *

Nahum and his unit drove to a gathering point at Jalameh junction. A freezing rain poured down on them. Mud was everywhere. Their coats didn't fit. When it came time to sleep, they weren't able to all fit into the overcrowded APCs. For those left outside, it was too wet and cold to sleep.

In the morning, the Regimental Commander briefed them. "Your mission will be to open up an entry point into the city of Jenin through the *Sabaah el Heir* neighborhood.. We've received confirmed intelligence that there's a 200 kg booby trap buried on the side of the road leading into Jenin. Your mission will be to find the explosives, neutralize them, and neutralize the enemy cell operating the detonator."

Unlike the other infantry units, they wouldn't be fighting house to house. They would be totally exposed, traversing the main thoroughfares. A booby trap is a fairly simple affair: a hole is dug in the road, explosives are buried, the hole is filled up. If the road is paved, a patch of asphalt is reapplied over the hole. In Israel, such a patch would have been easy to identify. But in Jenin, the roads were bumpy and full of potholes and patches. The only way to identify the booby trap would be by the thin wire poking out of the ground. If the booby trap were on the side of the road and hidden by tall grass, it would be almost impossible.

Shay gathered the men for a company briefing. We're *Milu'imniks*, thought Nahum. We speak our mind. If we have a question, no matter how unseemly, we don't hold back. "Isn't this the sort of work that's usually done by dogs?" he asked Shay.

"Definitely." Shay replied. "But the canine units are tied up in other operations, and won't be available for this assignment. So for today, we're them."

"What kind of damage can a 200 kg bomb do?" asked another soldier.

"Well, here's a good way to look at it," Shay explained. "A 200 kg blast can easily lift a tank off the ground."

4:00 am. It was time. They were all tense after the briefing. Nahum felt his churning emotions overflowing into nervous tears. He went to the far side of the APC, out of view. He wasn't embarrassed, but didn't want his tears to affect the others.

He felt a hand on his shoulder. It was Eddy, the machine gunner. Eddy had immigrated from Russia seven years ago. He was in his early twenties and massively built. Nahum always thought of him as older than himself.

"We're all nervous" he said. "But I'm sure it's worse for you, you have a small child. Don't worry, we'll look out for each other." Eddy carried the 40 lb. heavy machine gun as if it were a toy. Nahum liked having him nearby.

"Remember what you said on the first day." Eddy reminded him.

It was his medic's contribution to the opening pep talk. "Guys," he said, "We're going back without a single casualty. Anyone who wants to go home, goes home. Remember that." Now it seemed ages ago.

The tension became physiological as they approached the *Sabaah el Heir* neighborhood. Men felt pressure to relieve themselves but the procession of APCs had to keep moving. They used plastic bags. Nahum heard over the radio that Yariv, the X.O., was already injured. They were still 200 meters away from the entrance to Sabaah el Heir, but within sniper range. He hadn't heard any shots. What could have happened? He ran to Yariv's tank and climbed onto the turret. The hatch of the tank's turret had slammed shut on Yariv's hand. He was in severe pain.

"You'll be OK, it's only two broken fingers, " Nahum said. He strapped Yariv's fingers and ran back to his APC.

At the entrance to Sabaah el Heir, the APCs drew into a circle and Shay assembled the men in the center for final orders.

"I'm leaving two APCs here, with their crews, for backup. The rest of us are going in, with a tank escorting us." They started walking towards the neighborhood. Nahum was in one of the entry teams. Eddy was alongside him. Nahum noticed that he was walking with a limp.

"Eddy, what happened?"

"Nothing really. I guess something went through the sole of my boot."

He was pumped so full of adrenaline that he hadn't even felt the steel spike of a roadblock tooth-strip penetrating his boot.

"You should go back. You'll need a tetanus shot."

"No way. It's nothing." He stopped limping.

Nahum heard a pulsating noise from above. The sun was beginning to rise, and the welcome sight of a Cobra helicopter watching over them took form in the dim light. It felt good, being watched over so attentively, but also gave him pause: he had never been in an operation with helicopters overhead before. This was a new order of magnitude.

Nahum kept to the right of the main road. From the left, came a yell. "Military tents in front of us!" They were drawing near some sort of military compound, with a main building surrounded by tents. Nitzan, the platoon commander, motioned for Daniel and Nahum to follow him into the compound. Nitzan had been in the States when he heard about the callup. He took the first flight back.

Nahum fired warning shots and ran into the compound. The shots drew them out of their anxiety back into the moment. Nahum lobbed a grenade into the building. No response. They entered. The building had been occupied until quite recently. Coffee was still brewing on the burner. Some sort of training school, Nahum figured. Uniforms and ammunition sat in piles around the room. They were starting to flow. They moved beyond the tension.

With some of the tension dissipated, one of the men needed to relieve himself.

"Do you have any toilet paper?" Nahum realized that he had prepared for almost every bodily eventuality.

"Here, use a gauze bandage."

"Cover me." Nahum stood between the soldier and the building, moving from window to window with his rifle sight. Undignified, he thought, but highly necessary.

A hundred yards beyond the building, they came to a fresh patch of asphalt near the side of the road. A double strand of black wire protruded from an asphalt patch and led into a field of tall wheat. Soon it would be harvest time, and the stalks were waist high. Hunching over, Shay broke into a run. He chased the wire into the field, Daniel and Nahum huffing to keep up with him. It lead nowhere. They radioed the tank commander to loose a stream of machine gun fire into the asphalt patch, but the bullets flattened and bounced off the paved road.

"It's a dummy," said Shay. "Let's move on."

In the middle of the operation, Daniel's telephone rang. It was the unit liaison office.

"Daniel? I'm calling to inform you that you've been called up for emergency reserve duty." The clerk's tone was officious and overly formal. Daniel decided to have some fun with the young soldier.

"Called up?" He held up his cell phone so that that the ak-ak-ak of machine gun fire from the direction of the refugee camp could be heard clearly.

"I can't really hear you too well," said the clerk. "There's a lot of static. I think we have a bad connection."

Two hundred meters further down the road, they came upon another wire. This time, the double wire protruding from the asphalt patch ran up a hill. They sprinted after the wire. It was exhausting. Nahum had a 40 lb pack of medical equipment on his back. The wire went over fences and through backyards. All twenty of them followed, climbing and jumping after it. They ran in total silence. They expected an ambush at any moment. Finally, in the backyard of a small house, they came upon the terminus. One wire was connected to a car battery. The other wire hung loose.

They wound up a large spool of wire and brought it down the hill so that the Engineering Corps could detonate the explosives buried beneath the road. There were shots in the distance, but no telltale pinging of bullets nearby. They continued on to the end of the road, still encountering no resistance. At 2:00 pm, they returned to the APCs and parked them around a house, creating a semi-enclosed area between them. They sat in the enclosed area and broke out their rations. The mission had been completed. They headed back to the gathering point at Jalameh junction.

At 4:00, they saw three enemy gunmen in the distance, their faces hidden in scarves. They charged them, but the gunmen quickly darted into the village of Jalameh within pre-1967 Israel. Although Jalemeh was notorious as the "way station" for numerous terror attacks, Nahum's unit had no authorization to enter. They stopped at the entrance to the village.

Shay called them together at the gathering point.

"Tonight, we'll have a more difficult mission. We're going to join a police SWAT team. There will be a special op in the village of Tubaas, near Jenin. The SWAT team will be picking up three "heavies", including the local head of Hamas. We'll form a perimeter around the village and deal with any resistance that comes our way."

The village of Tubaas was a notorious Hamas stronghold. The entire village was armed to the teeth. In the hours preceding the mission, the men checked and rechecked their equipment. They checked their vests to make sure no grenades were missing, and checked the sides of the APCs to make sure no sand had leaked out of the sandbags. Half an hour before they were to leave, there was a change in plans. The mission was postponed. Their new mission: to find a decent hideout from the cold, driving rain.

*　　*　　*

Nahum's paternal grandfather, Saba Haim, was a survivor of Auschwitz. His eldest son Joseph, a strapping youth, would sneak out at night and steal food for him from the guard dogs. One night, Joseph was caught by the guards, beaten senseless, and left naked to freeze to death in the snow. Saba Haim waited until the soldiers had left and dragged his son's unconscious body to the only hiding place that was covered from the bitter cold: the cesspool in the outhouse. Saba Haim and Nahum's Uncle Joe were the only members of the family to survive the holocaust. Saba Haim's wife and three other children perished. After the war, Saba Haim amassed a small fortune selling army surplus in the Bergen Belsen Displaced Persons camp. He remarried and made *Aliyah*. Years later, he appeared as a witness at the Eichmann trial. Saba Haim never learned Hebrew. To his last days he spoke only Yiddish. He was a tormented soul, plagued by nightmares and outbursts. Nahum thought of him as a volcano. Savta Eva, Nahum's grandmother, also suffered from deep mood swings and spent much of her days in bed. Uncle Joe, unable to find work in the new country, left for America.

Nahum's maternal grandparents made *Aliyah* from Bulgaria. His grandmother, Savta Loti, set sail on the 'Salvador', a rickety, overloaded Greek steamer. It was 1946, and the British were still barring Jewish immigration into Palestine. The ship was denied entry, and sank off the port of Tel Aviv. When the ship began sinking, the passengers donned life vests only to realize that they were defective – they had been stuffed with straw. Savta Loti didn't know how to swim. She had very long hair, and her tresses caught on a board as she was drowning. She pulled herself up by her own hair, and held on to the board for dear life. Eventually, she washed ashore in Tel Aviv. Her father, a powerful swimmer, had swum ashore earlier. Upon not finding his family, he returned to the water and drowned himself.

Saba Moni, Nahum's maternal grandfather, made *Aliyah* in 1933 and worked as a stevedore in the new Tel Aviv port. He was mountain of strength who also spoke five languages. Nahum inherited Saba Moni's thick frame. At age 17, he placed second in a national weightlifting competition. Still, he was no match for Saba Moni. With one lung lost to emphysema, Saba Moni could still easily overpower him in arm wrestling.

Once, after running home to avoid a fight, Nahum received a severe scolding from Saba Moni. "You're a coward." The words stung. Saba Moni told him stories of Bulgaria, where he had taken on ten or more anti-Semitic bullies. Although he didn't always win, his opponents always came away badly bruised. Saba Moni was stubborn to the point of stupidity, Nahum consoled himself. Nahum had been outnumbered. Fighting hadn't made sense.

There were other voices within Nahum that demanded equal time. Fear was not necessarily a bad thing, they weighed in. It sharpens you. It makes you smarter. Fear breeds awareness.

"You're a coward." He wanted to prove Saba Moni wrong. I'll be more sophisticated. More successful, he averred inwardly But still, the nagging question -- will I be as true?

Sometimes Nahum looked within himself, searching for seeds of the past. He was certain that he had inherited the hot passions and insatiable ghosts of his father and grandfather. He could feel them building up within him. When they took hold of him, they took hold of him completely. He wondered what his legacy would be to his own son. Would it be *his* legacy? Or the legacy of those who had come before him. He resolved to have a say in the matter.

Nahum grew up in Ramat Gan, a suburb of Tel Aviv. As a teenager, he was macho like Saba Moni, expressive and uninhibited like his mother. His father pressed him to study, but he had no interest in academics. He wanted to spend time with his friends and his music. He sang lead in a rock band and played trumpet in the school orchestra.

It was a split life. On Shabbat afternoon, he was a scout leader in the local *Tzofim* troop. At night, he dressed up like David Bowie and went to sing with his band, Vertigo, at the Penguin club in Tel Aviv. He had a Mohawk haircut, wore makeup, black lipstick, and penciled kohl circles around his eyes. A makeup girl soaped up his Mohawk until it stood in spikes.

Nahum's father loved to hear him sing, but didn't want him to become too carried away with his music. It would impede his studies. When Nahum was sixteen, his band was approached by a local label for a record deal. Nahum's father stepped in. Enough was enough.

There was a big fight, and Nahum left the house to live with Ran, his band buddy. But Ran turned out to be a psychopath, and after a month Nahum came home. That night, his father broke down in tears. "All I want is for you not to make the same mistakes that I made." It didn't help.

Nahum enlisted in an anti-terror unit specializing in undercover operations. After boot camp, he was posted to "Hotel Sivan" in Ramallah. 'Hotel Sivan' was the euphemism given to the building that served as the army barracks in the center of the hostile city. Each night, Nahum's anti-terror unit would enter the nearby refugee camp and round up suspects. There was never much time for sleep, and no one was ever in a very good mood.

One afternoon, Nahum was dispatched to the roof of Hotel Sivan for sentry duty. In those days, stones and firebombs were their daily bread. The "sticky bombs" were particularly dangerous. The enemy would mix glue and kerosene together in a wine bottle to create a homemade variety of napalm. They would aim at the soldiers' feet. When the bottles burst, the soldiers would be splattered with burning contact cement. The glue would stick to the soldiers' uniforms, burning. Once, Nahum saw a sticky bomb spatter the hood of one of their jeeps. The jeep veered out of control and overturned. The driver was severely injured.

A crowd was gathering around the hotel. A man darted out of the crowd, poised to launch a sticky bomb in his hand. Nahum fired a shot over the man's head. It hit the wall next to him. The bomber continued, undeterred. The next shot went right through his head. The glue bomb exploded on the wall behind him.

Nahum froze. He had never killed a man before. Did I have the right? he questioned himself. Who gave me that right? He couldn't stop trembling. He heard a hysterical, alien giggling bubble up from within him, the reflexive, irrational giggling of a child caught in a forbidden act. He was thankful that he hadn't seen the man's face.

Nahum's first one week leave was after a straight month of special ops. A soldier had just been kidnapped and murdered. His parents were nervous when he told them he'd be heading home via hitched rides and buses. He was in his usual sleep-deprived, trance-like state when he left the base Friday morning. He ran into his childhood friend Guy, from the Border Police, on the bus to Ramat Gan.

"Guy, do me a favor, wake me up in Ramat Gan." Nahum's head fell forward and he was dead to the world. When he awoke, it was Sunday morning. He didn't even remember having gotten off the bus.

When the bus arrived in Ramat Gan, his father was waiting at the stop. He spotted Guy in his Border Police uniform.

"Are you Guy, Nahum's friend?"

"Yes." Guy led him to the seat where Nahum was slumped over, fast asleep.

"Here, help me lift Nahum into the car," said Nahum's father.

"But how did you know that I would be on the bus," Nahum later asked him.

"I just had a feeling and I came."

His father had never been a particularly strong man, but somehow he had lifted Nahum into the car and up the stairs into bed.

Special ops often involved donning disguises. Because he was short, Nahum usually ended up dressing as a woman. He loved the adrenaline rush of going in undercover. It reminded him of his days in the rock band, only the stakes were life and death.

Nahum was chosen for Officers Training School, but instead opted to become a combat medic. I've learned just about all there is about taking a life, he thought to himself. Now I want to learn how to save one. After his training, he was posted to a mountaintop outpost in Lebanon. He finally had time on his hands. He began to think, to write, to dream of a life after the army. His purpose in life, he decided, would be to create a family unit, a wife and children. He began writing letters to his future beloved, although she didn't yet exist in his life.

He slept well. The view from his mountaintop outpost was breathtaking. Every now and then the outpost would be shelled, but compared to Hotel Sivan it was heaven on earth.

After the army, Nahum completed his high school education and went on to take a degree in Business Administration. In the business world, Nahum came into his own. He was energetic and quick to form friendships. Soon he was appointed second in command for the Israeli subsidiary of a Korean conglomerate. He began to flex his muscles as a dealmaker, and relished every minute of it.

He particularly loved his *Milu'im* unit. His company commander, Shay, was 37 years old but still looked like a regular soldier. Of medium height and slight build, his dimpled, bespectacled features reminded Nahum of a cabbage patch doll. Nahum was drawn to Shay's calm and approachable style of leadership. He was unflappable. They always kept in touch, even in civilian life, and even looked for ways in which to create business dealings between their respective companies.

August, 2001. Nahum was back on the outskirts of Ramallah again, this time in Reserve Duty. It was the usual four: Shay the company commander, Eran, the Lieutenant C.C., Daniel, and Nahum. They were the *hapak*, the Company Commander's squad, the gang of four. They always drove together in the C.C. jeep, always patrolled together. They were inseparable. An alert had been received that a wounded civilian was being brought to the Adam roadblock outside Ramallah. A van arrived and the driver went around to the back and opened the double doors. A teenager lay moaning in pain, his body riddled with bullets. Nahum asked the driver, the victim's brother, what had happened.

"Clan war."

The youth's upper thigh was bleeding profusely. Nahum couldn't detect an exit wound. The bullets had lodged in his femur. Tremors shook Nahum's body as he bent over to attend to him. He felt exposed. Things weren't always what they seemed to be. His friend Ohad had recently bent over to help an old woman pick up the vegetable basket she had dropped. A young girl ran up behind him and stabbed him in the lower back. Now he was paralyzed.

The victim's thigh was severely swollen. Nahum applied a tourniquet and administered an IV. He pressed a bandage onto the wound. Visions of Ohad flashed through his mind, but he pushed them away.

"Don't worry", Nahum reassured him. The young man's color returned as the fluids entered his system. He was on the verge of going into shock.

Azor Li. Azor li, the youth said in Hebrew. Help me.

"Don't worry, *caparah*. We're here to help."

The border police arrived. The vehicle turned out to have been stolen in Israel. It was full of bullet shells.

Nahum reflected on his balance sheet with the Almighty. He had taken a life. Now he had saved a life. In either case, could he have done anything differently?

CHAPTER 20 Mimounah

From the concrete frames of the "clerks' houses", Shneor and his unit watched the sun rise. The platoon stayed there all of that first day. The buildings were on the outskirts of the city. They were open and vulnerable, requiring everyone to be constantly on guard from every direction. They were cut off from any source of electricity. Nowhere to charge their cell phones.

With each passing day, they inched towards the center of the camp, tightening the noose. A single platoon would venture forth to take a house and then the entire company would join them. Shneor's platoon was a smaller "professional" platoon of twenty men specializing in Dragon missiles. They moved well together. Shneor and Ronen Al-Shochet were the platoon's two medics.

Shneor tried to suppress thoughts of home, but sometimes there was no use. What if I don't come home, he would catch himself thinking. He would be leaving a life behind. He tried to liberate himself from those thoughts. Being too cautious can be deadly, he reminded himself. Sometimes you have to take risks.

Whenever possible, Shneor studied in *Hevrutah*, one on one study sessions, with Yoram Levy who always brought xeroxed pages of *G'marah* with him to reserve duty. In civilian life, Yoram studied Torah every evening late into the night. He worked at a pharmaceutical company and had passed over numerous promotions in order to make time for his family and his studies. Shneor felt dwarfed by Yoram's encyclopedic knowledge of the scriptures. He generally agreed with Yoram's interpretations but even when he took exception he didn't feel learned enough to argue with him. He considered Yoram a *Tzadik*, a truly righteous soul.

Five nights into the battle, an APC arrived and they were finally able to charge their cell phone batteries. Avner Yaskov waited for a lull in the fighting before calling his newlywed wife, but as luck would have it a mortar round landed in the middle of their conversation. Dror used text messages exclusively.

Yoram Levy had brought his *tfillin* and they took turns praying with them. Eyyal Azuri, the machine gunner, had loaded up with snacks. Whenever things calmed down, he would break out refreshments for the entire platoon. Danny Meizlish, one of the younger soldiers, was in perpetual motion. Always running from lookout to lookout. They called him the "energy bomb". At one point, he motioned to Shneor that he needed to speak to him in private.

"Shneor, I feel fear."

"It's natural. We all feel it. We just have to control it."

"It's not that kind of fear. I'm not afraid of anything happening to me. I'm afraid that I might freeze under fire. I'm afraid that I might let you guys down in battle."

"I know you Danny," said Shneor. "You'll do fine."

Chanoch was nicknamed "babyface". He was one of the quieter soldiers in the platoon and was about to be married. Like Danny, he seldom dropped his eyes from his rifle sights. None of the soldiers had ever been under such concentrated fire before. It's danger and claustrophobia together, thought Shneor. He felt the pinpoint stares of thousands of rifle sites being trained upon him.

They took a four-story house. Preventive fire. No answer. It looked empty. Inside, they found twenty people hiding in the kitchen. They tried to calm them down, warning them before each round of fire. They made space for the men to pray. They gave candies to the children. Dror spent all day pouring over maps, looking out the windows in search of the next house.

A gunman wired with explosives ran towards them. Shots rang out. Yuval Altshuler was the quicker of the two. The gunman crumpled in the alleyway. For a few seconds they waited for the blast, but it never came. Enemy snipers were everywhere. Shneor and the other soldiers crawled beneath the window sills to avoid detection. The fire on the house was relentless. They couldn't identify the source. Hanoch finally figured it out: they were being fired upon from the minaret of a mosque. Dror requested approval to have a tank take out the sniper's nest. The response came back negative. No firing on mosques, no matter what the circumstances.

Between 5 and 7 pm each day the soldiers held their fire. Ziv, who spoke Arabic, would call out on the megaphone that anyone who wished to come out unarmed would not be harmed. On the radio, there were constant alerts when civilians were spotted, advising the soldiers not to fire in their direction. "Civilians to your left, don't shoot." Sometimes it was just a ploy. More than once, armed gunmen charged out from the center of a group of civilians, firing at the soldiers.

*   *   *

Troops were gathering near Bet Horon, the small community outside of Jerusalem where Yossi Ezra lived. A jeep full of religious soldiers, spotting *kippah*-clad Yossi, asked if he could spare a bottle of wine for *Havdalah*, the ceremony ushering out the Passover Holiday. It turned out that they were *Milu'imniks* who had studied at Or Etzion. Fellow students of Gadi. Yossi dialed Gadi's cell phone. He left a message. "Call me. There are some friends of yours here from the yeshivah." Gadi would already be in Jenin, his phone turned off, thought Yossi. Their cell phone batteries would be running out, and they would be saving the electricity for outgoing calls. Already inside.

*   *   *

Still with his disabled APC, Doron heard on the radio that everyone else was already in the Jenin refugee camp. He wondered when the last time was that the rest of the company had eaten. The platoon's food supplies were on the back of Doron's APC. He tried to contact Maor, the Platoon Commander, to see what the food situation was, but couldn't get him on the radio. The original plan had been to bring in a day's worth of food. Then the APCs would come with replenishment. But the fighting had turned out to be much too fierce. APCs couldn't make it to where the troops were holed up. Too many makeshift bombs and booby traps.

That night was the *Mimounah* celebration, the traditional North African ceremony marking the end of Passover. Families opened their homes to all comers, offering sumptuous spreads of *moufleta*, sweet crepes, and marzipan cookies . Doron called his parents to wish them the traditional Mimounah blessing in Moroccan Arabic, *Tirbhu wa'tsa'adu*. May you profit and be blessed. Doron's mother burst into tears.

"Where are you? We're hearing horrible things on the news."

"Don't worry, I'm outside Jenin."

"I don't believe you."

"I'm still trying to get us a tow out of here," said Yoav. At 7:30 pm, an APC with towing gear came to take the disabled vehicle to the field hospital three miles back. Under cover fire, the squad scrambled into the APC and rode back to the field hospital. Finally, there was food. They ate ravenously, and fell asleep in the back of a troop carrier.

3:00 a.m. An intelligence alert. Three suicide bombers were spotted on their way to the field hospital. Doron and his squad were the only infantry there. They spread out to form a perimeter around the tents, and took turns at guard duty. As they stood guard, a crew of APC technicians worked through the night on their vehicle.

CHAPTER 21 The Qas's Son

In Ethiopia, as the youngest son of a *Qas*, Mulu had his hands full on Passover. The Seder ceremony would take place in the *masgid*, the House of Prayer, where the village elders and representatives from each family gathered to hear Mulu's father, the village religious authority, recount the story of Passover. Then his father would bless the wine and matzot. Invariably, something would be missing, a salt shaker or knife, and Mulu, the gopher, would dash home to fetch it.

Mulu's father was also a *Shemagille,* a village elder. Not every *Qas* was necessarily a *Shemagille*, but in the village of Abba Antonis in the hilly Gondar province, Mulu's father held both distinctions. Soon, the comportment appropriate for the son of such a distinguished personage would be expected of Mulu. But not yet. Mulu loved to play his *washent*, the traditional Ethiopian shepherd's flute. There was no set music for the *washent*. He played what he felt. It wasn't considered a particularly dignified pastime. The *washent* was for shepherds and entertainers. Mulu's father never played the *washent*.

At harvest time, Mulu joined the other village children threshing wheat on the village threshing floor while someone scratched his bow on a *masenqu*, an Ethiopian stringed instrument, in the background. After the communist revolution, when the land was redistributed, they all received larger plots. Mulu and his older brother worked the fields while their father traveled from village to village teaching Hebrew.

Because their father had a teaching salary, they received smaller fields than the other villagers. Nobody minded. It was still much more than they had before.

Their dream was of Jerusalem. Mulu imagined a Jerusalem covered with sand. He had seen a small burlap bag of sand in the *masgid*. He was told it was from Jerusalem. On Yom Kippur, the villagers would pour a bit of the sand over the roots of the Grar Tree which grew outside the prayer house. Everyone would take turns sprinkling out a few grains of sand. The largest branch of the Grar Tree pointed towards Jerusalem, they said. Mulu remembered seeing the sand sparkle. He imagined that all of Jerusalem would sparkle like that.

In 1984, Mulu's two oldest sisters left on the trek to Sudan that would take them to Jerusalem. Rumors soon came backk from Sudan that it was no longer safe. That route was closed. The family moved to Addis Ababa, the capital city. In 1987, at age 14, Mulu arrived in Israel.

When they arrived in Israel, the shock was so great that he forgot the images of a sparkling city. For the youngsters, there were more pressing problems. Mulu left home to study in the Yemin Orde Youth Village. But the adults didn't forget. In Ethiopia, they had been accustomed to fasting on Thursdays to purify themselves. Now, in the new country, Mulu's mother made a ritual of ascending to Jerusalem every Thursday.

The other Ethiopian teenagers at the Youth Village already knew enough Hebrew to watch TV. "Are you in a special class?" Mulu asked them.

"Of course not. We're in the same classes as everyone else." It seemed to Mulu that it would take him an eternity to catch up.

His first assignment was to summarize an article. He copied the entire article word for word. Over time, he began to unlock the language.

There were young female soldiers to help the students with their homework in the afternoons. Soon, his Hebrew flowed.

During his second year in the Youth Village, Mulu finally visited Jerusalem. It was the Youth Village's annual Jerusalem Trip. There was no sparkling sand, and it was far from a City of Peace, but he felt uplifted nonetheless.

He chose a technical track. Together with matriculation, he learned a trade. He spent an additional year after high school honing his skills as an electrician.

Mulu's father wasn't recognized as a rabbi in Israel. Instead, the local religious council retained his services as a spiritual counselor. He was dispatched as a roving marital counselor to help Ethiopian couples resolve their disputes. Once, an elderly couple arrived at the Rabbinate to request a divorce. They were in their seventies. Mulu's father steered them each to separate rooms, and then conversed with each separately. He began with the wife.

"He never does anything around the house," she complained.

"Did he ever do anything around the house in Ethiopia?" asked Mulu's father.

"Of course not, but that was the old country. I see what husbands do here in Israel. The husbands of my Israeli friends are very helpful."

"Very well," said Mulu's father. He left to confer with the husband.

"This is beneath my dignity," the husband protested. "She never would have asked me to do these things in Ethiopia."

"Well, this is a different place," explained Mulu's father. "Perhaps you can help her with a few small things."

"I'd rather get a divorce."

The *Qas* suggested to the husband that he take a mop and pail and help his wife clean the floor. But with a twist. He should make sure to spill the dirty water all over the floor and knock over as many things as possible with the mop. She would appreciate his good intentions, but in all probability he would be relieved of his duties. The couple never returned to the Rabbinate.

Then came the army. There was something about the immunization shot that first day in the *bakum* that drove home to Mulu the fact that he was no longer in control of his life. Then the uniform. He wasn't even the same person anymore. All of a sudden, his *Tzabar* friends, never much for paying attention to their teachers, were following orders down to the most minute detail. The instantaneous transformation was a mystery to him. He had always taken his own ingrained serenity and discipline as a given. It was his culture. But to watch his Israeli peers turn from *rosh kasheh* -"hard heads" - to disciplined soldiers was nothing short of magical.

Mulu had never been a trouble maker. In Ethiopia, the discipline was severe. Their teachers beat them freely. In the army, he enjoyed the fact that he was no longer the only one who wasn't *hatzoof.* Brazen. He liked the army's pervasive egalitarian culture. Everything was based on ability and desire. He felt unconditionally equal, as he had in the Youth Village.

Mulu initially wanted to join a combat unit, but the army needed electricians and he had already taken a one-year deferment to acquire that specialty. He went on to specialize as an APC electrician.

There were all types in Mulu's unit in the Ordinance Corps. There were those who came from the advanced placement academic track, and those who hadn't made it to high school. He developed strong friendships in the army. His bunkmate Eran was his best friend. They took turns visiting each other's homes on leaves.

Perhaps he should have insisted on a combat unit, he later reflected The APCs never seemed to break down, and there was little to do. He transferred to a vehicle electrician unit where there was more work. He liked the climate there. Everyone took initiative. Alex, a Russian immigrant, was their Company Commander. Mulu loved the way his mind worked, and how he pulled them all together. Alex didn't like it when one person would finish his job and then take a nap.

"Start together, finish together," he would say. "Work together and it will always pay off for everyone." He treated them all with the utmost respect. He never abused his authority, never settled petty scores with anyone. If there was negligence or slipshod work, Alex never went out of his way to find the perpetrator. He had a saying, "Shit always floats to the top." He knew how to wait. But he went out of his way to make sure that Mulu and his fellow soldiers were motivated.

Alex noticed that their leave rotation left more soldiers than necessary in the base on Shabbat. He created a rotating schedule that gave everyone more leave time. But there was an understanding. If anything came up, people would voluntarily cut short their leave. It worked. No one ever argued with him. The soldiers knew he was on their side. There was nothing he wouldn't have done for them, and they for him.

Mulu's base was near Eilat, and the dry climate reminded him of the mountains of Ethiopia. For peace of mind, Mulu still loved to play his *washent*, the traditional Ethiopian shepherd's flute. He carved it from a bamboo stick his brother had brought him. At night, he would play the background music for his fellow soldiers' backgammon games. The three years passed quickly.

After the army, Mulu spent a year in a college preparatory course at Hebrew University in Jerusalem. He loved the city's variegated diversity, the ancient buildings, the traditional garb. The old and the new. He particularly enjoyed the city's great variety of headdresses: *kafiyyehs*, *shtreimels*, knitted *kipot*. Mulu didn't feel different in Jerusalem. Everyone was different.

The year in Jerusalem was his first real exposure to the day-to-day tension between Muslims and Jews. It was a riven city, a city of discord. Growing up in Ethiopia, his family had many close Muslim friends. The tension disturbed him deeply. In Ethiopia, when he had first seen a picture of the Dome of the Rock, he assumed that it was his people's Great Temple. Later, when he learned the truth, he couldn't imagine how two peoples could be so intertwined and in such disharmony.

His four years in the Youth Village so soon after arriving in Israel had postponed his inevitable encounter with the religious-secular rift in Israeli society. In those early years at Yemin Orde, the Jewish holidays punctuated his existence as they had in Ethiopia. The male students all donned *kipot,* the female students all wore ankle-length skirts. It was a school uniform. It didn't signify a world view.

After the Youth Village, he and the other Ethiopian graduates found themselves in a society divided along religious-secular lines. In Ethiopia, there had no such differentiation; no such culture war. It weighed on Mulu. He understood both sides, but didn't want to lose his individuality in either.

From Jerusalem, he went on to study Sociology and Political Science at Bar-Ilan University. At Bar-Ilan, things were much more uniform. The students were very serious. He missed Jerusalem.

In *Milu'im*, he and his fellow electricians were attached to a different unit on each stint of reserve duty. He missed the cohesiveness of his regular army days, the teamwork that Alex had engendered. He didn't feel that same feeling of egalitarianism. The same guys always reported for duty, the same guys always found a way out.

Now, in Jenin, it felt like the days of his regular service again. Mulu and his fellow APC technicians reached the roadblock that signified the departure from pre-1967 Israel. They put on helmets and bulletproof vests, inserted magazines into their rifles. Up until the roadblock, Mulu had felt fear. Now he felt something else. It was that "beyond fear" feeling, that sensation of hyperawareness. Anything can happen. Too much to think of. It was his first time in a combat situation. The freezing rain drenched them. The men were silent, the routine complaining noticeably absent.

CHAPTER 22 Hear O Israel

Thursday, April 4. Gadi Ezra arose early, full of energy. Wrapping himself in his *tfillin*, he prayed *Shaharit*, the Morning Prayer, in the predawn darkness. The previous night, he had called Galit.

"Perhaps we should get married right away, right after this is over," he suggested. Now he was full of resolve.

Gadi's platoon prepared to take another house. They worked their way down a steep incline towards the center of the Jenin refugee camp. It was still early morning. A heavy mist -blanketed the yards and alleyways . Eliraz, Gadi's Platoon Commander, went first. Nissim Ben David, the officer from the Giv'ati Brigade who had cajoled he Battalion Commander into letting him join Battalion 51 for this operation, leapfrogged past him as Eliraz lay down a base of cover fire.

"I'm right after you, Eliraz," called Gadi Ezra.

"No, wait. I'll call if I need you. Cover us from the second floor." Eliraz didn't want too many men exposed before they determined if the next house was safe or not. They could barely see ten feet ahead in the heavy morning mist. Gadi went upstairs to cover them.

"I'll yell if I need you," Eliraz called to Gadi. Nissim Ben David peered beyond the corner of the alleyway to see if all was clear. A machine gun burst caught him squarely. He collapsed backwards. Eliraz ran to get a stretcher, then ran back to Nissim. He tied Nissim to the stretcher. He couldn't tell if he was breathing or not. A cold, wet mist covered everything. Eliraz couldn't tell where the shots had come from. When Nissim was securely tied down to the stretcher, Eliraz called to Gadi. Gadi ran to the stretcher together with the company medic and another soldier. Quickly, they lifted the stretcher and prepared to mount the ascent back to the house. It was steep and slippery. This wouldn't be easy. The fire was becoming more concentrated now. The next burst caught Gadi and the medic. They fell, together with the stretcher.

At first no one was aware that Gadi was badly hurt. The bullet had caught him in the neck, but the bleeding was internal. The medic was writhing in pain, and Eliraz attended to him first. Finally, Gadi said in a soft voice, "Eliraz, I need help." Then the Shma. Hear O Israel, the Lord thy G-d, the Lord is one. He hung onto each word as long as he could. "Shma....Yisrael...." Then silence.

The heavy fire continued. Eliraz attempted to drag Gadi up the slope but the fire was unrelenting and the stones on the steep incline were damp and slippery in the morning dew.

Avihu raced down the incline towards the shooting. He couldn't tell if Gadi and Nissim were still alive or not. Time after time, he had vowed to himself that not one of his men would ever be left behind, dead or alive. He peeled off his flak jacket. For what he was about to attempt, he would need to be totally unencumbered.

Eliraz was struggling with the now unconscious Gadi. "Quick, on my back," he said to Eliraz. And then, hunched over by a weight far greater than his own, Avihu sprinted up the incline.

When the evacuation was complete, Avihu joined Yaniv, the Lieutenant Battalion Commander, for a quick rest on what looked like an abandoned engine block .

"What's this thing we're sitting on?" He asked Yaniv. They both peered around the back of the metal debris. Avihu spotted some wires snaking out of the back of the hunk of metal. He jumped up. They were sitting on a 50 kg explosive device.

*　　*　　*

The *Pal-Sar* leapfrogged from house to house, sometimes no more than two or three a day. They assumed they were behind schedule, but Regimental Command came on the radio to congratulate them on their progress. "You guys are leading the charge so far!" It was then that Hanoch understood how long this operation was going to take.

For Hanoch this was where the *asimon*, the payphone token, dropped into place. When an idea takes hold, when all suddenly becomes clear, the token is said to have fallen. The realization now set in that this was going to be a war where all sense of time would melt away. This wouldn't be like regular *Milu'im*, where he counted the days until going home. Here, they had no idea when life as they knew it would resume. Their mission was to clean out the camp's nest of terrorists, but they had no deadline. Caution was the order of the day. Their progress would be excruciatingly slow. In five days, Hanoch and his men would advance only 700 meters. They would work slowly, painstakingly. Towards the end of each day, they would engage in the inevitable debate. Another house?

The natural instinct was to stay put. Not to venture out into the alleyways. The next house could wait until tomorrow. It was in these critical moments that Oren, the Company Commander, showed the power of inspired leadership. Somehow he always found within himself the strength to prod his men onwards. "After me." And they always followed. Hanoch marveled at Oren's leadership. It was something that defied analysis in the mundane terms of the business world. In civilian life, Oren was a computer technician. What was it within each one of them that made them follow Oren, Hanoch wondered. Each house they entered immediately became the most comfortable place in the world. A haven one could easily occupy forever. Yet they followed him without a second thought. It seemed like the most natural thing in the world. Each time he said, "After me", no one hesitated.

Hanoch had known Oren since their regular service together, but he had become someone new this time around. He had matured overnight. In their regular service, he hadn't seemed to care about anything. Now he cared about everything and everyone. He spent hours patiently listening to all and reassuring them that he understood their viewpoint. He always attempted to forge a consensus. Failing that, he would issue a directive but make it clear that he had factored everyone in.

We're a hard group to lead, Hanoch reflected. Most of the soldiers were opinionated academics. Leadership had to come from personality and professionalism, not from rank. Oren somehow knew when to bring an interminable argument to an end with a terse, "*Tistmu et hapeh*." Shut your traps. "Right now, you'll have to do what I say. Afterwards, we can argue about it." It was so contrary to Oren's gentle nature. Perhaps, for that very reason, when things reached a boiling point and he had to give an order, everyone accepted it.

One thing they never discussed was politics. It just didn't seem to matter. On the need for this particular operation, they were all in agreement. One soldier, a bus driver who had survived a bombing attack on his bus, had gained a reputation as somewhat of an extremist. Oren decided that it would be best if he stayed in the command post. Throughout the operation, soldiers trickled in, many having arrived from abroad. In spite of their good intentions, Oren assigned them all to the command post.

"No one comes in the middle of the movie," he said. "Anyone who wasn't in on the opening salvo, I don't want." Hanoch had no doubt that many of Oren's decisions saved lives.

The *Hapak*, the C.C.'s squad in Hanoch's company, stayed together the whole time: Oren, Hemi the X.O., Hanoch the Pathfinder, and Ari, Oren's radio man. Each step in the operation took hours. Calling in for tank support and then coordinating with the tank once it arrived could take half a day. Actual sleep was out of the question. They caught catnaps in between advances.

The exposed dashes between houses took place in slow motion, each precarious instant seeming like an eternity.

"Here's where the door should be."

"There's no door."

"Here, it's bricked up."

"There's a door, over there."

"No look, wires. It's booby trapped."

"Mortar round on the door. 1-2-3. Fire!"

In a living room, coughing in the swirling dust, sat an elderly man and two elderly women. The soldiers helped them to a side room, and moved the furniture to the sides of the room to keep it clean. The entire platoon poured into the house, all thirty men. The sounds of exploding shells and *mit'anim* never stopped. The screams of helicopter missiles presaged their impact.

A recon unit mistakenly identified the house as suspect, and a tank shell slammed into the porch. Hanoch heard the telltale whistle, and then all of the windows blew out.

Napping soldiers jerked awake. Some ran for the door, others jumped out the windows. They thought the house had been identified by the enemy and was under attack. When it became clear what had happened, they reassembled in the house and prepared to move on. Hanoch radioed their position to all nearby units to make sure they had the coordinates. His earplugs were no longer of any use to him. All he could hear was a ringing noise.

The door of the next house was wired. Hanoch called in a D-9, and it tapped the door with its shovel. A ferocious blast blew the door off its hinges. At the next house, Hanoch attached an explosive brick to the front wall. The brick exploded, but the wall turned out to be a support wall. The front of the house collapsed. He and the men were trapped, forced to circumvent the collapsed house in the exposed alleyways. He called in a tank to provide covering fire. They moved on.

They entered a house and heard footsteps on the upper floor.

"Stop! Stop!" One of the soldiers yelled. The footsteps continued, now descending the stairs. No one was in the mood for taking chances. Gideon fired a shot up the stairs at the approaching footsteps. When he saw what had happened, he fainted. At the top of the stairs stood an old man, apparently deaf, bleeding from his arm. Moshe, who was standing behind Gideon, managed to catch hold of him as he slumped. But Gideon was heavy. Moshe broke his fall, but couldn't hold up the weight of Gideon and his equipment. They both tumbled to the ground. The medic immediately attended to the old man. He stopped the bleeding and hooked up an infusion to prevent him from going into shock. Gideon came to and threw all of his energy into the rescue effort. He radioed the command post for an APC to evacuate the old man. The old man fluttered in and out of consciousness. For the entire time until the APC arrived, Gideon never let go of his hand.

Whenever he entered a house, Hanoch thought of his own house and how he would feel if soldiers invaded it. He and the other soldiers understood the necessity of searching the houses thoroughly, but took great pains to leave everything as they found it. Often, in the closets, they found plastic bags filled with Israeli shekels. They left them intact. They made sure to leave behind their own canned rations in the houses, even those that were uninhabited.

They moved on to a new house, no different than the others in its decorations. Posters of suicide bombers plastered the living room windows and walls. A placard with the image of a suicide bomber hung near the telephone like a takeout menu. The house belonged to a young couple with two small children. Supplies flowed more easily from the command post now, and Hanoch had them send in diapers for the small children. They shared their rations with the family.

*   *   *

From their tank radios, Stu and his fellow tankfighters had followed Battalion 51's entanglement second by second. Able to hear but not see the fighting, they felt constrained and stymied. They wanted to help, but the alleyways were too narrow for tanks.

A makeshift barricade of sand and barrels blocked the main road. Adi, the C.C., was asked to fire on the barricade. He fired a shell, but the resultant debris still blocked the road. They moved forward. A huge explosion rattled the tanks. Everyone assumed that one of the other tanks had fired a shell. A flurry of confused accusations bounced around the airwaves.

"Who shot that? Who gave an order to fire?"

"It wasn't us. We thought it was you…."

Ilan, Stu's commander, jerked his eyes away from the periscope. He and the driver had been momentarily blinded by a white flash. No one had fired. Adi must have tripped a wire or driven over a mine. There was no damage. A storm of rocks and debris from the explosion rained down on the tanks. Finally, Adi's voice came over the radio. "Carry on." Everyone breathed a sigh of relief.

"*KodKod*, did you go over an explosive device?" asked Ilan.

"Seems so."

"Are you OK?"

"Affirmative. Carry on."

A major push forward was to begin. Adi went to Ginat to receive new orders, then briefed the squad leaders. Ilan came back and went over the mission with Stu. They drove forward a hundred yards, infantrymen behind them. The main road ended in small open square flanked by a large building. Adi took his tank left around the square. Shay, another commander, took his tank right to cover him. Sporadic gunfire was coming at them from the upper floors of the large building. The tanks fired a few shells at the building from fifty yards. The gunfire continued. The infantrymen raced into the building. The voice of the platoon commander came over the radio.

"We're up on the second floor now. They're above us. Fire a *heavy* on the third floor."

"You mean a shell?" The tank commander wasn't sure they had ever felt the impact of a tank shell so close. "Heavy" was tank speak for a shell. Perhaps infantrymen used a different jargon. He wanted to be sure.

"Yes, *heavy*. Fire."

The tank commander was still hesitant. "I really wouldn't recommend that."

"Fire! Fire already!" the platoon commander insisted.

The tank fired a shell into the third floor. The platoon commander came back on the radio. It took him a few moments to get his voice back. He was coughing heavily.

"Don't shoot another one. Repeat, don't do that again."

"You guys OK?" The tank commander felt a little guilty. Perhaps he shouldn't have assumed that the infantryman knew what he was asking for.

"We're recovering. We'll be fine. "

The tanks turned on their smokescreens. White smoke filled the open square, and infantry poured into the building. The tanks continued pouring machine gun fire into the third floor.

Generally, smokescreens meant that D-9s, the giant bulldozers, were on the way. When a large mine or explosive device was discovered, the tanks would often detonate it with a shell, and then the D-9s would come in to clear away the debris. One of the D-9s ran over a 30 kilogram mine, enough to demolish a truck. The driver didn't even notice.

After that, the tanks split up. One or two tanks accompanied each infantry unit. Whenever an infantry unit identified a source of fire, they would call in from their vantage points within the buildings. If a tank had a straight shot at the source of fire, the task fell to the tank. If not, it fell to the helicopters. The accuracy of the helicopters was mind-boggling. They could place a missile in a single window from over two miles away.

Stu and one other tank accompanied the Naval Commando unit. Every few minutes the tank rode over a mine or a makeshift bomb would be thrown at it. One tank counted over thirty bombs and mines that day.

"I feel like a sitting duck," the commander of the other tank radioed. "We should move to a better spot."

"No big deal." It was one of the naval commandos. "Where's the fire coming from?"

The tank commander detailed the coordinates of the sniper. A few seconds later, the commando came back on the radio.

"OK, I just took care of it. You can relax now."

Stu found himself in awe of the unflappable calm of the Naval Commando soldiers. They were a different breed, an army within an army, he thought to himself. Theirs was a different culture, a different language. They dispensed with the formalities of radio code names, addressing each other by first names on the radio. For internal communications, they used their own wireless devices.

Other units interacted differently with them as well. Instead of going through the usual cumbersome chain of command to call in helicopter fire, they called in their support directly. There were none of the myriad questions that would inevitably follow an infantryman's call for a missile.

"I understand you want a missile on the building in cube 3129," Stu heard one of the helicopters confirm with a nearby commando.

"Affirmative."

"Which window?"

The commando told him which window. The helicopter puffed out a wisp of smoke as the hellfire missile found its mark. Boom. Done.

Stu watched as two Naval Commando soldiers went to place an explosive brick on a door. Just as they were about to blow in the door, they spotted a woman sitting with two children nearby. They approached the woman and her children to calm them down and move them out of harm's way. A sniper bullet caught one of the soldiers in the leg, severing his femoral artery. Immediately afterwards, an exploding booby trap sprayed the other soldier with shrapnel.

* * *

David Zangen remembered the wounded Naval Commando's light blue eyes. "Don't worry. I'll be back tonight, the young soldier said with a twinkle. But it was serious. A helicopter was called in to evacuate him to Rambam Hospital. The doctor who would accompany him in the helicopter asked the medic to remove his thumb from the wound. A fountain of blood spurted from the severed femoral artery.

His friend's face had been sprayed by shrapnel. He would require surgery, but was back the next day. They have strong will, thought David. It was his job to temper that will with judgement. He remembered the time that his own eye had been injured in a detonator accident. He too had wanted to be back the next day. It was that devil-may-care will that was the essence of being a young soldier.

The will of these young soldiers strengthened his faith. These were the bones and spinal cord of the Jewish people. It filled him with new strength to see how fervently these soldiers believed in their mission and how meticulous they were about executing it in the most humane manner possible. All of the reservists felt it.

It was the same sense of hope that he often felt as a pediatrician. For David, Pediatrics was a glimpse into the future. You're not just postponing the inevitable, he told himself. He felt life's continuation unfolding in his hands.

His heart fell when the next two casualties arrived. He was good friends with Dr. Yakov Ezra, whom he affectionately called "Jaques". They were both the Chief Medical Officers of their respective regiments, and worked at the same hospital. But there was nothing that he could do for his friend's baby brother. It was too late.

CHAPTER 23 Bending the Rules

Dr. David Zangen, Jerusalemite, pediatrician, and man of faith, felt himself in need of a booster shot. If only understanding could be administered by injection.

It wasn't a crisis of faith exactly. His faith was implacable, resolute. But he longed for an understanding that would make the past year's brutal chain of events look like something other than cruel divine providence.

His colleague, one of the head nurses at Hadassah hospital, had lost her husband to a brain tumor a few years back. David had always admired her fortitude and bright, cheery disposition. She was left widowed with four daughters. But her life seemed to be straightening itself out again. Three of her daughters were already married, there were grandchildren and joy again. And then one Saturday evening her youngest daughter decided to join her friends for a pizza on King George Street at the Sbarro Pizzeria.

Now, ever since the bombing, he was filled with unanswered questions as he passed his colleague in the hallway. Why her? Why in such a cruel way? She was such a righteous woman, always such a source of strength for others.

His faith and his practice of medicine were inextricably intertwined. Sometimes, when administering an injection to a crying infant, he would remind himself that such was the lot of mankind, able to perceive only the pain but not the hidden meaning of tragic events.

He constantly reminded himself how little he truly understood. It was what made him an extraordinary clinician. In coaching interns, he would first teach them to hang back, to spend a few minutes in quiet observation before rushing in to care for a young patient.

He was enormously sensitive. He taught his interns how to enter the world of a child. "Don't enter their space. Watch for a few minutes. Observe the parents and the child together. Look into the child's eyes. Does he look away? Does he meet your gaze? Try to radiate warmth. You may learn more in those few moments of observation than in the entire exam."

If an intern moved too quickly to the stethoscope, David would take him aside. "You've missed the main thing," he would caution them. "Observe the eyes, the rate of breathing, the relationship with the parents. Then the child will look at you differently."

There was another byproduct of the dim view that he took of the totality of human understanding: he maintained a healthy regard for intuition. His heroes were those who were sensitive enough to access their own intuition and courageous enough to act upon it. In that regard, there were none greater than his grandmother, Savta Rivka.

At age seventeen, David's grandmother read the writing on the wall in her native Poland. Certain that nothing good was awaiting the Jewish population there, she departed for Holland. Shortly before the deportation of Dutch Jewry to concentration camps in World War II, her husband traveled to Switzerland to pave the way for bringing the family there. But the war broke out, and Savta Rivka was left to her own devices for the entire war. It fell to Savta Rivka to bring her family through the war. In Nazi occupied Holland, the Jews were called upon to report to 'work camps'. "I don't believe it," she declared. "What kind of work camp wants five year old girls?" She had no doubt that these were extermination camps, even though many in the Jewish community refused to believe the rumors. She cared for her husband's niece as well as her own children. One day, the head of the local Jewish community called. He was attempting to fill the daily quota for the "work camps".

"You don't have to send your own children," he said. "You can send your niece."

"Have you sent your own daughter yet?" she fired back.

When the Nazis came to check her house, she hid in a mental hospital. Somehow, through her connections with the Dutch resistance, she and her family survived the war. Her daughter, David's mother, met David's father in a Zionist youth group in Holland. His parents had perished in Auschwitz. Together, they made *Aliyah* to Israel in the 1950s.

When eight years old, David visited his grandmother in Holland. By then, she was a well-known retailer of apparel. She took him on a buying trip to Amsterdam. He marveled as his grandmother quickly and intuitively selected the merchandise that she knew would suit her customers' taste. It was done in an instant. Merchants chased after her down the hallways, attempting to interest her in something else. But she knew what she wanted.

Those were the qualities that David most admired in her, the qualities he most wanted for his own children. They were the intuition and determination of Rivka, the biblical Rebecca. She had no doubts when she chose to go with Isaac, her husband. When he appeared at her family's watering hole, something inside her told her to give water to all of his retinue, not just to him. Likewise in raising her son, the forefather Jacob. She knew when rules needed to be broken.

David followed an atypical path for an army physician. Instead of taking a deferment for his medical studies, he entered the armored corps and became a Lieutenant Company Commander. During a training exercise, he was seriously injured by an exploding shell detonator that almost cost him his eyesight. After the army, he decided to pursue a medical career.

Much of his pediatric practice was devoted to the treatment of juvenile diabetes patients. Some came from Bethlehem and Nablus, with no money for medicine. They all had his phone number 24 hours a day. Sometimes the calls in the middle of the night would be in Hebrew. Sometimes in Arabic. He found solutions for them all.

*   *   *

The evacuations were excruciatingly slow. The field hospital in Ginat, the Command Post, had seen little use. By the time the wounded reached the field hospital, there was often little to be done. Either they were immediately evacuated via helicopter, or it was too late.

The further the soldiers penetrated into the refugee camp, the harder it became to attend to the wounded in the field. The medics were being picked off by snipers as they attended to their fallen comrades, and the alleyways weren't wide enough for APCs to reach the wounded.

David became furious at the lack of adequate evacuation routes. He insisted to Regimental Command that some houses be demolished in order to create wider evacuation routes, but the demolition of houses still seemed politically untenable. The army was different than the hospital. In the hospital, he was the final authority. Here, he was merely an advisor.

Jerusalem was a small town for its veteran families, and David Zangen was no stranger to the corridors of power. He had a phone number that he knew he could use if the need ever arose. But he would be circumventing his superiors. Could he bring himself to jettison protocol? He wondered what his grandmother, Savta Rivka, would have done.

He made the call. "Listen, something has to be done here. We can't keep fighting without proper evacuation routes!" he fulminated. "There's no alternative. Some houses might have to be shaved, but we need decent evac routes."

"I'll take care of it," said the voice on the other end of the line.

CHAPTER 24 The Rabbis' Tent

The APC seemed to be repaired, so Doron and his squad prepared to go in. Yossi, one of the older soldiers in the company who owned a bakery, filled his car with *pitot* and met Doron's squad at the Saalem intersection. Doron devoured one pitah after another. He hadn't tasted bread for the seven days of Passover, and these *pitot* were still warm and moist. On the radio, they followed the company's progress. They were making good headway, without any casualties yet.

Hagai, the Liaison Officer, motioned to Doron from his tent. He had a serious look. Eyyal, as usual, didn't miss a beat. "Everything OK?" he asked Doron.

"Hagai wants me."

"Want me to come?"

"No, it's OK."

Doron entered Hagai's tent. Hagai spoke in a low tones.

"We have two dead from Golani Battalion 51. One is named Ben David. No one knows which unit he belongs to. Do you know anyone named Ben David?"

"Of course, Yaron. He's in our platoon."

"What does he look like?"

"Tall. Thin. A goatee." Yaron and Doron were friends. They nicknamed him "Ben Da." Doron doubted it could be him, it didn't make sense. His platoon wasn't yet in the thick of the fighting. Besides, what would he be doing fighting with Golani?

A group of army rabbis had arrived to perform the grim work of identifying the casualties. One of the rabbis asked Doron to come in and identify the body. The sight of the black-clad rabbis with rubber gloves caused something to snap within Amzaleg. He began screaming at them.

"What are you doing, walking around here! Wait where you're supposed to wait! Don't walk around among us!" He looked as if he might attack them. "Don't walk around among us!!"

The rabbis apologized and entered one of the tents. Eyyal, watching from the side, approached Ohad, who had been closer to the Liaison tent, to fill him in.

"Who is it?"

"I'm not sure. Forget about it."

"Tell me!" he pressed him.

"They think it's Ben Da."

Eyyal and Ben Da were childhood friends. Eyyal approached Doron as he entered the makeshift morgue. "Just make a sign when you come out of the tent. Yes or no. I'll wait over here." He was holding on to APC for support. His knuckles were white.

Inside the tent, an army psychologist asked Doron if this was his first time identifying a body. Doron recalled Saba Nissim's funeral. He had been called upon to identify the body.

"Prepare yourself for the difference here," the psychologist said. "The soldiers were severely shot up, and the bodies haven't been cleaned.". Doron felt tears welling up. He helped lift the first body. It was extremely heavy. The hair was so matted with blood that Doron couldn't make out its color. The face was still covered with a blanket.

"That's definitely not Ben Da."

"No, it's not. It's a Golani soldier named Gadi. We've already identified him."

Doron was totally focussed on the other body. He heard the name "Gadi" but somehow didn't make the connection to his friend and former student. It registered somewhere, but not in his immediate consciousness. They lifted the body of the second soldier, Ben David. The build fit, he was tall and thin. Two witnesses from Golani stood beside him, together with a female clerk.

"Are you going to be OK?" her supervisor asked her.

"I've done this before," she answered.

"Who can identify the officer Ben David?" the Rabbi asked.

"The what?" Doron had to be sure.

"The officer, Ben David."

Ben Da was a sergeant. It wasn't him.

"His name is Nissim Ben David," the rabbi continued. But no one here can identify him. Doron ran out and signaled to Eyyal. Negative. The color returned to Eyyal's face. He took a long swig from his canteen, and ran to tell the others.

Doron was curious as to who this soldier was. As he later found out, Nissim Ben David had been an officer of the Giv'ati Brigade, in charge of training reservists. When the fighting broke out, he received special permission from the Golani Battalion Commander to join Battalion 51. He hadn't been called. He had gone in on his own.

*   *   *

Duchan, the C.C. of the Auxiliary Company, picked up Leibovich at the hospital. They drove to Ma'aleh Efraim, a small town in the hills above the Jordan Valley, to pay a condolence call on Roman's parents. None of the soldiers had been able to visit them yet. Roman's parents wanted to hear the story of how their son had fallen. Leibovich choked back tears as he told the story of the gun battle in the hallway. He would always see Roman as he had been moments before his death, smiling and confident. "I've got your ass covered, Leibovich."

On the way back to the hospital, Duchan received a call on his carphone from one of the other Company Commanders in the Battalion. He turned on the speakerphone so Leibovich could hear. "Duchan, it's Koby. Gadi's hit. I can't talk now." Leibovich heard shooting in the background . He felt tears streaming down his face.

Back in his hospital room, as they parted, Leibovich said to Duchan, "Whatever it is, call me. Tell me what happened." Fifteen minutes later, Duchan called. "Gadi's dead."

Shot full of painkillers, Leibovich heard the news in a fog. It didn't seem to make sense.

* * *

Thursday afternoon. Gadi Ezra's sister Vittoria was bathing her youngest child when the doorbell rang downstairs. Her six-year old son ran down to answer the door. "Ima, it's Miri and someone else," he called up, unsure of what to do next. "I don't know any Miri."

She wrapped her youngest in a towel and came down, glancing quickly through the peephole. Two female soldiers in uniform waited silently on the doorstep. Her hands trembled as she opened the door. The air seemed to rush out through the open door, leaving only a suffocating emptiness in its wake. She didn't know Miri either, but she knew exactly who Miri was.

* * *

Kobi Danieli, Gadi's childhood friend from Bat Yam, was in Jerusalem when he heard the news of Gadi's death. A friend's brother was in Gadi's unit and had called from Jenin. He immediately drove to Gadi's house. No one was there. He went to the Ezra family's pharmacy. Solly, Gadi's father, was working behind the counter. Kobi froze. Solly didn't know yet. Had he seen him? He would guess that something is wrong. He couldn't' be the one to tell him. He ducked out the doorway and ran across the street, taking cover in the shaded entrance of an apartment building. Where was the City Officer threesome, the officials whose job it was to provide the grim tidings? An hour passed, each minute an eternity Kobi called Rav Ruja, their high school principal. Rav Ruja would know how to get the City Officer here fast. "Where are the army officers? They have to tell the family before someone else does!"

One of Gadi's aunts came to the pharmacy. Solly proudly showed her the newspaper picture of Gadi peering out through a hole in the *Mukatt'ah* compound wall.

"Why is Gadi's picture in the paper?" asked a young nephew. "Is he dead?"

At that moment, the City Officer officials arrived. Always in threes. A civilian, a doctor, and an officer. From outside the pharmacy, Kobi watched the scene unfold. It was like watching a silent movie that ended when Gadi's father fainted.

Kobi feared for Gadi's mother. A woman of strong faith, but so gentle, so fragile, thought Kobi. How would she survive this? She was in Jerusalem that afternoon, praying at the Western Wall. When she arrived home at 7:00 pm, she was pleasantly surprised to find the door unlocked. Solly would still be at the pharmacy at this hour. Gadi must be home!

She opened the door and beheld the tear-streaked faces. "Hear O Israel, the Lord our G-d, the Lord is one," she whispered.

*   *   *

Doron's APC was stuck again. This time it was the electrical system. "It's obvious the Almighty doesn't want us in there. We'd better not go against his wishes," concluded Amzaleg.

"It's obvious Amzaleg doesn't want us in there," said Doron. Amzaleg chuckled.

An empty APC was headed towards the Jenin refugee camp to bring food to Golani. Doron approached the driver. "I have to get in there tonight. We have soldiers in there and they're running out of food and ammunition. Just bring us to the edge of the camp, we'll go in on foot from there."

They loaded up the food and ammunition on their backs, enough for eighty soldiers. The alleyways were too narrow for APCs. At 1:00 am, Li-Ad and Moti met them at the entrance to the camp. They were overjoyed to see them.

"We were worried about you!" shouted Moti as he gave Doron a bear hug.

"About us?"

"Yes, about you. We heard that your APC got stuck."

Doron, Yoav, and the rest of the men followed Li-Ad's platoon. But Li-Ad and his men were already familiar with the neighborhoods, and the gap between the two groups began to grow. Halfway there, they became separated. Doron radioed Li-Ad, and he came back to collect them. Finally, they reached the houses that had already been swept. The Hebrew letter "Chet", for *hanit*, or "spearhead", marked those that the *Pal-Han* had secured. It had taken Doron's platoon an hour to travel only 400 meters. They reached the house where the rest of the company, eighty soldiers, billeted themselves for the night. Doron was able to get a couple hours' sleep.

CHAPTER 25 Simple Text Messages

Friday, Apr. 5. Itzik ran up to Doron and gave him a bear hug. "Good to have you back! Have you spoken with Liron?"

"I called her from the field hospital."

"But you didn't tell her we were here, right?"

"Of course she knows we're here. She always knew that this is where we'd end up."

"I can't believe you!! You told Liron what we're doing here?? " Itzik was incredulous. He had tried to keep the worst from his own wife. The two wives were often in touch. "Now I'm sure Miri knows!! I can't believe you told her!"

"But all I told her was that we were in Jenin…"

"All? That's *all* you told her? All they're hearing on news right now is horror stories from Jenin. They have no idea what's really going on here. I never would have told Miri that I was in Jenin."

There was coffee in the house. Amzaleg awoke early to brew coffee for the entire company. In the gentle light of the morning, Doron saw that the walls of the house were covered with posters of suicide bombers. The coffee tasted good, and in this house it didn't bother him as much that it wasn't army issue. He borrowed *tfillin* from Ehud and prayed *Shaharit*, the Morning Prayer, among the beatific stares of the suicide bombers. That morning, many of the secular soldiers asked for instruction on how to pray with *tfillin*.

The houses began to flow into each other as they moved towards the center of the camp. With each new house, three or four of them would take turns being the "entry cell," responsible for gaining entry and securing the first room. It was Amzaleg and Uzi's turn. Amzaleg affixed a "leech," a magnetized explosive brick, to the metal door. A thick steel bolt ran down the middle of the metal doors, and usually the blast would bend the bolt enough to blow the door inwards. Some doors were too thick though, and wouldn't budge. Then they would go through wall.

This time it worked. The door blew inwards and Amzaleg charged into the dust-filled room, shooting at the ceiling. Generally, the blast was enough to stun anyone inside. Amzaleg staggered back out of the house and collapsed against the wall. The blood had drained from his face and he was trembling.

"My G-d. My G-d," Amzaleg kept on murmuring. A couple and their four young children were huddled together on the floor, wide-eyed with fear. "If anything happened to those children, I wouldn't be able to live with myself."

"What luck, what luck, what luck," he mumbled to himself over and over. He went back into the house.

After that house, he was a different Amzaleg.

They swept a total of seven houses that day. They weren't in any particular hurry. One of the houses sported a remarkably complete collection of suicide bomber posters, some ensconced in ornate shrines.

One of the shrines housed a large poster of Wafa Idris, the first female suicide bomber. There was a poster of the bomber who had blown up the Matza restaurant in Haifa only days before. Doron suppressed the urge to do damage. Part of him wanted to leave a sign that they had been there. A warning that they could return at will. It was difficult for all of them to pass among the shrines of the *suicide bombers*. It was more like a surreal stroll through an alternate universe, one where all that was profane had become holy.

The houses of the higher ranking police officers were easy to identify. Aside from the uniforms, they were the only ones with expensive entertainment centers and wide screen TVs. One such house, that of a police colonel, actually had a flush toilet, the only one they encountered in the camp.

At the third house, Doron affixed a "leech" to the door, and it blew in. Three adult men sat on the floor, along with women and children. Within the house, the soldiers found two holsters and police uniforms. They made a thorough search, and radioed in the identities of the men to Intelligence. Something felt wrong in that house. Intelligence radioed back that the men were not wanted. Doron had misgivings, but the orders were to move on.

"We're going to be back here. I can feel it," Doron said to Itzik.

*   *   *

Leibovich attended Gadi Ezra's funeral in his wheelchair. He was still shot full of painkillers. The crowd parted before him, but no one approached. All eyes seemed to be upon him, but no one made eye contact. "Look at him," their stares seemed to say. "The lucky one. He was only injured."

Later, at the grave, he and Galit remained alone. Leibovich handed her the photograph from his hospital room. He had never really spoken with Galit before. There had been too many people in the hospital room, and she and Gadi had been in a world of their own. "This is yours. I never got to give it to Gadi." She looked at it and smiled for a moment.

He wanted to share something with her, an inkling of how much he had cherished Gadi. He had been able to talk to Gadi about anything. It was like Gadi had divided himself up into little pieces and passed himself out to everyone. Nothing he could think of seemed adequate. He decided to share his final memory of Gadi, storming the room at the end of the hallway. "When Roman was killed, he wasn't afraid of anything," he said. "He rescued us under fire."

* * *

Rafi rarely slept. When not on patrol, he made the rounds, talking with small groups of soldiers. He shared his insights with them, they shared their views with him. Sometimes he strengthened others, sometimes he came away strengthened.

He paid a visit to the company that had lost their C.C., Moshe "Moshik" Gerstner. It was late afternoon. The soldiers of the company were still in heavy mourning. Many were new reservists in their early twenties. They related to Rafi how important Moshe had been to them. How much they missed him. How they had lost their confidence when he was killed.

In one of the houses that he entered, a gun battle had recently taken place and many of the windows were broken. He found a group of soldiers busily picking up shards of glass off the floor and collecting them in pails. The family was upstairs. Some of the soldiers were mopping up the floor. Rafi was astounded. He was amazed at their level of care, even in such a hostile environment.

Rafi spoke to them of the historical weight of their actions. Of how important the success of this operation had been to Moshik. Moshik himself had only been 32.

Yehudah, the new, younger C.C., later told him that his talk had been important to the soldiers. They came away strengthened. He had returned their motivation to them. He was gratified to have been able to touch them, to lessen their pain.

In Givat Oz, the supply personnel worked round the clock loading and unloading food and ammunition. They had been working like dogs, but were over six miles from the actual fighting. They didn't feel a part of things. They too were soldiers of Regiment 5, and Rafi wanted them to know how important their work was to the regiment.

He went to speak to them on Shabbat evening, before prayers. He took a full hour and a half to provide them with a complete briefing on everything that was happening in Jenin. How the soldiers on the "inside" felt. How the commanders felt. For days afterwards, whenever any one of the supply personnel spotted Rafi, they would thank him for his talk. His words made them feel more a part of things. They were always forgotten, seldom did anyone pay attention to them. It meant a lot to them that Rafi had not only shared facts with them, but his emotions as well.

He spoke with the rabbis of the Army Rabbinate in the field hospital. There were forty of them, thankfully many more than were needed. Some had been brought to evacuate the bodies of dead enemy gunmen, but many of the corpses were booby-trapped and they weren't able to approach them.

It filled Rafi with exhilaration to watch all of the care packages flowing through Giv'at Oz. In the Yom Kippur War, Rafi had sent a care package to a soldier. He had written a note to the soldier in pencil. " Be healthy.

Watch over us. Come home soon." He had received a reply from the Sinai. "Thank you!" Now the notes were printed on laser printers with ornate graphics. Out in the field, Rafi was happy to see soldiers writing responses.

*   *   *

Hanoch's platoon split into squads. He entered a new house with a squad of seven. The house was inhabited. They separated the men and women according to local custom, and checked I.D.s. It turned out that two of the men, in their mid-thirties, were wanted by Intelligence. He soon found out. An APC arrived to deliver them the General Security Services.

"Here, take this," he said to the driver, handing him his wallet. What did he need it for? The weather had changed now, and it was hot. The water main to the camp had burst, and they had no drinking water.

"Bring any water?" Luckily, they had. The APC backed up to the door of the house, and under the watchful eyes of the tank, unloaded supplies. They then guided the two men, bound and blindfolded, into the APC.

The squads reassembled at the end of the day. They were sixty men now, and they needed to find a house big enough. It was too late to venture into unchecked territory, so they opted to return to the house they had occupied the previous night. Hanoch heard the radio crackle. It was Intelligence.

"Get ready. There's a man walking your way from the house next door. He's strapped." They took up positions in hushed whispers. Maybe returning to this house wasn't such a good idea. It was a long half hour as they waited for the figure to appear. It was almost totally dark now. Finally, they heard a blast. Another company spotted the bomber walking in the adjacent alleyway and fired. He had only partially detonated himself.

It was a sleepless night. Their approximate position had been identified. Hanoch half stood, half slept, the entire night. It was too dangerous for cellphones. He could only listen to his voicemail and send text messages. There were increasingly insistent messages from those who didn't know that he was in Jenin. The bank, asking why he hadn't come in to pick up his new credit card. The gardener, asking why he hadn't sent him his check. The world outside of Jenin was continuing as normal. He sent Efrat the same text message every evening. *Hakol Beseder*. Everything's all right.

*   *   *

Doron and the *Pal-Han* identified countless booby traps. Eli and his "sixth sense" proved invaluable. He had discovered over ten booby traps himself. He caught sight of a suitcase by the side of a house.

"Booby trap," he announced calmly. Ivan, standing next to him, told him to relax.

"Everything to you is a booby trap."

"Move away, Ivan." Ivan took a few leisurely steps back. Eli fired at the suitcase. The bomb was far larger than he had surmised, and the explosion was deafening. The blast sprayed Eli's face with shrapnel and burst his ear drums. He was evacuated by helicopter. But four hours later, the men heard him on the radio.

"This is Old *Kodkod*. I'm coming back in."

Itzik turned to Doron. "That's what I call tempting fate."

"Would you come back?" Doron asked him.

"Me? Definitely." Not a moment's hesitation.

Doron didn't feel as certain. "I don't know what I would do."

Eli had three children and a pregnant wife. While in the hospital, he had seen news reports of four injuries in Jenin. He was excited when he rejoined the company. "Hey guys!! We're on the news!"

At 4:00 pm, Doron called Liron to wish her a *Shabbat Shalom*.

"Your brother just came back from Gadi's funeral."

"Gadi?" It hit him. "Oh my G-d. Gadi Ezra. It was *him*. He was in my hands."

Doron called his mother to wish her a *Shabbat Shalom*. She sobbed hysterically. "Where are you? May the Almighty watch over you." He asked how his father was doing, how his legs were. He had suffered two strokes, and had taken a fall on the first night of Passover which had left him weak.

"He's fine, *Omri*." My life.

Doron had to hang up. It was getting dark and they needed a better resting place for the night. The house they had been assigned wasn't ideal. It was exposed from four directions. Maor decided to look for a more secure house.

*   *   *

Rafi had never felt himself such an integral part of a large historical event. From the hill on which the regimental command post rested, he looked east and saw the Jenin refugee camp. Looking west, he could see all the way to Afula and even Haifa. This is a war on our homes, he thought. We're going into the snake's pit and grabbing the snake by the head.

Rafi was in charge of all of the units surrounding Jenin. His area was called the "lower hill". By the third day, when prisoners began to stream out of the refugee camp, he was put in charge of all of the arrests. It was his unit's job to make sure that all who exited the camp were checked for explosives. He had two full companies under his command, with two tanks. Many civilians emerged from the camp unescorted; he had to make sure that they weren't concealing any weapons. He and his men needed to frisk all of the men coming out of the camp. The fear was that gunmen would charge out with their weapons and begin firing, or that there would be a suicide bomber in the crowd.

The decision was taken not to check women and children as they emerged from the camp. They were the scariest.

A nine-year-old boy approached them. Rafi and his men were thirty yards away, warily eyeing him through binoculars. They called to him to stop. Apparently he didn't understand. Their instincts forced them to train their sights on him. Every hour there were new alerts on suicide bombers approaching them out of the refugee camp. All of a sudden, Rafi had a flashback. It was the famous picture of a young Jewish child, hands raised, with German soldiers aiming their rifles at him. "This is enough," he said to himself, lowering his rifle. The soldiers continued to shout to the boy to raise his hands. Finally, he did. Rafi knew that he couldn't have acted differently. Even if the boy had reached into his shirt and pulled out a detonator cord, Rafi wasn't sure if he could have brought himself to shoot.

He called Ma'ayan to wish her a *Shabbat Shalom*.

"Hi Ma'ayan. What are you up to?"

"I'm daddy's little soldier. I'm taking care of *Ima*." She was always strong on the phone, but according to her mother she would cry at night. Maybe Abba wouldn't be able to kill all of the terrorists. Maybe one of them would kill him.

The battle was going very slowly. The troops were encountering fierce resistance, and progress was much slower than expected. The regimental staff met Friday night to ponder next steps.

"We're at the junction of two dangerous myths," said Rafi. "If we stop now, the other side will claim that they stopped us. If we continue, they'll claim that there was a massacre. Let's face it, the myth of a massacre is going to be propagated anyway. But the first myth is much more dangerous. It could have much wider implications. Jenin is the "Capital of Terror." If our regiment, reservists mainly, is the one that takes it, we'll be sending a strong message about what reservists are capable of. That message is for Baghdad and Damascus."

*   *   *

Battalion 51 took two more casualties, Matanya Robinson and Shmuel Weis. This would be a difficult evacuation. To reach them, Avihu would have to cross an alleyway ringing with the ricochets of sniper fire. He gingerly extended one of his maps beyond the corner that shelterd him to gauge the accuracy of the fire. A burst of withering sniper fire immediately perforated the map. His next test would gauge the competence of the snipers. He poked the nose of his flashlight a few inches beyond the wall that concealed him, into the alleyway. It was immediately shot from his hand. Still, he would have to find a way. He was not going to leave a single soldier behind, dead or alive.

The evacuation proceeded under unrelenting fire. Finally, when it was over, Avihu, drenched with sweat, sat down with his radioman on a stoop to rest. Shots rang out, and bullets slammed into the brick wall two inches from his ear. He and the radioman jumped around the corner, into an alleyway. He was unharmed, but bullets had never passed so close to him before. He was shaken. He was being watched over, he reminded himself. But that was close.

* * *

During a lull, David Zangen and some twenty other soldiers tried to pray *Kabbalat Shabbat*, the prayers welcoming the Sabbath. As the service began, he was called away to take attend to Marom Fisher, a severely wounded Golani soldier from Battalion 51. It was too late. When he returned to the prayers, it was time for *Kiddush*, the blessing over the Sabbath wine. Two more dead arrived.

He couldn't concentrate on the liturgy. He offered a prayer in his own words. "Dear G-d, these are the best of our youth. So please take care of them. Help me make the right decisions."

CHAPTER 26 A Psalm

Darkness settled. They nailed carpets to all of the windows, plunging the hideout into complete darkness. The carpets provided scant protection from sniper fire, but they made them less visible and made it slightly harder to lob grenades in through the windows. It wouldn't stop an exploding grenade, but would serve as a barrier if the timing wasn't perfect. Shabbat had begun.

A nearby Golani platoon came on the radio. They were taking incoming fire and weren't able to identify the source. Maor looked at the map. The *Pal-Han* was the closest force to the Golani platoon. He decided to go out in search of the sniper and chose eight soldiers for the detachment. As they left, Doron recited Psalm 121, which asks the Almighty for protection. "A song for on high, I raise my eyes to the mountains, from whence will come my salvation?....May the Lord protect your going out and your coming back."

The moment they stepped outside, fire opened up on them from all directions. Maor identified the closest source of fire, and led the detachment in that direction. Barak Cohen, the machine gunner, sprayed fire ahead of them.

As they covered each corner, Maor radioed for all forces to stay inside. They tossed grenades, sprayed machine gun fire, and moved forward. Even Maor was surprised by how quickly they were progressing towards the house from which the sniper had fired. It was almost too easy. Maor affixed a magnetized brick to the door of the house, and shouted *Alukah*! Leech. Itzik, in Maor's detachment but a number of meters away around a corner, thought he heard Maor yell *"alunkah"*, stretcher. Maor must have been injured. Itzik radioed in for a medic. The medic was with Doron in the house. Doron opened the door to go out with him, and bullets ricocheted off the metal doorway. They were pinned down in the house.

Maor's leech didn't work. This door was of thick metal. The leech blew a hole in the door, but the bolt remained in place. Silence. Maor spotted a back door to the house, slightly ajar. He pulled out the pin of a grenade and was about to toss it into the open crack. Something gave him pause. There was something strange about this door. And the silence. Why weren't they being shot at? The snipers seemed to be shepherding them towards that door. Maor held the grenade ready, and had Itzik shine a flashlight on the door. It was wired with enough explosives to take down the entire building. If he had as much as pushed the door open, the entire detachment would have been wiped out. They backed slowly out of the alleyway. The sniper fire started back up, heavier than before. It was now clear that the trap had been discovered, there was no longer any reason to hold back. It would be hard to make it back to the house now. Barak resumed fire with the machine gun, with Itzik covering him from behind. All of a sudden, Itzik's magazine was empty. A gunman popped up behind him and fired at point blank range. A bullet grazed Itzik's cheek. He dove forward on the ground, allowing Barak to fire over him, spraying the gunman. They made it back to the house without injury, save Itzik's cheek wound. But it was going to be a long night. The enemy had an approximate idea of where the platoon was now, even if they didn't know the exact house.

Enemy gunmen were firing into the house two doors down. The walls shook as they tossed in a *mit'an*. Everyone wanted to return fire, but Maor and Doron motioned for everyone to be quiet. There was a burst of machine gun fire into the adjacent house, and another *mit'an* exploded in the yard outside. Still, no fire through their windows. Doron prayed that Effy Cohen, who was stationed at the window closest to the yard, would decide not to return fire. Silence. Doron prayed a prayer of thanks.

Later , Eli came to tell him what had happened. "When the bomb went off, I instinctively raised my rifle to fire, and it jammed. In ten years in the army, I've never had a rifle jam on me before, until now." It was a miracle. If he had fired, the platoon's position would have been given away, and they would taken heavy incoming fire and bombs.

They didn't sleep at all that night. Itzik, Maor, and Doron, in full gear, commandeered the double bed, but they were too wound up to close their eyes. Itzik, his face bandaged, had a question that had been nagging at him.

"Who are you going to kiss first when you get home? Your wife or your kids? I mean, who do you love more, your wife or your kids?"

"I couldn't tell you," Doron answered. "I think I'll kiss my wife first, but it doesn't mean I love her more."

"I know your type. You're like one of those types who comes home and immediately makes conversation with his wife," said Itzik. "Maor and me, we're not like that. First, we check if there's a soccer game. Then, we see if there's anything on the news. Only then, if she happens to pass by, do we make conversation." Everyone laughed.

They were all in full ordinance vests. It was a tight squeeze. "Man, look at how close we're sleeping to each other," said Maor. "I don't even let my wife sleep this close. I'll give her a hug, but then I need my space."

After a while, Doron got up. Staying in that house had been a mistake.

They were on the ground floor. He felt totally exposed. He passed among the guards to make sure they were alert. With the first glistening of dawn, he prayed another prayer of thanks. He had never been so glad to see morning come.

CHAPTER 27 The Long Call

Saturday, April 6. Shabbat morning. Hanoch and his squad approached the next house. They had taken fire from the house next door and anticipated trouble. Surprisingly, the owner of this house spoke Hebrew. Hanoch asked him to knock on the door of his neighbors' house and tell them to come out.

"I can't. They're bad people. If I do, they'll shoot me."

Hanoch pointed to a spot around the corner from the doorway. "Then stand over there and call to them to come out."

A few elderly people emerged. They weren't the ones Hanoch and his men were looking for. The squad retreated to the shelter of the previous house, and Hanoch called in a helicopter, code name *Rikud*. Dance. Hanoch could see shadows flitting across the walls through two of the second story windows of the other house. He consulted his maps.

"*Rikud*, this is *Afshara*. Do you see house 1752?"

"Affirmative, I have it in sight."

"Good. Bring down two missiles from the east." He signaled to the helicopter from the window to make sure they were aware of his position. "Do you see me?"

218

"Affirmative. Firing." The helicopter fired two missiles. Hanoch heard two reports but didn't see anything.

"I don't see anything. Repeat, I do not identify a hit."

"Relax. I put them right through the window. They went through the north wall, on the far side of the building." *Rikud* sounded offended that Hanoch had questioned his marksmanship.

"Sorry, *Rikud*. Don't take offense."

"None taken."

Hanoch and his men stormed the house. It was an explosives lab. The components of *mit'anim* were everywhere: barrels of TATP, ammoniac, propane tanks, and an assortment of metal pipes. Hanoch found a Xerox of an article from an Israeli newspaper about last month's operation in Jenin. The title of the article quoted a soldier as saying "We were sent here to die." Hanoch resolved to send the Xerox to the article's author so that he would understand where demoralizing articles like that ended up. This had been Hanoch's first time witnessing a missile strike from up close. He was underwhelmed. He admired the accuracy of the missiles, but their blast was little better than a grenade. There was no sign of the two men on the upper floor. One of the missiles had left a hole in the wall, perhaps they had escaped through it.

Hanoch still hadn't spoken to Efrat since they had entered the camp. He couldn't bring himself to call her. Efrat had a special way of getting him to spill his guts to her. He had never been able to hide anything from her, and he couldn't bring himself to tell her what he was going through. Your head has to be "inside" an operation, he reminded himself. Otherwise you're a danger to yourself and your buddies. He continued to send her text messages every day. *Hakol B'Seder*. Everything's OK.

They reached a crowded backyard, and called for the twenty or so people within to come out. All except three men emerged. The squad entered the yard, all rifles trained on the three men. Their hands were in the air, but still they didn't move.

"Lift your shirts," Hanoch called out.

The first two lifted their shirts. The third man remained motionless, then dropped his hand and pull at a cord under his tunic. Itzik, the machine gunner, mowed all three of them down with a burst of machine gun fire. The third man was strapped with explosives, but apparently hadn't had quite enough time to complete the wiring and connect his detonator switch. The soldiers had to jump over the three bodies to enter the house.

That night no one spoke. They expected a retaliation. Hanoch had been able to recharge his cell phone battery for a few minutes on the APC that came to collect the prisoners. He received his first phone call from Efrat.

"I can't talk now, I'll call when I can," he said. He couldn't pour out everything that was in his heart in front of sixty men.

Yoel, one of the soldiers in Hanoch's squad, asked to use his cell phone. There was little charge left in the battery, and Hanoch had hoped to save it for an emergency. But there was something forlorn in Yoel's look, and Hanoch couldn't bring himself to turn him down. Yoel sat in the corner and carried on what seemed like an endless conversation. Hanoch felt an urge to remind him that the battery was running low, but something held him back. He was reading from a small notebook into the phone. What could be consuming all of his remaining minutes, Hanoch wondered. Stock quotes? Bets with a bookie? Not likely, Yoel was a *kibbutznik*. What could be so important for a kibbutznik? After what seemed like an eternity, Yoel brought the phone back to Hanoch.

"I really appreciate that. My mother just passed away and I had to dictate the eulogy to a friend of mine."

CHAPTER 28 Breakfast in Bed

Sunday, April 7. Doron's unit spent the night in a house inhabited by a couple with three teenage sons. The family was sequestered in the bedroom, the platoon stayed in the living room. Outside the house, there was a food pantry. The family asked permission to get food from the pantry. It was too dangerous. Outside, bullets were flying everywhere. Instead, the men shared their rations with them.

Uzi, an irrigation engineer, warned them all against using toilet paper in the bathroom. He explained that there was no plumbing in these houses, and that toilet paper would immediately clog the septic system, creating grave health risks. He meticulously scrubbed the bathroom to guard against dysentery.

In the morning, they asked the family's permission to prepare coffee. They brought a tray of coffee to their room. "*Ajeeb*! Amazing," said the wife to Mizrahi, the sniper, who spoke Arabic. "I've never seen a man prepare coffee before. And by the way – who cleaned the bathroom? It definitely wasn't my husband."

*   *   *

A dilemma arose in Ginat. Nearby was the main reservoir for Jenin. There was one main water pump, powered by gasoline. There was concern in the command post that the gasoline would run out and the water would stop pumping into the city. The municipal liaison to the army said there was a tanker full of gasoline in the city that could come to fill up the pump.

Rafi stopped to think. Could he let the truck enter Ginat, the command post, full of personnel and vehicles? What if it was booby-trapped? The pump was about to run out. Rafi and his crew finally found a roundabout path for the truck to take. They evacuated the entire area in preparation for the truck's arrival. But then there was a change of heart on the part of the municipal representatives. They decided not to send the truck. The army finally arranged for an Israeli tanker truck to refill the pump. Rafi hadn't wanted to bring about a water shortage, but he didn't want to undertake unnecessary risk, either.

*   *   *

During the *shivah*, the seven days following Gadi Ezra's death, the Ezra house in Bat Yam overflowed with people. Gadi had touched a multitude in his short life, and they all came to pay tribute.

Yossi Ezra thought of his last night with Gadi, the night of the Seder. He had had little patience for Gadi's thoroughness that night, but now he viewed it differently. Thank G-d he got to do it his way, he thought. He had prayed *Ma'ariv* as he wanted, and performed the Seder as he wanted. Thank G-d for that.

Avihu Yaakov arrived with a carload of other soldiers from Battalion 51. They came directly from Jenin, and his uniform was still covered with the blood of the dead and wounded. As he paid his respects to Gadi's family, one of the other soldiers began to tell the story of Gadi's evacuation. Avihu silenced him. "It's not for here, " he whispered. Many of the soldiers wrote lengthy inscriptions in the Guest Book for visitors to the *shivah*. Avihu signed it quickly, and was gone.

*   *   *

That day, Hanoch and the *Pal-Sar* made their best progress yet. Thirty houses – over 100 yards. They were almost at their target, Intersection 25 near the center of the camp.

In one of the houses they found two elderly women and eight young children. The soldiers entered the large back yard. One of the women began shouting in Arabic, "Flee! Flee! The army is here!" Immediately, gunfire rained down from the surrounding houses into the back yard. The soldiers took cover in a corner of the yard and returned fire. Two gunmen were killed, the rest fled. The elderly women spoke to the children and they began to cry. From the sound of the gunfire, Hanoch assumed. He reached into his flak jacket and pulled out some of the M&Ms his brother had brought from the States. Two of the children gingerly approached and took some. One of the elderly women scolded them and threw the candies on the ground. Hemi understood a bit of Arabic. "She's telling them that we're trying to poison them and if that doesn't work we'll shoot them," he translated. They moved them inside the house.

The incoming fire resumed. It was time to find a better house. "What number is that house over there?" asked Hemi. Hanoch looked at his map. Every house was numbered. If he made a mistake, they could find themselves the target of friendly fire. A gunman peeked out from an alleyway to take a shot, but one of Hanoch's men was quicker. The gunmen crumpled to the ground. Faceless hands reached out from within the alley to drag him back.

They entered the yard from which the two snipers had fired. There were large vats of TATP explosive powder and a Kassam II missile and launcher in the back yard. They exploded the powder and took the Kassam launcher with them. They moved on to another house, but it had too many doors and windows to make a good lodging for the night.

The next house had only one door, so they decided to call it a day. Regimental Command radioed again to congratulated them on their progress.

CHAPTER 29 The Traveller's Prayer

Monday April 8. Doron and his men returned to the police colonel's villa. It too was plastered with posters of suicide bombers. It had already been taken, but they were ordered to give it a more thorough search. Yevgeni found a cache of documents in the basement, which the Intellligence officers found quite interesting. The soldiers had been out of water for quite a while. Doron boiled water from the storage tank on the roof, and they drank.

In the next house, Amzaleg discovered a large room with two older women and thirty or so young children. The children were wide-eyed and hungry.

There was a *pitah* oven out in the back yard, with sacks of flour next to it. "Why don't you go out and prepare some food for the children," Amzaleg asked.

"Can't. Forbidden." The woman replied.

"Come with me." Amzaleg signaled to the lookouts watching the back yard, and motioned for her to follow him. For the next two hours, he served as her bodyguard as she kneaded dough into little balls and baked them into *pitot*. When the replacement unit arrived to take up positions in the house, it was redolent with the aroma of fresh pitah bread.

"Man, does that smell good! Where are the *pitot*?", one of the soldiers asked Amzaleg.

"What are you talking about?" said Amzaleg. "I don't smell any pitot."

The soldier regarded him quizzically.

"Come here," said Amzaleg. "I'll show you something." He grabbed the soldier by the arm and dragged him to the room full of children, munching silently. "There," he said. "Now tell me you still want *pitot*."

The soldier was silent as he beheld the crowded room. "My G-d," he finally whispered. "So many children."

At the next house, they received an unexpectedly warm greeting. Eyyal announced their presence and the door opened to reveal the owner of the house, Mr. Majid, beaming broadly at them. He seemed genuinely overjoyed to see them.

"What's so funny?" asked Maor.

Mr. Majid spoke good Hebrew. "I'm just happy you're here. Stay for a while. Make yourselves at home. As long as you're here, we won't get hit by missiles."

There were three adult men in the house, together with women and children. The soldiers separated them and checked I.D.s. Amzaleg asked the women if they needed to bake *pitot* in the back yard, to which they enthusiastically answered in the affirmative. He accompanied them to the backyard. An argument ensued over whether or not the family would agree to accept payment for the *pitot*. Amzaleg finally prevailed upon them to accept payment, with a proviso that they bake enough for the second platoon. The deal was done.

A sniper fired at them from the house next door. They called in missile strike from a helicopter, but the sniper fire continued. They then called in tank fire, and the house next door was reduced to rubble.

"You see why I'm so glad that you're here?" said Mr. Majid.

David, one of the younger soldiers, snapped pictures whenever possible. Neither Doron nor any of the older soldiers had any desire to be in David's photo album. For the veteran soldiers, both secular and religious, there was still something unlucky about snapshots before or on the field of battle. Doron didn't consider himself superstitious, but he still didn't want to be photographed. Too many such photos ended up being developed posthumously. The younger soldiers seemed to have less of a hangup about being captured on film. It was David's first *Milu'im*.

"Come on, Doron, take a picture with me," David pleaded with a smile.

"Find someone else."

David had Yevgeni photograph him. Doron got angry with them both. "Don't let me see you two goofing off again until we get out of here," he snapped at them.

*   *   *

Ginat became the site of frequent pilgrimages by IDF generals. The Chief of Staff himself passed through four times to monitor the operation's progress. One general, inquiring into the morale of the soldiers, asked if a rotation of leaves had begun yet.

Col. Didi Yedidiah, the Regiment Commander, smiled ruefully. "Leaves? No one's taken a shower yet."

* * *

The making of bombs was a widespread cottage industry, Rafi observed. The houses were littered with all sorts of bombs in various stages of assembly. It was amazing to see how people went about their daily lives surrounded by explosives. He tried to picture the typical bombmaking family. Did they put these things together at night while watching TV? Nothing was what it seemed. Many of the booby traps had been hidden in garbage bags, soda cans, and myriad other mundane props. There were no "innocent" objects. In one of the houses, they found a photo album filled with pictures of young children gotten up with explosive belts. The oldest was 11 years old.

From their APC, Rafi and his soldiers spotted a man nearing them, pushing an older man in a wheelchair. They were headed out from the camp towards the city. On Sunday, they had received an alert that there would be a suicide bomber in a wheelchair. The description had been given in painstaking detail. They knew his name and physical description; the victim of a bombmaking "work accident", he would be old and hunched, with an amputated arm and leg. He would be accompanied by one or two men. White hair, white beard. "He is to be considered extremely dangerous. Heavily armed and strapped with explosives. The goal of this cell is to detonate themselves and take with them as many soldiers as possible."

The old man reached the yard of a house. Rafi and his squad rolled out of the APC 15 meters from where the man sat. Rafi was the closest to him. There were three other family members with him, and they sat in the shade of a gazebo. He had all of his hands and feet.

"It's not him," said Rafi.

* * *

After each house had been swept, Doron found his thoughts drifting back to his family and his students. But running between houses, the only ones in his thoughts were Itzik, Maor, and the other eleven members of his squad.

It was here in Jenin, sprinting from house to house, that Doron came to understand the wisdom of the Rambam. Once, he had viewed the Rambam's words as detached and impractical. Now, he was certain, they were the key to his survival. If he were to allow fear to paralyze him, then it would destroy him. He marveled that the Rambam, who had never fought in a war, could have arrived at this truth.

He stopped speaking with his children, even when he had recharged his cell phone battery. Whenever he spoke with Adi and Shoham, it was Amir's children that he pictured in his mind. Each conversation with them killed a little part of him. He kept the conversations with Liron to a minimum.

"Liron, are you OK? Are you strong enough?"

The previous night's experience taught the *Pal-Han* two things: no more ground floors, and no more night operations. Doron and his fellow soldiers owned the days, the enemy owned the nights. The night protocol was absolute: no flashlights, no standing, talking only in whispers. For almost a week now, they hadn't been able to shower or change their clothes. They hadn't even taken off their boots.

That night at 3:30 am, orders came through for a night mission. Rumor had it that high-ranking American dignitary was about to arrive in Israel and things had to be accelerated. Maor called Asi, the C.C., on his cell phone to question the wisdom of a night operation.

"Asi, I thought we had agreed that night operations don't make sense here. It's problematic. I'll do whatever you say, but this is a serious problem."

An order was an order, but soon it would be dawn. Perhaps, offered Asi, there was a way of postponing the sortie until first light. "Look, stay inside for now. The other Golani force has to get situated first, and it'll be light out by the time they're in position."

After he hung up with Asi, Maor called Itzik and Doron over. "There's no way we're going back out at night. I'll find a way to make sure it's light by the time we go out. I'm not going to risk lives for geopolitics."

*   *   *

Monday Night was *Erev Yom HaShoah*, the evening before Holocaust Memorial Day. Hanoch and the *Pal-Sar* felt the need to hold some sort of ceremony, but there could be no candle lighting or other traditional means of commemoration. Thirty of them stood in a circle in the living room of a small house. In whispered tones, the men surprised each other with their readiness to speak and share experiences. Emotions flowed readily. Hemi read from a prayerbook with the aid of a dim red flashlight. They talked about the connection between the Holocaust and what they had been doing this past week. Some told of their parents' and grandparents' escape from the Holocaust. Others told of their pride in being able to fight back in a way that their parents and grandparents in Europe never were. In civilian life, Hanoch had never attended a Holocaust ceremony that lasted more than ten minutes. Theirs lasted over two hours.

*   *   *

Dror Bar took out six candles, one for each of the six million Jews that had perished in the holocaust. "We're in Jenin to prevent what happened fifty years ago from happening again," he said. Yoram Levy read Psalm 83.

"G-d, don't be silent. Don't be quiet.

Your enemies are threatening.
Others are conspiring against your people.
To decimate them. No memory will remain.

After the ceremony, Dror asked the soldiers to share their future plans.

"How do you see yourself in life? What is a meaningful life for you?" he asked Yoram Levy.

"For me, it's studying Torah." Some of the soldiers shared their career plans. Some spoke of family. When they were finished, Dror made an announcement.

"We're going to sleep a bit now until the next house. In all probability it will be our last." They were thirty yards from the center of the camp now. Shneor felt relief. The end was in sight.

At 4:00 am they cleaned the house and made ready to take what they hoped would be the final house.

Platoon 8, Shneor's platoon, went to the house occupied by Platoon 7 to drop off their heavy things before taking the next house.

"Let's say the Traveller's Prayer," said Shneor. He couldn't explain why all of a sudden he felt that need. He hadn't felt it before the taking any of the other houses. Somehow, he felt that he was about to embark upon a journey that was more significant than the others.

CHAPTER 30 The Bathtub

Oded Golomb, Shneor's Company Commander, had received a citation for bravery in Lebanon. He was meticulous to the point of fanaticism when it came to preparation. Before, as Lieutenant C.C., they had called him the "Company *Ashkenazi*" for his reserved, considered manner. As Company Commander, he had come into his own. He was different now, thought Shneor. He had become much more outgoing, a social force in the unit. He organized barbecues for the company and did whatever he could to raise everyone's spirits. In spite of the traditional "distance" between soldiers and their commanders, he was everyone's friend. Like Dror, he hardly ever slept. On the morning of April 9th, he decided to accompany Shneor's Platoon 8 on their final sortie.

Some units preferred the daylight, but Shneor's platoon preferred to move at night. They crept silently through a narrow alleyway. The final house was only thirty yards ahead of the house where Platoon 7 was holed up. It was a two-story house. Dror and Oded entered. The house was empty. A poor way station, the two officers decided. Too many windows. The rest of the platoon stayed in the alleyway to cover them.

They decided upon a house a few doors down. Oded put a "finger" on the door of the new house. He called out before blowing in the door.

Shneor and the others took up positions in the back yard. They heard a shout from the other side of the house. It was Dror.

"*Nitkalnu!*" Incoming fire. He must have seen something, thought Shneor, because no shots had been fired yet. Then, a fraction of a second later, all hell broke loose. It was 5:45 am.

The air was filled with cries of the wounded. Shneor fired off three magazines. It was his first time under direct, heavy fire. There was no cover. He was directly in front of the windows from which they were being fired upon. Those to the right and to the left of him were mowed down. Avner Yaskov, Eyyal Azuri, and Reuven Magnajji fell. Reuven and Shneor had studied together at the yeshivah, and had served together in their regular service. After two minutes of continuous fire, there was a momentary lull. Ronen, the other medic, covered Eyyal Azuri with his body as he attempted to attend to him. Yoram Levy, with a pack of twenty grenades on his back, had taken a bullet through the side of his head. He sat on the ground, his head slumped to the side, his body propped up by the grenade pack. His seemed to have nodded off to sleep. Shneor saw the hole in the side of his helmet. The grenade pack was intact. If it had been hit, it would have taken out the entire platoon .

Roni Drori threw grenade after grenade. Sputtering fuses streamed back at them through the air like fireworks as an endless barrage of makeshift bombs rained down from the windows into the yard where they were trapped. Later, they would call that yard "the bathtub". Hemmed in by walls spouting fire on all sides, it slowly filled with the blood of Shneor's brothers.

The sun was rising. Shneor tasted a bitter taste in his mouth, bile rising from deep within. An emptiness descended upon him and sucked him dry of all feeling. He became an automaton. Avner Yaskov emitted a final gurgling sound and fell still. All around him, the souls were leaving the bodies of his brothers. It was a thing that couldn't be stopped. His friends, one by one, were floating away. He thought of his family and immediately banished the thoughts. He focused on the task at hand. What could be done right now? In the distance, he heard Dror's voice, calmly calling out orders. "Louder, Dror!" he called to him. "We can't hear you back here."

He heard a whisper behind him. "I'm wounded in the leg." It was Reuven Magnajji.

"Come on, let's take Reuven," said Eyyal Zimmerman, the young, long-haired radioman. Shneor and Zimmerman pulled Reuven behind a low wall, out of the line of fire. Shneor applied a tourniquet to Reuven's leg as Zimmerman radioed for help. From behind the low wall, Zimmerman returned fire towards the windows.

The young soldiers from Platoon 6 ran towards the yard. The older soldiers affectionately nicknamed them "the kids". Ofer, their platoon commander, dispatched them towards the yard. Menasheh Chabah, the machine gunner, asked Dror where to begin shooting from. Dror sent Shneor to take Menasheh back into the yard and show him which windows to fire at. Shneor watched in awe as Menasheh positioned himself directly in front of the windows, lifted up the massive gun and began pouring fire into the building. Where does that kind of courage come from, Shneor thought. In the darkness behind the building, he couldn't quite glimpse Menasheh's face.

Oded, the C.C., was down. He had taken a bullet to the chest. Shneor and Ofer carried him towards the gathering point that had been set up for the wounded a few alleyways over. He was still alive, but Shneor could tell that he was in his death throes. Before they reached the gathering point, Oded fell still.

At the gathering point, Shneor set to work on Oded, attempting to resuscitate him. It was too late. Two soldiers arrived carrying Dror Bar's lifeless body. Shneor assumed that all of the other wounded were being carried back as well. But the minutes passed and no more wounded appeared. They were all still back in the yard. He approached Avi Attias, the Lieutenant Battalion Commander , and requested to form a detail to go back in after the wounded. Kobi Azoulay, the officer in charge of the rescue squad, arrived as they were speaking.

"Wounded? Where? Let's go!"

Shneor led Kobi and three other soldiers back to the yard. Kobi ran ahead. As they ran down an alleyway parallel to the yard, they caught sight of a figure across the main street. In the early morning light, they couldn't tell if he was friend or foe. He seemed to be in uniform, with a standard army issue flak jacket. "Israeli Army!" Kobi and Shneor shouted. The gunman was just as stunned as they were. "*Wakef*!" he shouted in Arabic. "Halt!"

Shots rang out from the upper floor of the original house that they had chosen not to occupy. Bullets pounded into the stone wall behind Koby Azoulay, tracing a dotted line in the wall. One bullet caught him in the shoulder and exited from his chest. Shneor's detachment fell back. It was now 7 am.

Menashe Chabah spotted Reuven behind the low wall. He took up a position behind the wall and continued firing at the windows. "We'll have you out of here in no time", he said to Reuven. Next to him, Zimmerman the radioman lay dead. After the last of his ammunition was gone, Menasheh tried to drag Reuven to safer ground. He too was shot and killed.

Reuven was now the only soldier left alive in the yard, hidden behind the low wall. Gunmen emerged from the building directly across from him. He heard them counting the bodies in Arabic. They began dragging three bodies away from the yard. Reuven removed a grenade from his belt and popped the pin. Clenching the live grenade in his hand, he resolved not to be taken alive.

Zeev Iluz, the commander of Platoon 7, moved from house to house houses towards the yard. Eyyal Yoel and two others were ahead of him. A booby trap exploded, killing Eyyal. Iluz knew that every inch of the room he must traverse was wired. But he was determined to reach the vantage point afforded by the second floor balcony. He made his way gingerly through the booby trapped room in which Eyyal Yoel lay dead. Helicopters were in the sky above, but the opposing forces were too intimately enmeshed. It was like a chess board. If only he could make it to the second floor balcony, he could direct their fire from his radio.

Lidani, a sniper, saw one gunman dragging the body of a soldier and another gunman covering him. He noticed a bulge in the second gunman's pocket. A grenade. He shot at the pocket and scored a direct hit on the grenade. The gunman exploded.

The chain of command was decimated. The Company Commander, the Platoon Commander and all of their successors had been killed. Now it was each according to his own initiative.

Shneor brought his detachment back to the gathering point and reported to Avi Attias. "We can't get in via the alleyway. We need an alternate route."

"Go back in via the houses now," instructed Avi. Shneor's assignment was to assess the damage. He was joined by Sar, one of the medics from Platoon 6, and six other soldiers. They reached the yard at 7:30 am. The faces of the dead were already white. They were frozen in place where they had fallen. A yard of statues. Shneor and Sar tied the dead onto stretchers, covering them with blankets, and carried them back to the gathering point. Torrents of blood poured out of the dead soldiers' uniforms when they lifted the bodies.

Roi and Hezi, two of "the kids" from Platoon 6, caught sight of Reuven lying behind the wall. He was barely conscious.

"Watch out, it's live," said Reuven, nodding weakly towards the grenade in his hand. His knuckles were white. Roi slipped the pin back in and they carried him back to the gathering point. When he saw Shneor, he reached up from his stretcher and grabbed Shneor's shirt. Tears streamed down his face. "They're all dead," he wept. "All of them."

He heard an officer addressing a group of reinforcements, preparing them for what they were going to encounter in the yard.

Special Forces arrived with dogs to search out the wounded who had been dragged away. No one knew if they were dead or alive. At the gathering point, Shneor gingerly removed Yoram Levy's grenade pack. He could see the hole where the bullet had entered. A miracle.

"You're wounded too," a soldier said to him at the gathering point. He had taken shrapnel to his temple and leg, but hadn't noticed. He was bleeding profusely from both wounds.

Shneor went back into "the bathtub" three times. This is the *correction*, he kept on reminding himself. The correction of Joseph's Tomb. The correction of the past year and a half of violence. He was in reserve duty when Madhat Youssef died at Joseph's Tomb. The incident left him deeply shaken. The agreement had to be understood: you risk lives to save lives. The entire army was based on that. It was an absolute, not subject to calculation or optimization. If there are wounded, you go in. Without that absolute, everything falls apart. Nobody would be willing to risk their lives anymore. Time after time, he forced himself to go back.

CHAPTER 31 Day of Rumours

Shneor was able to call Orah at noon. "Orah, I'm OK. I just wanted you to know that. I'll talk to you later." Orah knew that he was in Jenin, but thought that the reservists would be behind the regular soldiers, not out in front.

She heard a tremor in his voice that she had never heard before. His was always the soothing voice of calm. "He's my epidural," she always said when he held her hand during childbirth.

The country was awash in rumors. Something terrible had happened. No one knew the exact details. 11:00 pm. Orah still hadn't heard back from Shneor. She went to her neighbor's house.

"My brother-in-law is in Jenin," said her neighbor. "He has a cell phone, he can talk. Let's call him."

"Do you know someone named Shneor?" she asked her brother-in-law. "Tell him that his wife is looking for him."

"There are too many units here. Do you know what company he's in? What battalion?"

Ora didn't know those things. She ran back to the house to look at Shneor's telephone list on the refrigerator. Then she saw the names. The names on the list were the same names that she had been hearing on the radio. It was then that she knew that the terrible thing had happened to Shneor's unit.

Finally, Shneor called.

"Shneor, can you tell me what happened now?"

"Not now."

"It was your unit, wasn't it? It was all your friends."

"I don't know exactly how I'm still here."

*   *   *

The *Pal-Sar* set out that morning to link up with the rest of the battalion at Intersection 18. Hemi, Oren, and Hanoch sat with the Battalion Commander and reviewed their progress thus far. They set up a map room to plan their route for the coming days. At 5:45 they were shaken by a series of massive explosions followed by a barrage of machine gun fire. Oren and the Battalion Commander sped off in an APC to evacuate the dead and wounded.

The APCs came back laden with 13 corpses. The room next to the map room was designated as a temporary morgue until the bodies could be evacuated. Hanoch tried to concentrate on their coordinates, but he couldn't stop thinking about all the death in the room next to him. He had to speak with Efrat. As always, they kept it short.

"Some soldiers have been killed. Pretty soon, you'll know more than me. I'm OK."

"Do me a favor, call your mother," said Efrat. "She's on pins and needles."

He called his mother. "One second," she said. He waited a bit on call waiting. It had never been easy for her to express emotion. She came back on. "I had thought this was over years ago," she said. "I thought I wouldn't have to worry about my sons anymore."

On the news program that night, Hanoch's father-in-law seemed disheveled and shaken. He wasn't his usual polished self. Friends feared that it was because something had happened to Hanoch. Efrat's phone rang endlessly.

"Have you heard anything? Nobody knows anything. I read on one news site that the Chief of Staff was killed." She began to understand that no one on the outside had the foggiest idea of what had happened. They were all feeding off of the Internet rumor mill.

Hanoch received 24 text messages that day on his cell phone. What's happening? How are you? Where are you? *Ten Siman*. Give a sign.

*   *   *

Platoon 2 in Doron's company went out just before dawn. Li-Ad, the platoon commander, blew in the door of a house. He saw a booby trap and detonated it. Everyone's eyes burned, and the smell of tear gas was everywhere. The soldiers began to fear that some of the booby traps had been mixed with poisonous chemicals. Li-Ad radioed in that he was about to sweep the house.

All of a sudden, they heard a massive burst of machine gun fire that seemed to go on forever.

"Why is Li-Ad shooting so much?" Maor asked. "Isn't he overdoing it a little?"

But it wasn't Li-Ad who was firing. A message came over the radio to halt all fire. A platoon from Battalion 7020 had been ambushed. Three soldiers were missing. A while later, the Regiment Commander came on the radio. "Despite a tough blow on our front, the mission is not yet complete. We are going to press on according to our original plan."

Doron and his soldiers still didn't know exactly what was happening, but it sounded grave. Eyyal used his cell phone to call one of his relatives that worked in IDF headquarters.

"Any idea what's going here?" he asked.

Only later would they find out that the shooting they heard was the ambush of the company from Battalion 7020 in which 13 were killed. They stayed put that day.

At ten in the morning, Doron called Liron. "I don't know what you know so far, but I'm OK. If you hear something later on, just know that I'm OK."

Doron's brother came to the Saalem intersection looking for him. He heard that there were 13 missing soldiers, and called home to see if Doron had called in.

"Have you heard from Doron?"

"No, why?" Doron's father answered. No one had told him anything yet.

Doron's mother worked as an assistant principal in a Bat Yam elementary school. After reading on the Internet that 13 reservists had been killed in Jenin, the principal of the school became panicked. Unsure of what to do, she decided to have a social worker collect all of the children whose fathers were in Reserve Duty into one classroom in order to calm them down. Doron's mother came into the office while the principal was giving instructions to the social worker.

"That makes no sense," said Doron's mother. "It will only create more hysteria. Wait for more specific news. What have you heard, anyway?"

"Thirteen soldiers have been killed in Jenin," said the principal.

Doron's mother fainted.

Liron called Doron's father. "Doron's OK," she said.

"What do you mean he's OK? What is everyone talking about?"

Ohad, stationed at the command post, later told the other soldiers what it had been like in the rear lines. "We were sure it was you guys," he said. "We heard it was reservists, and we knew you guys were out ahead of everyone else." At the Saalem intersection, where the press was assembled, panic ensued. Reporters demanded a press conference but the IDF wasn't ready yet. No information could be released until all of the families had been notified.

Amit, another soldier in Doron's company stationed at the command post, overheard one of the reporters threatening the IDF spokesperson. "You don't want to tell us what happened? No problem. We'll help you decide that it's time to hold a press conference." The reporter called his office. "Put a story out on the Internet that the Assistant Chief of Staff was killed. We'll have a press conference real soon."

*　*　*

Friends had been calling Ravit all day long, fueling her hysteria. "Did you hear? Twenty reservists were dead and two kidnapped." The phone rang again. "Can you believe it? The Chief of Staff was killed!" Ravit tried to call Nahum but couldn't get through. By the time the fifth friend called her, she exploded.

"Enough already!! Do you want to give me a heart attack?? You're all going to kill me with your good intentions. I can't find anything of what you're telling me on the news."

The most disturbing rumor was that soldiers had been kidnapped. Ravit thought of the two soldiers who had been lynched in Ramallah. With each passing hour her panic grew. This was the blackest day she could remember.

* * *

In the early morning when the 13 were killed, Rafi was in Ginat. At first light, he raced to the refugee camp to make sure the monitor units were in place. From there, he called the Regimental Command Post to arrange equipment for the evacuation of the wounded. A Naval Commando unit went in to storm the house where the three missing bodies had been dragged to. It was then that the decision was taken to bring in the D-9s to raze the remaining stronghold.

CHAPTER 32 Show and Tell

Stu's conversations with Judy were always very short. Thankfully, on the day of the 13, he was home on 24-hour leave. It was odd and jarring. He had just spent 24 hours in a tank, rocked by explosions. Now, a scant two hours after clambering out of his tank's back door, he was sitting comfortably in his living room. Maya and Yaeli, his nine- and seven-year old daughters, were beside themselves with pride. Their English words and Hebrew syntax often had a poetic ring. "Daddy is fighting the bad people. He's going to 'save on' us." Their teachers talked to them about war. After the operation, Stu and Judy had a parent-teacher meeting with Maya's teacher. Maya, their eldest, had grown up a lot during that month. She was much more responsible now.

Yaeli begged Stu to drop her off at school in his uniform. "Will you wear your *madim*? Maya and Yaeli always spoke to their parents in English. They peppered their speech with Hebrew when a word arose that wasn't a part of their parents' American experience. Will you bring your *neshek*?" Your weapon. It broke Stu's heart to turn her down, but he couldn't bring himself to oblige her. He didn't feel that weapons and uniforms were things to be proud of. Not that he wasn't proud to serve in the first Israeli army in 2000 years. But this isn't something we're doing out of choice, he thought. He didn't want to draw attention to himself. He didn't want little children milling around him. He wanted no part of military worship.

Judy put a different spin on it. Pride wasn't such a bad thing if it served as a buffer against fear. For the children, it gave them a positive way to deal with a difficult situation. There was solace to be found in the pride they took in their *Abba*. There were only one or two other children in the school whose daddies were in *Milu'im*. "*Abba* is away, but we're proud of what he's doing."

But still, Yaeli desperately wanted him to bring his *neshek*. "Yaeli, a gun isn't a toy," said Stu. "Not even Ima can touch it." Guns had become a necessary part of the landscape. But the children had to learn that they're not playthings.

"How many bad people did you kill, Abba?" asked Maya. He changed the subject.

*   *   *

The *Pal-Han* changed their methods in the wake of the ambush. They decided to send only one soldier into a house at a time, instead of three or four storming in. It was slower, but safer.

The fear of death, which had left him throughout much of the operation, returned to Doron. Tuesday they took only two more houses.

That night, supplies arrived. It had been getting bleak, as all of the food and ammunition had to be carried in on foot. One can of tuna had to suffice for four men. In carrying in the supplies, the priorities were clear: first water, then ammo, then food.

A newspaper made its way to their current hideout. The men couldn't believe their eyes. A member of Knesset called the events in Jenin a "massacre". A famous Israeli singer was quoted comparing the soldiers to the Nazis. Tel Aviv was only an hour away, but did they have the slightest idea of what was happening here? Doron wondered. During the entire ordeal, Doron and his fellow soldiers had thought that they were risking their lives in order to underscore their country's humanity. They had paid an exorbitant price for waging such a surgical campaign. Now they were being accused of inhumanity. Nothing seemed to make sense.

CHAPTER 33 The Furnace

The Tubaas operation was back on track. The weather had gone from one extreme to another. Now the sun was beating down on them full force. They were to head towards the village at 5:00 a.m.

Nahum knew Tubaas well from his days in the Anti-Terror unit. Nine years ago, they had entered Tubaas in search of Yihyeh Ayyash, the notorious Hamas bombmaker known as "The Engineer." That night, luck had been on his side.

Now, they surrounded the village, 4 APCs and 4 tanks. There were only five men in each APC. The passages between the houses were just wide enough for a tank to pass through, and those cars unfortunate enough to be parked in the alleyways did not fare well. They didn't want to do any damage, but the need for tank cover soon became self-evident. A booby trap blew the tread off of one of the APCs, taking it out of commission. They were now down to three vehicles.

Nahum's APC took up a position next to the village mosque. Automatic weapons fire rained down on them from all directions. Exploding *mit'anim* rocked Nahum's APC, all the while raising the temperature within. He opened the hatch to get his bearings. Bullets immediately ricocheted off the open hatch and into the APC. He slammed it shut. They were being fired upon from such close quarters that the tank couldn't angle its cannon up high enough to silence the fire. They were sitting ducks.

Eran, the Lieutenant Company Commander, decided that enough was enough. He and another soldier, Davidson, jumped out of the APC and made a run towards the nearest building. Nahum heard a burst of gunfire. Eran and Davidson hit the ground. Eran was hit. He was bleeding profusely from his leg. A bullet had fractured his femur. It wasn't clear whether or not Davidson was hit. Two more soldiers jumped out dragged them back to the APC.

"I'm OK, I'm OK," Davidson said. "Take care of Eran." Davidson hadn't even noticed that he was hit. He had taken two bullets, one through the shoulder and one through the side.

Nahum heard the report over the radio. "We have two *flowers*." Two injuries. "One is the *second*." The *second* was Eran, the Lieutenant Company Commander. He had to get to him, thought Nahum. He would be losing blood and would need a tourniquet.

Eran was like a brother to Nahum. More. He was one quadrant of Nahum's four-part self: Nahum-Shay-Eran-Daniel.

"Cover me!" Nahum called to Adi, one of the other soldiers in the APC. He opened the hatch and crawled out. A firebomb landed on the tank next to them and it caught fire. Nahum scrambled back into the APC for a fire extinguisher and began spraying the tank as Adi returned fire towards the balconies above. Nahum found it impossible to make his way back out of the APC again. Each time he tried to crawl beyond the APC hatch, he was driven back by increasingly accurate fire. The "pings" were right by his ears. He dropped back into the APC and pulled the hatch shut.

"My rifle! My rifle!" It was Adi. His rifle was caught in the hatch. He pulled it out and they slammed the hatch shut not a moment too soon.

A makeshift bomb shook the vehicle. The heat within the APC was becoming unbearable. Sweat poured off of them in rivulets. There was no room to maneuver. It was impossible to undress. The best Nahum could do was to cut off some of his underclothes with his combat knife. It didn't help much. They guzzled water endlessly to cool down, but the temperature kept rising. "I think we're going to fry to death in here," said Adi.

It was a furnace. The bullets had become the lesser of two evils. They flapped the hatch open and shut to drive some air into the compartment. If a bullet found them, so be it.

The medevac APC collected Eran and Davidson. They were evacuated by helicopter to Rambam Hospital in Haifa. The Battalion Commander came over the radio.

"A weapon was left behind. We need to retrieve it."

They drove closer to the spot where Eran and Davidson had fallen. Nahum opened the hatch to retrieve Eran's rifle. A hail of bullets ricocheted off the hatch. He could feel the impact of each bullet on the vehicle. The APC shook violently as another makeshift bomb landed.

"You can't go out now. No way." Adi pulled him back in.

Ram, the APC commander, pulled off his communications helmet. "Fine. I'll go out then." He headed for the hatch. Nahum pulled him down onto the metal bench next to him.

"Ram, you're not going out either. This is ridiculous. There's no way you'll ever make it to the weapon. And I'm not coming after you. What sense does this make? We gave them twenty thousand rifles at Oslo, and now you're going to get yourself killed retrieving *one*?"

A partial lie. Nahum knew he would have gone out after him

Ram still wasn't convinced. "If you're afraid, then I'll go out. You have a young child. I don't." Others joined in with Nahum. "Ram, you're not going out." He remained undeterred until Nahum proposed an alternative.

"How about if we just run over it? That'll take it out of commission." They agreed on flattening the weapon. But in the end, there were cement blocks obstructing the vehicle's path to the rifle. They couldn't get to it.

A report came over the radio. The SWAT team had completed its mission. A cell of six Hamas gunmen had been liquidated, but at a terrible price. A stray bullet had killed a female doctor in the village. The SWAT team piled into the APCs and they headed back to base. They received word that Eran was in stable condition, but still the mood was somber.

Their bodies were numb with pain. They had been squatting on the metal APC benches for hours and their haunches were black and blue. The fear was gone. The pain had burned it away.

CHAPTER 34 The Day After

Wednesday was the day of funerals. There were so many funerals that only a handful of soldiers could attend each one. Shneor and Orah met in Petah Tikvah at Dror Bar's funeral. Shneor had asked her to bring newspapers. Now, he went over each face with her. He needed to see the face of Menashe Chabah. He had only known him for three minutes in the dark before Menashe was killed. He hadn't seen his face in full light. Shneor had only said one sentence to him, "Here's where they're shooting from." And Menashe, without another word, took up a position directly in front of the windows and began firing the heavy machine gun.

Orah melted in tears the entire day. Shneor did not cry at Dror's funeral.

"He was an amazing man," she said after the eulogy. "That ceremony he conducted the night before he died," she said. "Even in battle, he kept his men connected to their past."

"It was his last will and testament," said Shneor.

Shneor tried to picture Dror's unique smile. It's how our forefather Jacob must have looked, Shneor thought. He saw the two as connected. "On in days", Jacob was described at the time of his death. This, Shneor had been taught, was how Jewish tradition described the death of one who had truly lived. One who had truly lived all of his days, one who could go in pride before the Almighty. That was Dror. On in days.

After the funerals, the soldiers met back at Giv'at Oz, the kibbutz that served as the logistic and administrative center for the Jenin theatre of operations. The Battalion Commander addressed them. "We're going to continue moving ahead," he said. "Slowly."

Some of the soldiers asked whether it might not be a good idea for the unit to get a few days of rest. Inwardly, Shneor disagreed. He hoped that the unit would stay together for these next few days. He wanted to be with his brothers. He wanted to hug them. Not to be separated from them. His healing would only be found at the site of the wound. He needed to be with those who were there, those who stood with him in that yard.

*   *   *

Nahum received a 48-hour pass. Before going home, he first went to Haifa to visit Eran at Rambam hospital. Eran's father was a physician there. Eran was awake, in traction, and an attractive young woman was massaging his feet.

"Wow. Being injured has its privileges." Nahum's attempt at humor barely disguised his discomfort. He hadn't been able to rescue Eran. He hadn't been able to get to him.

"Nahum, meet my sister Galit," said Eran.

"I tried to get to you, Eran, but I couldn't," he blurted out. Tears streamed down his cheeks.

"Come here, Nahum." Eran hugged him and kissed him on the cheek. "I know, I know you tried, " he said. " There was nothing to be done. It was just a bad scene."

Nahum continued on to his parents house where Ravit and Ron were staying. They went for a walk on Shenkin St., Tel Aviv's little bohemian district. Nahum carried Ron, now two months old, close to his chest. Ravit held tightly to his arm. The cafes were still empty, but he felt a sense of security and pride in the knowledge that the streets of Tel Aviv were safe for the moment. Our forces are in *their* cities now, he thought. Our cities are safe.

He looked at Ron's little face. Nahum had been gone for two weeks and now they barely knew each other. Two weeks are a long time in the life of a two-month old, thought Nahum. For him, they had been an eternity.

*   *   *

Golani Battalion 51 took another hit. Gedaliah Malick, the Battalion Commander's radio operator, was killed by a sniper two houses in front of Doron and his men. They heard the battalion commander calmly directing the evacuation and calling in tank fire on the radio. "That guy must have nerves of steel," thought Doron.

Ofek Buchris was a highly unconventional Battalion Commander. His was a moving command post, always as far forward as the most advanced of his troops. He reached every house that his troops entered. Even many of his platoon commanders weren't as far forward as Ofek was.

For the *Pal-Han*, this was the final stretch. They had one more open space to cross, a wide boulevard, before reaching their target: a mosque near the center of the camp. The boulevard seemed dangerously wide. They tossed smoke grenades and fired at possible sniper positions as they sprinted across. One by one they slipped into the mosque amid heavy fire. It was 10:00 am when they reassembled inside. They were joined by Golani Battalion 51. About two hundred soldiers in all. Ehud took out his *tfillin*, and soldiers took turns praying. Nissan, the engineer, hadn't prayed with *tfillin* since his Bar Mitzvah. He asked Doron to remind him how.

The mosque was full of Hizbullah audio cassettes for the minaret loudspeaker, decorated with impaled and bleeding Stars of David. Food arrived. Doron felt uneasy as the mosque became strewn with refuse. He collected food cans and candy wrappers. Incoming fire opened up on them again. Yevgeni the sniper climbed up a bookshelf to survey the scene from a high window. Books tumbled to the floor. Doron picked them up. This was a place of worship, bleeding Stars of David or not. It had the musty book smell of a synagogue. He imagined how he would feel if foreign soldiers were occupying his small synagogue in Bat Yam.

In the evening they billeted themselves in a house adjacent to the clump of buildings that formed the final stronghold. The D-9s were lumbering into position for the denouement. A man stood in front of his house, a gaping hole where a tank shell had found its mark. "Who will fix this?" he shook his fist at Doron. "Who will fix this?"

They were two APC squads in the house, roughly 25 men. On the kitchen floor lay a sack of zuchinis, still edible. An argument ensued over whether or not they were allowed to cook them. Some insisted that it wasn't allowed under any circumstances. Others said it was permissible as long as money was left. The religious soldiers disqualified themselves, as the pots and pans weren't kosher. In the end, it was decided to cook the zuchinis and leave money. They would rot in a few days anyway. They left 20 shekels. Some were angry at those who ate. Some were angry at those who refused to partake. "This is ridiculous," pronounced Amzaleg. "Twenty shekels for a bag of zuchinis? You guys probably just set a record in this town."

* * *

Nahum and his unit, their APCs in a line, headed for the center of the Jenin refugee camp. It was now a ghost town, but bursts of fire still rang out. There was sporadic sniper fire from the rooftops, and an occasional bullet made a "ping" as it hit their APC. In the center of the camp, the "tough core" of 36 gunmen still fired at them from within a small group of buildings. It was a small stronghold, only 70 meters by 70 meters. They took up positions in houses around the besieged area. Using bullhorns, they called for the gunmen to come out.

In the house that Nahum and his team occupied, there were posters of suicide bombers on all of the walls. Each poster featured the name of the bomber, the attack perpetrated, and the date. Nahum noticed an open Koran on one of the tables, with a newspaper clipping on the open page. He had learned to read Arabic in high school. It was an authorization from a *mufti* for women to carry out attacks.

Night fell. They had to stay alert. Enemy gunmen made an occasional dash from inside the besieged buildings, and they had to keep them from reaching the surrounding houses.

So many hungry children. Nahum wanted to hug them, to tell them that everything would soon be better. But both sides had been warned against contact with each other. Nahum saw 14-year-olds with Kalashnikovs but couldn't bring himself to shoot at them. How can you shoot a 14-year-old? thought Nahum. He has his whole life ahead of him.

The soldiers brought in more food than they knew they would need, in anticipation of providing aid to the locals. They tried to give food to the children, but the they refused it. They had been told it was poisoned. The men left cartons of food by their houses. There hadn't been any special order to that effect, but they decided that it was the right thing to do. They were there to fight terror, not children.

The D-9 bulldozers were gargantuan. Each shovel the size of a living room, thought Nahum. Three of them began snorting and eating away at the clump of buildings where the gunmen were still holed up. At first, the gunmen threw makeshift bombs from the windows in an effort to disable the D-9s. The bulldozers barely noticed the explosions. Nahum and the men called again on the bullhorns. "You have no chance. Come out with your hands up."

After the first house was leveled the gunmen filed out. In case any were wired, the soldiers ordered them to strip to their underwear before approaching. They lay their weapons down in a pile. Their bodies were covered with Hamas and Islamic Jihad tattoos. Nahum and his men bound their hands and blindfolded them. One had taken a bullet through the upper arm, and Nahum dressed his wound, applying a bandage to stop the bleeding. Nahum felt nothing.

*   *   *

Rafi and his soldiers were amazed to see sixty women and children approaching their roadblock from the direction of the refugee camp. The battle was already into its second week. Why had they stayed? The soldiers directed the ragtag group in the direction of the city. They reached another roadblock in the city, where they were guided towards one of the wealthier neighborhoods. The group wandered the city for ten hours, but none of the wealthier inhabitants of Jenin would take them in. At dusk, they returned to the camp. An IDF liaison officer asked that they be allowed to go to the Red Crescent School for Girls near the hospital. Rafi gave the OK. He felt for these unwanted wanderers. The inhabitants of the Jenin refugee camp were at the bottom of the local social ladder. Now he understood why they had stayed through it all. They had nowhere else to go.

Rafi positioned his unit outside the stronghold where the last group of gunmen surrendered. As they filed out, he contemplated the intricacy of their tattoos. He was actually surprised that they had surrendered so soon. A good deal of food and ammunition still remained within, but the sight of the D-9s had broken their spirit. These were the most extreme elements of three terror organizations. Rafi knew that they had been responsible for the deaths of many. They deserve only death, he thought to himself. But they're mine now. My responsibility is to deliver them safe and sound to the General Security Services.

Rafi radioed for a bulletproof "safari" truck to transport them back to the command post. He wanted the driver to come all the way into the center of the camp to guarantee the safety of the prisoners. The driver objected. He preferred that the prisoners come out on foot. He didn't like the alleyways. Rafi stood firm. He radioed for an APC to accompany the "safari". Some of the soldiers grumbled.

"That doesn't make sense. Why should we endanger the driver for the sake of the prisoners?"

"They're our prisoners now," said Rafi. "We're responsible for their safety. End of story."

Rafi thought of the Bible's skeptical take on leniency in such situations. "He who pities the cruel will ultimately be cruel to the merciful." King Saul spared Agag, king of the Amalekites, and ultimately Saul himself acted with great cruelty towards David and Jonathan. Perhaps I'm sinning here. Perhaps this is a mistake. Am I doing this out of lack of clarity? Am I erring as Saul erred? Does this make me a better person or a weaker person? What does one do when the army's ethical code is more lenient than the harsher dictates of the Bible?

* * *

From his tank, Stu saw a group of women and children walking out from the center of the refugee camp towards the city of Jenin. They were close to the final stronghold, the 70 meter by 70 meter bastion of rubble. They picked their way through the rubble. Stu couldn't believe his eyes. Where had they come from?

He found it difficult to watch the D-9s eating into the final stronghold where the last group of gunmen were holed up. No doubt, this was war; but still, the sight of a bulldozer tearing into a house affected him deeply. The walls were shaved off one by one. Here and there, a single chair fell over the edge of a floor where once there was a wall. Within was the furniture, undisturbed. Like the opening of a doll house, thought Stu.

* * *

At 7:00 pm, Mulu's technical crew was called in to replace an APC engine. They drove on a crane towards the stranded APC. He was still tense, but the presence of the other technicians calmed him. Etan, another Ethiopian friend of his, operated the crane.

Etan moved the crane in place over the APC. There were occasional shots, and flares lit the sky. Some of the older mechanics took cover inside the disabled vehicle. Etan stayed outside. "Don't worry guys. It's our side. They're just laying down some preventive fire." At 2:00 am, a young Ordinance Corps Lieutenant came running up to them. "Are you guys crazy?" he huffed breathlessly.

Etan calmed him down. "Don't worry, it's our side. Preventive fire." He had been making these crane runs for days and could identify the precise single shot fire of the Israeli forces from the crackle of the Kalashnikovs. After that, Mulu became accustomed to the shooting. If Etan wasn't worried, he wasn't worried.

Etan towed the APC to Katya junction, where the crew set to work replacing the engine. They worked around the clock until noon the next day. But the crankshaft hadn't been calibrated properly. When the driver started the APC, it lurched backwards and crashed into the crane. Luckily, no one had been standing in its way.

Under normal circumstances, this would have been cause for a serious investigation. But this was war. They extracted the engine again. Six hours later, they finally had it right. As they worked on the engine, the sole topic of conversation was the 13 who had been killed. It didn't make sense, everyone agreed. If the world was going to accuse us of war crimes anyway, why were we being so surgical about this operation?

CHAPTER 35 The Soccer Field

Thursday, April 11. Forces converged on the center of the refugee camp, a s70-meter by 70-meter square, from all directions "If an officer had run a training exercise like this, he would have been court-martialed," joked Didi Yedidiah, the Regiment Commander. Luckily, there were only one or two injuries due to friendly fire, none of them serious.

Yevgeni, one of the *Pal-Han's* snipers, spied a rifle barrel protruding from a window. He hadn't received any notification of friendly forces in that house.

"That looks like an M-16 barrel to me," he said.

"But that house isn't supposed to have friendly forces in it," said Mizrahi, the other sniper.

"I'm counting down," said Yevgeni. "3-2-….."

"Wait!" yelled Mizrahi. "I see a helmet. Don't shoot." It was a squad of Nahal soldiers. They had just taken the house, and the update hadn't come through from Regimental Command yet.

*   *   *

Rafi tried to call Ma'ayan every day or two while in Jenin. In the tumult of the past few days, he'd been unable to call. Ma'ayan left a message on his voicemail. "Daddy, I love you and hope you're eating well, wearing your sweater, killing terrorists, taking care of yourself, and taking care of your soldiers." In his spare moments, he played the message over and over again to himself.

*   *   *

Nahum and his unit moved out of Jenin to begin ambushes and set up surprise roadblocks in the surrounding foothills. They received an intelligence alert that a car bomb was headed for nearby Haderah.

By now they were half-crazed with fatigue. The orders were not to let any vehicles pass through the roadblock. Day after day, the same truck slowly approached the roadblock, made a U-turn, and drove away. Shay's antennae were up. "That damn truck is starting to irritate me," he said.

A small motorcade of three cars arrived at the roadblock. Two men sat in the front car. As the soldiers approached, they jumped out of the car and ran off in opposite directions. The driver was the faster of the two, and escaped into the nearby hills. The passenger was less fortunate. They called for him to stop but he kept on running. One of the soldiers opened fire. A bullet passed cleanly through the top of his head, opening up two holes in his skull. He lay bleeding, stunned but not unconscious, gripped by the intense euphoria that occurs when oxygen rushes into the brain cavity. His eyes half shut, he smiled blissfully as Nahum stood over him. Danny, the older medic, bandaged his wound. A helicopter was on the way to evacuate him to Rambam Hospital.

"I love you, *ahuuyah!*" My brother. "I promise you! I promise you! I'll never do another thing against Israel." He remained conscious for another forty minutes before fainting. At Rambam, he underwent cranial surgery. He returned to full consciousness three days later.

The Engineering Corps arrived to examine the abandoned car. It was crammed with TATP explosive. The back seat housed a huge propane tank. They moved Nahum and his men over 200 meters from the car before detonating it. The blast was deafening. Pieces of the vehicle landed over a wide radius. Had it reached an Israeli city, it could have brought death to an untold multitude.

Gil, one of the soldiers in Nahum's company, was a professional photographer. He wanted to catch the explosion on film from what he thought was a safe distance. He wore earplugs. The explosion was so powerful that it left him with total hearing loss for two days.

Before the war, Nahum had believed in a fluid, osmotic form of coexistence; the coexistence of two peoples passing freely among each other. He had hoped that perhaps Ron, his son, wouldn't have to perform the same sort of military service that he did. Now he saw everything differently. In the houses, he witnessed the bizarre rituals that had been developed around murder and bloodshed. The posters, the shrines, the candies for the mothers of the bombers. Now, he only believed in a coexistence that involved total separation. He could no longer imagine the two peoples living among each other.

*   *   *

Avihu took a firm stand against the taking "souvenirs" from the battle. Not even loops of *masbaxah* beads, the rosary bracelets that the older men would count behind their backs. Not even a soft drink or pitah bread from one of the refrigerators. And no graffiti on the walls. He commanded the soldiers to leave rations behind when leaving an inhabited house. He handed out ashtrays so that no one would leave ashes on the floor. He aimed to teach his men what he had stressed to Zohar, his sister. "Strive to leave every place better than you found it."

It reached his ears that despite his commands, souvenirs had been taken. He assembled the soldiers in a circle. "Anyone who has taken souvenirs, put them in the middle of the circle." A few soldiers stepped forward and tossed some objects in the center of the circle. Some of the soldiers hadn't been able to resist leaving their own inscriptions among posters of suicide bombers. "Likewise for those of you who wrote on the walls," said Avihu.

He set the punishment for those who had taken things or had written on the walls: they would not be joining the company on the next mission. For Avihu, there was no worse punishment than being left out of the action.

"We don't need any more souvenirs from Jenin. We already have plenty. Four of them." The company had lost four men in the fighting thus far. He didn't want to overwhelm them with guilt, but he wanted the battle ethic upheld. "These things aren't yours. You'll be taking home a lot from Jenin, but it won't be these little things."

*   *   *

The stronghold in the center of the camp had surrendered, but Hanoch's unit couldn't disperse yet. The non-religious among them, those who could travel on the Sabbath, took a bus to the Giv'at Olga amusement park where they met their families for the first time in two weeks. On the bus, Hanoch felt something that he hadn't felt in thirteen years, since his regular service – the euphoric mixture of gratitude and anticipation that would hit him just before a Shabbat leave.

They arrived at Giv'at Olga one night before their families. They all had beards, and hadn't showered or removed their boots for two weeks. Each time Hanoch scrubbed his hair a new stream of black sludge flowed out of it. He was glad that they had the night to prepare for their families.

Efrat related to Hanoch how the children had dealt with his absence. When asked where *Abba* was, his four-year old son, Assaf, would matter-of-factly reply, "He disappeared."

His daughter Ela, seven, already had a name for the disappearance: "*Abba* is in *Milu'im*." She instinctively understood that the circumstances required different behavior of her. She didn't indulge herself in her usual morning dawdling and finicky wardrobe session. She arose, dressed quickly, and ate her breakfast in silence. But when relatives questioned Efrat about Hanoch's whereabouts, Ela became angry. "Enough talking about Hanoch," she admonished them tearfully. "Just stop talking about him."

Hanoch was afraid that Assaf would be angry with him for disappearing for so long, but his son barely let go of him for a minute. Many of the families hadn't seen each other for years. "It's a shame that this is what it took to bring us together again," someone said.

*   *   *

Ofer, one of the men in Doron's company, arranged for the entire company to get a free night at the Meridien Hotel near Haifa. A local moshav donated the food. They got there a few minutes before Shabbat. Liron and the the children arrived. They hugged and kissed a thousand times.

For nine days after Doron left for Jenin, Adi, his daughter, barely spoke of him. At night, she would ask Liron if he had called, but otherwise wouldn't mention his name. Finally, on the morning of the tenth day, she awoke early and asked Liron, "Is Daddy still alive? I want you to tell me the truth."

Doron hadn't seen his family for twelve days. For those interminable twelve days, he hadn't been able to bring himself to believe that he would ever see them again. It had seemed like too wonderful a thing to hope for. Saturday night, his parents arrived, laden with leftovers from the *Mimounah* celebration.

This was his first exposure to television since the operation began. Watching the news was painful. Despite all of their precautions, the world was still accusing them of monstrous crimes. It was their first sortie from the bubble of Jenin.

* * *

Mulu and the other technicians took turns taking one-day leaves. It was "one on one" – if someone was late getting back, someone else wouldn't be able to leave. Everyone got back early.

Mulu arrived home for his one-day leave on Friday afternoon. He had lost track of time. He sat bleary eyed at his parents' house as they sang songs welcoming the Sabbath and his mother served the Sabbath meal. He hadn't yet told anyone that he was in Jenin.

On Saturday night, as he prepared to return, Mulu's father placed his hands on his shoulders and blessed him in Ge'ez, the ancient Ethiopic language of their prayers. *"Cher yimallesih, Egziabher yetabbekih."* May G-d bless you and return you whole.

This was much harder for them than it was for me, thought Mulu. He had buddies like Etan at his side. All they had was the television and the rumor mill to feed their anxiety. Earlier that week, Mulu's mother caught a brief glimpse of a bandaged Ethiopian soldier in a hospital ward on one of the news programs. She couldn't tell if it was Mulu or not. Everyone began calling her. Did she know who it was? Had she heard anything?

CHAPTER 36 Tending the Flock

Sunday, April 14. Doron and his men returned to Saalem junction. The intersection was full of well-wishing Israelis. They handed out falafel, *pitot*, and drinks. After the APCs were readied, Doron allowed himself to partake. The well-wishers had come spontaneously, from all walks of life. *Chabadniks* with books of Psalms. *Kibbutzniks* laden with food. Grandmothers with home-baked cakes. Young "hippies" with pierced ears and eyebrows, shaved heads and *sharwal* pants who handed out a pizza to each APC in the procession. The APCs rapidly filled with candy and food.

While Doron and his squad spent the weekend with their families at the Hotel Meridien, the mechanics had been working feverishly on their APC. When he returned on Sunday, they were just finishing up.

"Don't bother with this one," Doron said as they closed the metal plates. "This vehicle just wasn't meant to enter Jenin." Sure enough, it stalled again.

They took the APC that the unit had been using as a mobile warehouse. It had lighter armor and was vulnerable to RPGs, but was in good running condition.. They lined the sides with sandbags, and piled in.

Their mission would be to supervise the general curfew. They positioned themselves between the city of Jenin and the refugee camp. Doron's platoon took the third floor of the building that housed the Regimental Command Post, next door to the Regional Hospital. They would be in charge of guarding the command post and manning the roadblock next to the hospital. They searched each ambulance for smuggled weapons.

Doron found the searches disgusting. Everything had to be checked. Medical licenses, Incident Reports, Identity Cards. Patients had to be moved. Often they were elderly and near death. On numerous occasions, Doron felt close to vomiting. But there was no choice. A few weeks before, an explosive belt had been found in an ambulance on the outskirts of Jerusalem. It was been hidden underneath a seven-year old child.

An old man approached the roadblock with a white flag.

"You can lower the flag," Doron tried to calm him.

"I'm afraid," said the old man.

"Don't be. It's all right."

"No, not of you. Of him," he pointed to a sniper position. "And of him, and him." He pointed out the other snipers positioned around the roadblock.

The old man went into an explanation of why he had left the relative safety of his house. No one could make out exactly what he was saying. It seemed to be something about food.

"Don't worry, we'll bring you food," said Doron. The soldiers brought him some of their rations, but the old man remained animated. Doron, in his fragmented Arabic, tried to make out what he was saying. One of the words, *haroof*, was familiar to him. At the Seder table, Saba Nissim used to ask for one more *haroof*, one more rib of lamb. The man was asking to take food to his flock of sheep.

A young woman ran out of the hospital workers' hostel which had become the temporary displaced persons shelter. She was in her mid-twenties and wore a head covering. She spoke to Doron in broken English.

"Don't do something bad to him!"

"Don't worry. We're trying to help him. Make sure you bring him back before the end of our shift so we'll recognize him. *Matchafeesh*," he said to her in Arabic. Don't be afraid. Doron and his soldiers had drilled that simple phrase in all of its inflections. Feminine singular, *matchafeesh*. Masculine singular, *matchaafsh*. Plural, *matchaafuush*. The young woman accompanied the old man in search of his flock. Doron radioed ahead to all lookouts to let them pass. An hour or so later, now smiling, the old man returned.

* * *

After their 48-hour leave, Stu and his tank squad were assigned to an area next to the UNRWA Girls' School to the west of the camp. From their lookout, they saw some women, in their twenties, walking across a nearby open lot. One of them was carrying a bundle in her arms.

"Is that a baby?" asked Stu.

The gunner looked into his scope. "Looks like it."

They were a platoon of three tanks, attached to a paratrooper unit. Whenever he saw something that aroused suspicion, Stu called Anatoly, the paratrooper APC commander. His code named was *One Zap*.

"*One Zap*, there's someone coming your way."

It was mid-day, and the heat was stifling. As the soldiers approached, one of the women fainted. The young paratroopers were confounded.

Stu called his platoon commander, who called the Regimental Command Post. The directive came down. Keep her under observation, call a local Red Crescent ambulance, they'll come and get her.

For Anatoly, the orders were far too passive. The woman needed help now. He carried the woman and her child to a nearby house, then called his platoon commander. The platoon commander returned with a medic.

Stu felt uneasy. His view of the house they had entered was totally obstructed by a grove of olive trees. His job was to cover them. He radioed the commander of his tank platoon. "I can't see them. We're supposed to be covering them."

"Guys, we can't see you!" Stu screamed into the radio. "We can't see you. You're blocked by the olive grove. Get out where we can cover you!"

Anatoly responded on the radio. They were too busy. They were administering an infusion to the young woman who, as it turns out, had given birth the night before.

Stu's platoon commander was exasperated. "Great, guys. I hope you won't need that IV bag later."

The paratroopers were young, still in their regular service. The risks they were taking drove Stu and his cautious reservists up a wall. It was a different mentality. They're good boys, thought Stu. They care. But had they acted wisely? He wasn't sure. The liaison unit in the Regimental Command Post had called the local Red Crescent to pick up the young woman. They never arrived.

Stu called the APC. He wanted them back in his view. "*One Zap*. This is *Lulav*. We'll take care of this. Don't do anything foolish. Get back in view."

*   *   *

Monday, April 15. Doron's squad headed down to the roadblock at 3 am. A fresh tray of hot buns and grilled cheese sandwiches awaited them, courtesy of the command post. A civilian approached the roadblock from the nearby shelter. "There are lots of hungry children in there. Do you have any food?" Li-Ad, about to go off duty, gave him the tray of snacks.

"Where's the food?" the soldiers asked Li-Ad when they arrived.

"I gave it to the children in the shelter," said Li-Ad. "They're hungry." There was some requisite teasing.

"Sure, you took one for yourself and gave the rest away," Amzaleg teased him. But no one disagreed with his decision. They all would have done the same.

At the roadblock, they received an alert on a seven-year-old who had been booby trapped.

"That's it," said Eyyal. "I quit. I'm not shooting a seven-year-old. If a seven year old comes near this roadblock, I'm running away."

Before daybreak, a mother arrived on foot carrying her small daughter. The daughter seemed to have a broken leg. They were a procession of four: a man, the mother, the young girl, and a nurse from the Red Crescent. The little girl, five years old or so, was crying. They came from the direction of the city.

Doron let the women pass, and checked the man's ID.

"She fell in her house," said the nurse. Eyyal reached into his vest and brought out the goody bag that he had received at Saalem junction. He gave it to the nurse, who looked at him suspiciously. "For the girl," he said. "How many more children are there in the hospital?"

"A lot," said the nurse. Eyyal went into the APC and returned with all of the goody bags from Saalem junction. He gave them to the nurse. "For the children," he said.
She thanked him profusely. *Shukran, shukran, shukran,* she said over and over again in Arabic. Thank you, thank you.

That weekend, at home on leave, Eyyal was watching the Weekend News Magazine on Israeli TV when a familiar face came on the screen.

"Hey, I know that woman. It's the nurse from the roadblock! I gave her all of our goody bags for the kids in the hospital," he said to his family.

The interviewer asked the nurse what she thought of the Israeli soldiers.

"I think there is no emotion in these soldiers," she said. "They deserve to die. "

CHAPTER 37 Day of Remembrance

Tuesday, April 16. *Yom HaZikaron*, Israel's Day of Remembrance. In Ginat, the command post, Rafi assigned Gal, a 42-year old teacher, to prepare the ceremony. In the center of Ginat, Gal built a monument with 23 candles for the 23 soldiers who fell in Jenin. It was 5:00 pm when the ceremony began. They were only 800 meters from Jenin. Still within range for a sniper, thought Rafi. He requested that the candles be extinguished. Gal objected.

"We're not out of this yet," said Rafi. "We can't make ourselves a target."

They compromised on leaving one candle.

Gadi Ezra's letter to his girlfriend Galit had been discovered in his bureau drawer soon after his death. It struck a chord in the Israeli public and received wide publicity. Rafi read the letter aloud.

My Beloved Galit,

If this letter reaches you, it means that something has befallen me.

This morning I received word that the operation planned

yesterday will take place, G-d willing. I told you that the operation had changed and that it was not what it was originally supposed to be – because I didn't want to worry you, my dearest. It was very hard for me not to tell you the truth, but I preferred to do so rather than to drive you crazy with worry. "One can tell a lie for Peace," it is taught, and that also includes the peace of mind of the person that you love more than anything else on earth.

My beloved, I feel that on the one hand there is nothing that I would like more than to be with you, to love you, and to raise a family with you. But on the other hand, there is nothing that I want more than to go on this operation and deal such a great blow to the terrorists that they will never dare perpetrate another bombing or terror attack. That they will take into account that each time they commit an atrocity we will hit them in the most painful place possible and will be willing to pay the price. I am willing to be that price.

Do not be angry at me , my loved one, but in moments like this one must be guided by the greater good of the people Israel, and one needs to deal a blow to evil as if one has no private life. As it is written, 'In the armies of King David a conditional letter of divorce would be granted before going off to war.'

My dearest, do not forget: everything is for the best, and if this is what the Master of the Universe has chosen, so be it. To us remains the task of accepting it all with love.

Everything the Lord does is for the best. Everything is for the best, even this. I promise you that I am in the most wonderful of places, without suffering, without regret. My only sorrow is for those who remain – for you, for my family, and for my friends.

Spread the good news, my dearest one. 'Never despair, be only joyous.' That is what I ask of you, even if it is difficult.

I know that I can ask this of you, because I know well the joy and bliss that radiate from you naturally, those qualities with which I fell in love. They are what drew me to you when I first laid eyes upon you.

My dearest, my beloved. I love you and will always love you. Promise me that you will continue onwards, and will not allow Sodom to triumph. You be the triumphant one. That is what must be.

I will love you to all eternities, and will always be at your side.

The ceremony unleashed in Rafi wave after wave of pent-up emotion. He couldn't stop crying. He had been in charge of medical logistics, the monitoring all of the casualties and wounded. But somehow, it wasn't until Gadi's letter that it all became real to him.

Gadi's letter was a letter of farewell. He had appointed himself to a mission in the world beyond, thought Rafi. "I am willing to be that price." For Rafi, it was a sudden awakening. Until then, his focus had been on the completion of the mission. Now he was standing face to face with the terrible human price that had been exacted.

All of a sudden, it was too real.

CHAPTER 38 Independence Day

Wednesday, April 17. Independence Day. APCs arrived filled with journalists.

"Why are they coming in APCs?" Doron's soldiers asked him.

"For their safety."

"But that's not what they think."

"Doesn't matter. It's too dangerous for them to wander around in the camp on their own."

Doron had been eyeing a partially destroyed house near the roadblock for days. There was something menacing about the smoldering building. When he and his squad came on shift, he asked if the house had been swept. No one knew. Doron had Itzik go to the shelter to see if the house belonged to anyone there. Perhaps someone had a key.

Itzik entered the shelter. "Does anyone here have a key to that house?" Itzik pointed to the blackened building. Silence. He lifted his walkie talkie to his lips and pretended to speak to someone on the other end.

"OK, I can't find the key so you'd better send in the bulldozers...."

"Wait! Wait!!" A man jumped up from his seat, a jingling key ring in hand. "Maybe one of these will work."

"OK. Why don't you try it." Itzik didn't feel like taking chances. If the house was booby-trapped, the owner would find a way to tell him. The room that they entered first was scorched, and a disgusting burnt smell pervaded the house. In the kitchen, Doron found a car battery with some wires. Whatever was being prepared there had not come to fruition. The two-story building was empty.

That afternoon, the troops began moving out. Doron's company remained alone. Kalashnikov fire echoed from a distance. Asi radioed in to Regiment Command to see if it should be investigated. It was decided not to bother. At scattered points throughout the city, gunmen were firing temporary farewells in the air.

"It's not worth it right now." Asi said. "It's obvious we'll be back. I want you guys to be familiar with this route." Doron thought back to all the times that Amir had said that.

*   *   *

Rafi's first leave was Independence Day. He drove by a campground near Yokneam, full of civilians celebrating the holiday. Barbecuing, playing soccer. His eyes filled with tears. Two weeks ago, people had been afraid to leave their homes. Now it was safe. I had a part in this, he thought. But he was still a long way from being able to celebrate. The price for all this still weighed heavily upon him.

He heard a tune. *Our Little Country*, by Rami Kleinshtein. One of Rafi's favorite pastimes was the setting of Jewish liturgy to popular tunes. A few years back Rafi had set the *kaddish,* the Jewish prayer for the dead, to this tune. The *kaddish* separates parts of a liturgy. It praises the Almighty without mentioning death. "Our Little Country" spoke Rafi's love of Israel. Setting the *kaddish* to its tune closed the circle between his love of G-d and his love of Israel.

In this war, he reflected, some felt that they were fighting for the land of Israel, some felt they were fighting for the people of Israel. But above all else were the ethical standards. The impact was on the entire people of Israel. Afterwards, many said to Rafi "I'm proud of what you did." But even more said, "I'm proud of how you did it."

Before going home, he made the rounds of the hospitals. Afula, Haifa, Tel HaShomer near Tel Aviv, and Hadassah in Jerusalem. His first visit was with Dori, from Battalion 7020. Dori, one of the younger *milu'imniks*, had just returned from a long trip to India. Running between houses, he had been shot in the stomach.

Rafi didn't know what to expect. Dori's whole family was there. They seemed ill at ease. Suspicious, perhaps. They didn't know what he was doing there. But Dori was smiling from ear to ear. He didn't stop thanking Rafi and everyone involved in saving him. The doctor's intervention had been critical. The helicopter had been heading for Rambam in Haifa and the doctor attending to him had rerouted it.

"He'll never make it," the doctor had said. "We have to land now, in Afula." The two additional minutes that it would have taken to reach Haifa proved critical.

When he was wounded, Dori had somehow managed to crawl 15 feet out of the alleyway where he was shot so that those rescuing him wouldn't be exposed. His entire midsection was bandaged. He was already able to stand.

There were others there from Battalion 7020. Hanoch, whom his friends called "Babyface", was shot in the shoulder and somehow managed to change three magazines with one hand and keep on firing. Reuven Magnajji, who had been rescued still clutching a live grenade. Our people still has its determination, thought Rafi. Our will hasn't left us.

Rafi arrived in Jerusalem late in the afternoon. His daughter Ma'yan was staying with his parents. "*Abba*, I want to kiss you, " she said as Rafi was putting her to bed. She kissed him on the cheek. "*Abba,* you're my hero."

*   *   *

Thursday, April 18. Leaves were assigned in the *Pal-Han*. Uncertainty still hovered in the air and only three soldiers from each squad would be leaving instead of five.

The three soldiers in Itzik's squad who had been granted leaves decided to forego them. "We can't leave if Udi is stuck here. If G-d forbid anything were to happen to him while we're on leave, we'd never forgive ourselves," they explained to Itzik.

Itzik already had his bag on the APC. He hauled it off and gave up his leave for Udi, the one remaining soldier, so that four of them could leave together. Udi, a young soldier, was not yet married.

Itzik called his wife. She didn't believe him. "You're kidding, right? I know you're kidding. You're right outside the door, aren't you…." She ran to open the door. "Oh…I understand. Bye." He could hear her choking back the tears as she quickly hung up the phone.

Itzik called some friends to see if they could add his wife and kids to their weekend plans. He didn't want them stuck at home alone. Doron called his brother to see if he could come to Yemin Orde for a barbecue with Liron and the kids.

"Amir would have done it this way," said Itzik after the soldiers had left.

"I can't lead soldiers who are demoralized. I'd rather give up a few days at home than not be able to lead."

CHAPTER 39 Home

The day after he arrived back at Yemin Orde, Doron accompanied Liron to her ultrasound appointment. Afterwards, they took a walk along the nearby beach. It was windy, and the sea was turbulent. The beach was nearly deserted. He held Liron close as the waves crashed against the shore. With each successive wave, tiny droplets of spray reached his face. Everything can be washed away, it all seemed to be saying. All the hatred, all the depravity. Everything can be washed away.

At the Saturday morning service, Doron was called up for an *Aliyah*, the reading of a Torah portion. He made the blessing of *HaGomel*, a prayer of thanks for having been delivered from the jaws of death. "Blessed art Thou O Lord Our G-d who has bestowed good things even upon those undeserving and has bestowed only good upon me."

* * *

Mulu made a new friend this *Milu'im*, a Yemenite APC mechanic named Eliezer. Eliezer often asked Mulu to tag along on jobs, and they developed respect for each other's work. They enjoyed the same thick brew of coffee, and always prepared coffee together on the propane burner. It turned out that Eliezer lived right down the street from Mulu, so they took their leaves together and Mulu hitched rides with him. They were both surprised by the kind of music the other liked. Mulu assumed Eliezer would like Oriental music, but it turned out that they were both devotees of Reggae. Mulu played some of his Ethiopian CDs. Eliezer liked one of them so much Mulu let him keep it.

Eliezer had Ethiopian coworkers and neighbors but hadn't yet had a close Ethiopian friend. When Mulu told him that he had a college degree, he couldn't hide his surprise. "Really? You don't say." Mulu let it pass. It was a customary reaction, he got it all the time. Eliezer was a good man. Some day, looking back, they would laugh together about his unwitting lack of tact. They resolved to keep in touch after *Milu'im*.

* * *

A few days after his *Milu'im* were over, Hanoch was on a flight to the States for a one-week business trip. He had been out of touch with his American clients for almost three weeks now, and wanted to get things back on track. Over the Atlantic, he composed a letter recommending Oren, his Company Commander, for a citation. "He had the leadership required to fill a group of men with great motivation and determination," he wrote. "Looking backwards, those men are filled with wonderment at having managed to do the things they did."

Hanoch thought back. It was under that first round of fire that Oren became a leader. It was his calmness under fire that conferred that leadership upon him. It was in those few moments, in the olive grove, that the transformation took place.

Once back in Israel, Hanoch knew that there would be some major changes taking place in his life.

He wanted to spend more time with his family. In the past, he had arranged his split work schedule to spend more time with his children but now, after Jenin, it wasn't enough. He felt a strong need to have another full day at home, besides *Shabbat*, every week. An American weekend. He never thought that this would become the most important thing in his life, but now it was. He resolved to leave the structure of his job and start his own company. Perhaps Hemi would join him. He, too, had decided to leave his job in order to have more time with his family. They had fought well together. Hanoch was certain they could work well together.

*   *   *

Nachshon, Shneor's newborn son, came late. Two weeks after Jenin. He was born pale and needed help to take his first breath. This is my birth too, thought Shneor. I am being born again. He was overcome by the feeling that there hadn't been proper time to pay respects to the fallen. He felt a great debt towards his fallen brothers.

Throughout Orah's labor pains, Shneor whispered to her, "This is our answer." Messiah pains are like labor pains, he thought to himself. There are miracles that we don't understand.

After Jenin, everything became a miracle. Orah would find herself crying watching Shneor go about his daily tasks. Taking the children to the nursery school. Helping her set the table. For Shneor as well, everying felt different now. Every hug from his sons felt like a miracle.

As always, in Gush Qatif, there were gunshots at night. In the past he had always calmed others. "Don't worry. It's our side." Now he wasn't so sure.

Orah felt a strong need to reach out to one of the wives of Shneor's fallen brothers, to give them strength. She called Rachel Levy, the wife of Yoram Levy. She too was pregnant with her fourth. Orah's husband had come home, Rachel's had not. Both wept the entire conversation.

"I feel so close to you because of all Shneor told me about Yoram," she said. "He was so righteous."

A few weeks after Jenin, Shneor and Orah spent a Sabbath in Jerusalem with Rachel Levy and her children. Shneor set aside some time to spend alone with Yoram's seven-year old son Eden. He took him alone to the synagogue on Sabbath Morning. They discussed the weekly Torah portion.

"Look what I know how to read!" Eden proudly showed him how he could read from the prayerbook. "Let's go kiss the Torah!" Eden whispered excitedly as the Torah scroll was carried through the aisles of the sanctuary. Shneor recognized Yoram's contagious enthusiasm for learning in his young son. Yoram isn't over, Shneor thought in the synagogue. This is his continuation. Eden ran up and gave Shneor a long hug as they drew ready to leave. "*Abba*," he whispered to him. Father.

Shneor froze, unable to speak. In his previous life, perhaps he would have cried. In the past, he had wept over friends who had been killed. Somewhere, far away, he felt Eden clinging to him. But he had no more tears.

True thanksgiving, Shneor reflected, requires the blessing of bad things as well as good. Man understands so little of Divine will. One must mourn outwardly, but inwardly one needs to know joy. Ultimately, only man's myopia is responsible for his suffering.

He wondered when the next callup would be. All he could do now was wait. For his next reserve duty, to be rejoined with his brothers.

*　　*　　*

In Jerusalem, a man on the street approached Rafi for a handout. He had missed his ride home, could Rafi spot him bus fare? Rafi looked in his wallet. He had no small change. He gave the man a one-hundred-shekel bill. Before Jenin, he had been preoccupied with his financial situation. Now, money no longer held any importance to him. It seemed like something easy to do for a stranger. Compared to all that others had given, it seemed like a small thing.

Time was now of the essence. It was now of extreme importance to be punctual. In the past, Rafi had allowed himself a certain measure of tardiness. People always forgave him. It was one of his quirks. It was Rafi. He no longer allowed himself those little eccentricities that tested the patience of others. The two weeks in Jenin had wrung out of him his last vestiges of childishness. His actions during the operation had far reaching effects on the lives of others. Everything he did now mattered.

He knew himself much better now. "You never left the army," his former wife would tease him. It was said in jest, but it was true. It was a passion of his that they didn't share; she would suppress a yawn whenever he began talking about the army. On the next go around, he resolved, he would find a woman who would share his involvement with the families of the fallen soldiers and the wounded. Jenin had left a deep, indelible mark on him. It would always be a part of him.

Had he lost his innocence in Jenin? He hoped he still had a bit left. The experience had triggered a spiritual growth spurt within him. It greatly strengthened his desire to be close to others. To be a part of something significant.

Over the past year, it had been difficult to come to terms with events over which he had no control. The divorce. Losing his job. In Jenin, he learned to jettison the illusion of control. All of a sudden, he found himself doing things had never thought he could do. One can accomplish tremendous things when one isn't in control, he learned, particularly in large groups. With a common vision, great things are possible.

He began to devote much more time to volunteer activity and friends. He and his fellow soldiers from Regiment 5 formed an organization to commemorate the unit's fallen soldiers and perpetuate their legacy. Not long after the fighting was over, they began speaking to youth groups about the values that had come to the fore during the fighting in Jenin. Rafi was not always awarded a warm reception by the young audiences. Many were angry and confused.

"Is it true that the IDF bulldozed houses with people in them?"

"Is it true that the army prevented medicine from reaching the civilian population?"

"Is it true that the army used civilians as human shields?"

For Rafi, this was a new phenomenon. He had never before encountered youth who were looking for a way out of serving in the army. He was deeply troubled. The young people in these movements were the "cream" of Israeli youth. The phenomenon couldn't be dismissed as youthful frivolousness.

"I think that refusal to serve is an illegitimate means of expressing one's views," he told them. "It's the same with anything that runs against a national imperative, such as calls from extremist rabbis to not evacuate settlements should the government decide to do so. In both cases, there need to be consequences."

"But how can we put those who refuse to serve in jail? This is a democracy!"

"That's exactly the point. In a democracy, one needs to participate in the process, not abandon it. Democracy doesn't guarantee an easy way out."

It became very important to Rafi to get the message out. After the Madhat Youssef incident , he heard people say that the army didn't take care of its own. For him, Jenin had put an end to that. The circle of doubt that had been opened at Joseph's Tomb was now closed.

*   *   *

Nahum stopped working late in the evenings. Two weeks after coming home from Jenin, he bought a jeep. It was fully equipped with his first-aid gear. Some evenings, he and Ravit would pack up the jeep and head for the beach. Other times, they would take a walk in the neighborhood. On Sunday evening, a month after his return, they decided to check out the new stores in the small strip mall in Em HaMoshavot, their neighborhood in Petah Tikvah. It was a new neighborhood, full of young couples. High tech couples from Kiryat Aryeh, the industrial area nearby, who worked for Intel and TTI.

The shopping center sidewalk was crowded with parents and children sitting in front of Bravissimo, the Italian-style ice cream parlor and patisserie. Nahum was struck by the face of one of the fathers, beaming with joy as he played with his young daughter. Nahum picked Ron up out of the carriage and held him to his chest.

Nahum and Ravit turned right along the sidewalk towards the Gymboree play center. Ravit was dimly aware of a figure staring into the Gymboree. A young man in his twenties, swarthy, in jeans and white T-shirt. There was a security guard at the entrance to the Gymboree. The man turned away and walked towards Nahum and Ravit, towards the corner of the strip mall. Ravit took note of the man as he passed them. His front tooth was broken. He was mumbling to himself. Suspicious, she thought, and immediately caught herself. My paranoia again. I have to stop that.

They passed the Gymboree store and Nahum grew excited. "Look!! Kids are playing here!!" He grabbed Ravit's hand, pulling her towards the glass window, behind a concrete pillar. "Come on, let's watch the kids play."

Ravit was nonplussed. "I know, I know. I pass this place everyday."

A blast, followed by complete silence. To Nahum, accustomed to being shaken by detonations at close range, the blast sounded as if it had come from a distance. He looked off into the distance, towards the buildings of Kiryat Aryeh. He hadn't felt reverberations. "Where was that?" he asked Ravit.

Then he saw them. All around them, on the ground, people and body parts. The bomber had detonated himself a mere seven yards away. Only the concrete pillar had shielded them.

"I saw him! I saw him!" Ravit was hysterical. Ron, on Nahum's chest, began crying.

A switch flipped. Nahum became his combat medic self. Ravit grabbed his shirt as he ran towards the wounded. "Don't go! There might be another one!" He grabbed her by the shoulders, easing her to the ground behind the concrete pillar. He passed Ron to her and ran. As he ran, he pulled off his shirt and tore it into four strips. It was his light green Versace dress shirt, his favorite.

A two-year-old girl lay on her back, in shock. Her stomach was torn open and her intestines hung out. Her mother was nearby, one forearm nearly severed. Her arteries were still contracted from the blast and not yet spurting blood.

Nahum tied a tourniquet on the mother's arm. The young girl was breathing, but there was nothing he could do for her. Her eyes were open as he checked her for further bleeding.

"Don't touch her," he said to the mother. "Wait for the paramedics."

A large number of wounded awaited around the corner. An old man sat back in his chair, bleeding profusely from his legs and chest. He was in shock, his eyes closed. Nahum tied a tourniquet on his leg and checked for additional bleeding.

Nahum retraced his steps, looking for any serious injuries that he may have missed. There was a charred leg, barefoot, in jeans. The jeans of the man who had walked passed them. Behind a table, an overturned baby carriage. He had missed it on his first pass. A faint moaning. "My child. Help my child."

What a beautiful baby, Nahum thought. The little girl he had seen earlier playing with her father. Her skullcap was gone, her brain exposed. The father's face, covered with blood, was torn by shrapnel. "Help her. Please help her." So helpless, thought Nahum. He got to his knees. He recognized the signs. Her eyes were open, her breaths short. He knew there wasn't much he could do. He could try to maintain her breathing. Covering her nose and mouth with his own mouth, he attempted resuscitation.

Beyond the table, an old woman was lying still. A young man arrived and asked if he could help. "Check the woman. See if she's still breathing."

He came back. "She's not."

"See if there's a pulse on her neck."

He returned again. "No pulse."

Nahum gave him a strip from his shirt and pointed towards the elderly man to whom he had applied a tourniquet moments earlier. " See if he's bleeding anywhere else. If he is, press on the spot and let me know."

Three minutes had passed since the explosion. The first ambulance arrived. Nahum was still monitoring the infant's breathing. "Over here!" he called to the paramedic, a young woman in her twenties.

"There's nothing to do there," said the young woman. She placed her coat over the infant.

"Idiot!!" Nahum screamed at her. "Can't you see she's still breathing! Evacuate her right now!" He pulled the jacket off of the infant and grabbed the paramedic's collar with force. The young paramedic went into shock and began walking in circles.

The infant had stopped breathing. He attempted resuscitation once again, without success.

"Take her to the ambulance and evacuate her right now," he said gently to the father. The father's cheek was bleeding profusely, torn open by shrapnel. He carried his daughter to the ambulance and climbed in with her. Nahum coordinated the triage as the ambulances arrived. First the two-year-old girl and her mother. Then the old man. Then the rest.

Nahum went back to Ravit and Ron. His face was covered with the blood of the infant. He picked up Ron, still wailing, and took Ravit to a grassy spot fifty yards away. He tried to calm her.

"I saw him. I saw him." She couldn't stop trembling. She was confused.

"Here, give Ron some food," said Nahum. He hoped a task would calm her. It didn't. The paramedics suggested to Nahum that Ravit and Ron be evacuated as well. Nahum rode with them in the ambulance.

Three weeks later. Ravit answered the phone. It was Mrs. Tanenbaum, the wife of the man whom Nahum had treated. "He hasn't recovered yet, she told Ravit. He kept the strip from your husband's shirt as a souvenir. The doctors told him that he would have died without it."

*   *   *

Battallion 51 kept on the move. Two weeks after leaving Jenin, they were sent on an operation in Nablus. Avihu came home for a quick leave the Wednesday night before the operation. He remembered that he had forgotten to call Zohar, his younger sister, to ask how she had done on her college entrance exam.

"Promise me you'll call her to tell her I was thinking about her," he said to his youngest sister, Chen, as he prepared to leave.

Avihu called Chen "My look-alike sister". They were both redheads. On her birthdays, Chen often woke to find her room filled with balloons and a sprinkling of small trinkets. Avihu always saw to every little detail. This past Purim, Chen had needed a female soldier's uniform for a costume. He hadn't been able to get one on the base, so he made a special trip to a costume store in Haifa and bought her one.

He taught her to love the land. "Love the land and love it deeply," was his saying.. They both loved horses. Someday, they would raise one together. She would take care of it when he was in the army, and he would help out when he was on leave.

That evening, Chen was overcome with dread. She spent much of the evening alone in her room crying, and then ran out to hug Avihu before he left.
"Don't worry, Chen." He reassured her. "Don't worry, my look-alike sister."

In Nablus, Avihu and Ofek Bukhris prepared to storm a house in which a cell of enemy gunmen were holed up. Avihu crouched down, ready to spring inside once the door blew open. Ofek stood ready to follow. A sudden burst of machine gun fire tore through them both. Ofek, severely wounded, survived. Avihu was killed on the spot. It was the fifth of

May, the day of Gadi Ezra's thirty-day memorial.

*   *   *

Chen saw her older brother Amir at the door. She knew. She ran from the room.

"Our power is our children," Avihu had often said. The younger nieces and nephews were certain that there had been a mistake. How could anything have happened to Avihu? Everyone knew that he was the best wrestler in the world.

Thousands arrived for the funeral. "The worst thing would have been a purposeless death," said Gadi Yaakov, Avihu's father. "He died in the defense of our country.."

At the end of the *shiva*, the seven days of mourning, Gadi Yaakov assembled the family. There was a meeting, and minutes were taken. "We're now members of three families," he said. "The Naval Commando, Golani, and the family of the bereaved. Each person will mourn Avihu privately in his own way, but collectively, in the public space, I don't believe in erecting shrines. There won't be a black-framed picture of Avihu on our living room wall. His room won't be turned into a shrine." Avihu's room didn't need a shrine to bear testimony to his life. Each of the objects in the room told a story of its own. In one corner stood a pile of books, a hundred copies of *Fire in the Galilee*. It was the book Avihu gave to each of his soldiers on their birthday.

In Kfar Hassidim, the parents of a newborn infant asked if they could name their son after Avihu. Gadi Yaakov thanked them for the thought but demurred. "I don't want anyone to live in Avihu's shadow," he said. "I want everyone to hold his head high, looking forward."

Solly, Gadi Ezra's father, was one of the many speakers at Avihu's thirty-day memorial service. "Avihu, I heard about what you did for my son," he said, his voice breaking. "When I found out, I wanted to hug you. But it was too late. Now all I can do is salute you." As Solly descended from the stage, Gadi Yaakov, Avihu's father, wrapped his thick arms around him.

"You can hug me," he said.

CHAPTER 40 The Sleep of Angels

Someone was making noise. It sounded like crying. "Quiet, they'll hear us!!" Doron whispered. The noise continued. "Quiet!" he hissed. Still, the noise, louder now and more insistent. He grabbed for his rifle. It wasn't there. He felt naked and vulnerable. Where was his weapon?

He came to. It was his nine-month old son, Ofek, crying in his crib. He went to the crib and held Ofek to his chest. Tears streamed down his own face as he rocked his child to sleep. I will hold him forever, Doron thought. I will hold him until he feels real. I will hold him until I have reclaimed him.

He had been home for two weeks now, but every night he still awoke in Jenin. He wasn't able to sleep for more than an hour or two without awakening in a sweat. Each time he awoke, it would take him a number of minutes to gain his bearings. The other night, awakening to the sound of a helicopter, he was certain that he was still in Jenin.

While Doron was in Jenin, his short conversations with Liron gave him great strength. But she had concealed numerous things from him that she felt would have weighed on him unduly. Now that Doron was finally home, she brought him up to date.

"Ofek is much better now."

"What do you mean much better now?" asked Doron. Ofek had fallen out of bed on his head. He had suffered numerous asthma attacks and had needed inhalation every three hours.

"You think you're the only one with secrets?" asked Liron.

*   *   *

On *Shavuot*, the holiday that commemorates the revelation of the Torah on Mt. Sinai, it is traditional for students to study Torah all night long. The children of Israel wandered for fifty days before reaching Mt. Sinai. It was now a full fifty days after the Netanyah attack. Doron gathered the students in the dining hall for the night-long study session. The night's learning was dedicated to Gadi Ezra. Doron recounted stories from Gadi's life, and read a passage from Gadi's letter to Galit.

> *My beloved, I feel that on the one hand there is nothing that I would like more than to be with you, to love you, and to raise a family with you. But on the other hand, there is nothing that I want more than to go on this operation and deal such a great blow to the terrorists that they will never dare perpetrate another bombing or terror attack. That they will take into account that each time they commit an atrocity we will hit them in the most painful place possible and will be willing to pay the price. I am willing to be that price.*

At Gadi's commemoration, one of the eulogizers, a religious educator, had asked, "How can we be sure that we'll be able to raise students like Gadi in the future?"

Doron spoke to his students of his confidence in them. "Those of you here will act according to the same values that Gadi embodied. G-d willing, you will pass the test of Jewish values and ethics, G-d willing with a happier outcome." Both Gadi and Doron himself had come to combat units from homes overflowing with love. Doron told his students that he had particular admiration for those who came to combat units from difficult home situations. And in the future, he thought to himself, he and the teaching staff would once again have sleepless nights until their student soldiers came home safely.

Doron shared some of his own stories from Jenin. He told of making the *kiddush* on the last night of Passover; of praying with the troops before going into Jenin. He looked out over the multicolored sea of young faces. He remembered what he had felt that night, how connected he had felt to all of *Am Yisroel*, how close he had felt to G-d. The immigrant youngsters in the Village still felt different, set apart from the Israeli mainstream Doron stressed to them the variegated ethnic makeup of his unit. There were soldiers from all backgrounds in Doron's unit. "With helmets on, we're all the same," he stressed to them. "Sephardi, Ashkenazi, religious, secular."

They studied the Rambam's sentence from *Hilchot Melachim,* the passage that he had debated years ago with Itamar. He asked them what they made of it.

One of the *Tzabarim* raised his hand. "Just another illogical religious law, if you ask me."

Doron thought of countering, of sharing the awful truth that he had finally grasped in Jenin, but then thought better of it. The Rambam's words were now a part of him, an instinct, a spontaneous reflex. But could anyone ever grasp this truth without experiencing it? It was a lesson that he was in no hurry to teach. Their innocence would be over soon enough, he figured. For tonight at least, let them cling to it.

"When are you going to tell us some real battle stories?" asked one of the ninth graders.

He spoke with them of the ethical questions that arise in war. He told stories from his regular service in Jebaliah. The time that he was forced to back his vehicle into a crowd. The prisoner who was beaten. "Even if someone deserves a punishment, you still need to ask yourself – what kind of person are you if you mete out that punishment yourself? You need to ask yourself -- what kind of person will come home from a situation like that?" Doron said.

"So how *did* you come home from Jenin?" asked one of the students. "Are you still the same Doron?"

"I think so," he answered. "I hope so."

They studied until morning. At 7:30 am, he arrived home and fell into a deep sleep. It was the first time since Jenin that he had slept for more than an hour or two. He awoke in the afternoon. Liron was sitting on side of the bed, stroking his hair.

"You slept the sleep of angels," she said.

Acknowledgements

The interviews that form the basis of this book were conducted in May and June of 2002, immediately following Operation Defensive Shield. I wish to thank first and foremost the men who opened up their souls to me and the families of fallen soldiers who brought me in without hesitation. Many of the interviews lasted days on end. We often worked through the night. I will be eternally grateful to all of them for placing their trust in me.

There were many who helped bring about these interviews.

My first conversations were with Dr. Haim Peri, Director of the Yemin Orde Youth Village. This amazing institution could fill volumes by itself and indeed has served as a model for the care of youth-at-risk worldwide. Dr. Peri, a world-renowned child psychologist, is unique in his ability to draw from all walks of Israeli life in his spiritual weavings. More than anyone else, he helped make this book a reality.

General Elazar Stern, Chief Education Officer of the IDF, came to meet with me the night he heard about this project. General Stern was instrumental in providing initial encouragement for the project and in facilitating contact with the families of fallen soldiers.

My friend Ms. Gila Gerzon, Director of the USO in Israel and legendary "Mother of the Sixth Fleet," provided me with invaluable assistance in facilitating contact with official bodies. Her advice always proved dead on.

My friend and rabbi, Rav Mordechai Helfand of Brooklyn, was on call throughout the writing of this book, often many times a day. He was always there to fill in the blanks for me in his own ebullient manner.

Mr. Reuven Koret, of Koret Communications and israelinsider.com, was instrumental in keeping me on track. He pushed me to enlarge the scope of the project and was kind enough to bring his keen editorial eye to bear, as well as to provide the project with its first exposure on israelinsider.com.

My editor, teacher, and friend, Ms. Barbara Carlson, spent endless hours helping me convert this material from a collection of interviews into a narrative format. Her enthusiasm and endless patience never flagged.

Ms. Simona Pachter was instrumental in connecting me with relevant sources. Ms. Isabelle Smith was a wonderfully encouraging and instructive reader.

And throughout it all my own family, my wife Eve and daughter Isa, as always, overflowed with encouragement and support.

Glossary

Abba – (Hebrew) Father.

Aliyah – (Hebrew) Literally: an ascent. To "make Aliyah" means to immigrate to Israel.

Bakum – Literally: Intake and Selection Base. First stop for new army recruits.

Birkat HaGomel – Blessing made when one emerges whole from a harrowing experience.

Caparah – Literally: forgiveness, or: one in whose place I would die. Term of endearment.

Chabad -- the general by-name for Lubavitcher Hasidut.

Chabadnik – Follower of Chabad.

Daf Yomi – Daily page of Talmud study.

Falafel – Mideast staple made of fried chick peas.

Gibush – grueling stress test for applicants to elite army units.

HaGomel (see 'Birkat HaGomel')

Halachah – Jewish Law.

Havdalah – Prayer marking the end of the Sabbath or a Jewish Holiday

Ima – Mother

Kabalat Shabbat – Friday night prayers for welcoming the Sabbath.

Kadimah – Onwards!

Kaffiyeh – Middle Eastern headdress.

Kav LaHayim – Literally: lifeline. Volunteer program for terminally ill and impaired youth.

Kibbutz – Israeli collective settlement.

Kibbutznik – member of a kibbutz.

Kiddush – Blessing over wine made on Sabbath and holidays.

Kippah – Yarmulke. Skullcap.

Ma'ariv – Evening Prayers.

Madim – military uniform.

Masenqu – (Amharic) Ethiopian stringed instrument.

Mifgash Tzameret – Literally 'The Summit Meeting Place'

Milu'im – Reserve Duty.

Mimounah – North African celbration marking the end of Passover.

Minchah – Afternoon Prayers.

Mit'an (plural: *mit'anim*) – explosive charge of any sort.

Mufti – Muslim Religious Authority.

Neshek – weapon.

Pal-Han – Abbreviation of '*Plugat Handasah*': Engineering Company.

Pal-Sar – Abbreviation of '*Plugat Siyur*': Reconnaissance Company.

Pikuach Nefesh – The saving of a life.

Pitah (plural: *Pitot*) – Middle Eastern bread.

Red Crescent – Muslim Red Cross.

Saba – Grandfather.

Sabaah el-Heir (Arabic) – Good Morning.

Savta – Grandmother.

Shabbat – Sabbath. Jewish day of rest, lasts from Friday night until Saturday night.

Shabbat Shalom – Sabbath Greeting. Literally: 'A Sabbath of Peace'

Shaharit – Morning Prayers.

Sharwal – Druse baggy pantaloons.

Shavuot – Jewish Holiday that commemorates the revelation of the Torah at Sinai.

Shaheed – (Arabic) Literally: martyr. Suicide Bomber.

Shma – Jewish prayer that reaffirms the centrality of monotheism: Hear O Israel the Lord our G-d the Lord is One.

Shtreimel – Traditional Chassidic fur hat.

Tfillin – Phylacteries, used when praying morning prayers.

Tallit, tallitot – prayer shawl.

Tzabar (plural: Tzabarim) – Native Israeli. Literally: cactus plant (soft on inside, prickly on outside).

Tzav – Reserve Duty Callup notice.

Washent – Ethiopian wind instrument.

Yom HaZikaron – Day of Remembrance for casualties of Israel's Wars. Comes one day before Israeli Independence Day.

Yom Kippur – Day of Atonement. Comes ten days after Jewish New Year.

Major Avihu Yaakov, 24, fell on May 2nd in Nablus.